GMAT® Verbal Workbook

Sixth Edition

Other Kaplan Books on Business School Admissions

Kaplan GMAT Premier

Kaplan GMAT Math Workbook

Kaplan GMAT Integrated Reasoning Workbook

Kaplan GRE & GMAT Exams Writing Workbook

Kaplan GMAT 800

Kaplan GMAT Math Workbook

GMAT®
Verbal Workbook
Sixth Edition

The Staff of Kaplan Test Prep and Admissions

PUBLISHING

New York

© 2011 Kaplan, Inc.

Published by Kaplan Publishing, a division of Kaplan, Inc.
395 Hudson Street
New York, NY 10014

Printed in the United States of America

10 9 8 7 6 5 4 3 2 1

ISBN-13: 978-1-4195-5043-0

Kaplan Publishing books are available at special quantity discounts to use for sales promotions, employee premiums, or educational purposes. For more information or to purchase books, please call the Simon & Schuster special sales department at 866-506-1949.

Table of Contents

KAPLAN

kaptest.com/publishing

The material in this book is up-to-date at the time of publication. However, the Graduate Management Admission Council may have instituted changes in the test after this book was published. Be sure to carefully read the materials you receive when you register for the test.

If there are any important late-breaking developments—or any changes or corrections to the Kaplan test preparation materials in this book—we will post that information online at **kaptest.com/publishing**. Check to see if there is any information posted there regarding this book.

kaplansurveys.com/books

We'd love to hear your comments and suggestions about this book. We invite you to fill out our online survey form at **kaplansurveys.com/books**. Your feedback is extremely helpful as we continue to develop high-quality resources to meet your needs.

How to Use This Book

Welcome to Kaplan's *GMAT Exam Verbal Workbook*. You have wisely just purchased the most comprehensive book on the market focusing specifically on the verbal and writing portions of the Graduate Management Admissions Test (GMAT). Kaplan has prepared students to take standardized tests for over 60 years, longer than the GMAT has been around. Our team of researchers and editors knows more about preparing for the GMAT than anyone else, and you'll find their accumulated knowledge and wisdom here in this book.

This book is designed to benefit anyone who needs to increase scores on the GMAT, whether on the Verbal Section, the Analytical Writing Assessment (AWA) Section, or both. Perhaps you have already taken the GMAT, or at least a simulated GMAT, and you're comfortable with your quantitative score on the test, but you need to boost your verbal score in order to get into the MBA program of your choice.

If so, this book is for you. If you want a book that covers the entire GMAT, we recommend *Kaplan GMAT* or *Kaplan GMAT Premier* (with CD-ROM); for a book that focuses on math content and strategies for the GMAT, pick up a copy of Kaplan's *GMAT Math Workbook*.

This book is designed to raise your verbal score on the GMAT regardless of your present skill level. Some of our readers may have relatively strong verbal skills, but know they could still be scoring higher, while others may not be native English speakers and can use serious help with English grammar and idioms. This book is designed to help in either situation. And almost all test takers, no matter how proficient in English, can use solid strategies for dealing with the dense reading passages and arguments found on the GMAT, as well as techniques for writing superior AWA essays.

With this understanding of our readers' differing needs and skill sets, we have divided the book into several parts.

PART ONE: GETTING STARTED

The first step to a higher score is to know exactly what you can expect to find on the GMAT. In part one of this book, we'll provide you with background information on the different sections of the test, what they cover, and how they're organized. We'll explain how the Computer Adaptive Test (CAT) format differs from traditional pencil-and-paper tests in the way it determines your score, and how you can use the CAT format and scoring method to your advantage.

PART TWO: VERBAL STRATEGIES

Once you have the big picture, it's time to focus on the specifics of the verbal portions of the GMAT. Part two examines the three question types that constitute the 75-minute Verbal Section: Sentence Correction, Reading Comprehension, and Critical Reasoning. We dedicate a chapter to each, examining first the question format and then exactly what is tested by the question type. Finally, we give you our best Kaplan methods and strategies for handling each, along with plenty of testlike examples on which to practice. We also devote a separate chapter to "Reading the GMAT Way," which is designed to help you develop the very specific reading skills that you need to read Reading Comprehension and Critical Reasoning passages with better efficiency and understanding.

PART THREE: PRACTICE SETS

After you're comfortable with our Kaplan methods and strategies for handling Verbal question types, you'll want to try them out with more questions. The practice sets contained in part three contain hundreds of Sentence Correction, Critical Reasoning, and Reading Comprehension questions complete with detailed explanations. As you go through these, look for patterns of questions that you tend to get right and wrong. Take notice of your areas of strength, but focus the bulk of your studies on your areas of weakness. With sufficient practice, you'll be ready for anything that could appear on the GMAT Verbal Section.

PART FOUR: PUTTING IT ALL TOGETHER

Part four contains our best effort to replicate (on paper) the experience of taking an actual GMAT Verbal Section, mixing the Verbal types in the same manner that an actual GMAT would. Here's your chance to bring together all your newly acquired verbal strategies and get a sense of what the GMAT Verbal Section feels like.

PART FIVE: ANALYTICAL WRITING ASSESSMENT

Part five focuses on the essay portion of the GMAT, known as the Analytical Writing Assessment (AWA). It contains descriptions and examples of the two essay question types, along with an explanation of how the essays are graded and strategies for successfully completing each. Finally, you'll see sample essay topics and sample essays, along with a scoring guide that will enable you to see how your practice essays measure up to the GMAC scoring formula.

PART SIX: APPENDIXES

The appendixes contain additional materials to help you fine-tune your skills and address any verbal weak spots. We especially recommend that all readers take a look at the list of common GMAT idioms in appendix 3. There is also an extensive grammar reference guide, as well as a guide to usage and style that presents 16 principles of good writing and exercises to help you sharpen your writing skills. Spending time with these guides will help you develop skills that will serve you long after you've taken the GMAT. Good luck with your studies.

A Special Note for International Students

The MBA (Master of Business Administration) has become a degree of choice for businesspersons around the globe. Variations of U.S.-style MBA programs exist in Asia, Europe, and the Americas. In recent years, hundreds of thousands of international students have studied business and management in the United States.

As the United States increases its participation in the global economy, U.S. business schools are reaching out to attract exceptional international candidates to their graduate programs. However, competition for admission to prestigious programs is heavy and international students need to plan carefully if they wish to enter a top U.S. graduate management program.

If you are not from the United States, but are considering attending a graduate management program at a university in the United States, here is what you'll need to get started:

- If English is not your first language, start there. You will probably need to take the Test of English as a Foreign Language (TOEFL®) or show some other evidence that you are proficient in English prior to gaining admission to a graduate program in business. The ability to communicate in English, both verbally and in writing, is extremely important to your success in an American MBA program.

- You may also need to take the GMAT® (Graduate Management Admissions Test). Some graduate business programs may require you to take the GRE® (Graduate Record Examination) as well.

- Since admission to many graduate business programs is quite competitive, you may wish to select three or four programs you would like to attend and complete applications for each program.

- You should select a program that meets your current or future employment needs, rather than simply a program with a big name. For example, if you hope to work in the hotel and tourism industry, make sure the program you choose specializes in that distinct area.

- You need to begin the application process at least a year in advance. Be aware that many programs only offer August or September start dates. Find out application deadlines and plan accordingly.

- Finally, you will need to obtain an 1-20 Certificate of Eligibility from the school you plan to attend if you intend to apply for an F-1 Student Visa to study in the United States.

KAPLAN ENGLISH PROGRAMS*

If you need more help with the complex process of business school admissions, assistance preparing for the TOEFL or GMAT, or help improving your English skills in general, you may be interested in Kaplan's programs for international students.

Kaplan English Programs were designed to help students and professionals from outside the United States meet their educational and career goals. At locations throughout the United States, international students take advantage of Kaplan's programs to help them improve their academic and conversational English skills, raise their scores on the TOEFL, GMAT, and other standardized exams, and gain admission to the schools of their choice. Our staff and instructors give international students the individualized instruction they need to succeed. Here is a brief description of some of Kaplan's programs for international students:

General Intensive English

Kaplan's General Intensive English classes are designed to help you improve your skills in all areas of English and to increase your fluency in spoken and written English. Classes are available for beginning to advanced students, and the average class size is 12 students.

General English Structured-Study

For students needing a flexible schedule, this course helps improve general fluency skills. Kaplan's General English Structured-Study course employs the communicative approach and focuses on vocabulary building, reading, and writing. You will receive books, and audio and video materials as well as three hours of instructor contact per week.

TOEFL and Academic English

This course provides you with the skills you need to improve your TOEFL score and succeed in an American university or graduate program. It includes all the skills tested on the new test.

TOEFL Test Preparation Course

Kaplan's TOEFL course can help you learn test-taking skills and strategies to raise your TOEFL score. This course is for intermediate to advanced English learners.

GMAT for International Students

The Graduate Management Admissions Test (GMAT) is required for admission to many graduate programs in business in the United States. Hundreds of thousands of American students have taken this course to prepare for the GMAT. This course, designed especially for non-native English speakers, includes the skills you need to succeed on each section of the GMAT, as well as access to Kaplan's exclusive computer-based practice materials and extra verbal practice.

*Kaplan is authorized under federal law to enroll nonimmigrant alien students. Kaplan is accredited by ACCET (Accrediting Council for Continuing Education and Training).

OTHER KAPLAN PROGRAMS

Since 1938, more than 3 million students have come to Kaplan to advance their studies, prepare for entry to American universities, and further their careers. In addition to the previously mentioned programs, Kaplan offers courses to prepare for the SAT®, GRE®, LSAT®, MCAT®, DAT®, USMLE®, NCLEX®, and other standardized exams at locations throughout the United States.

Applying to Kaplan English Programs

To get more information, or to apply for admission to any of Kaplan's programs for international students and professionals, contact us at:

Kaplan English Programs
700 S. Flower, Suite 2900
Los Angeles, CA 90017, USA
Telephone: (213) 385-2358
Fax: (213) 383-1364
Website: www.kaplanenglish.com
Email: world@kaplan.com

| PART ONE |

Getting Started

Chapter 1: **About the GMAT**

Let's start with the basics. The GMAT is, among other things, an endurance test. It is a computerized test consisting of 150 minutes of multiple-choice testing plus two 30-minute analytical essays. Add in the administrative details, plus two 8-minute breaks, and you can count on being in the test center for about 4 hours.

It's a grueling experience, to say the least. And if you don't approach it with confidence and rigor, you'll quickly lose your composure. That's why it's so important that you take control of the test, just as you take control of the rest of your application process to business school.

Here are the basics.

GMAT FORMAT

The GMAT begins with the Analytical Writing Assessment (the AWA). You will be required to compose two different essays, typing them into the computer using a simple word-processing program. You are given 30 minutes for each essay.

One essay is the "Analysis of an Argument" topic, for which you'll have to analyze the reasoning behind a given argument, explain its weaknesses or flaws, and recommend how to correct them to improve the argument. Your own personal views on the topic are not relevant.

The other essay is the "Analysis of an Issue" topic. You'll have to analyze a given issue or opinion and then explain your point of view on the subject. You will be required to cite relevant reasons and/or examples drawn from your own experience, observations, or reading.

After the essay sections and an 8-minute break, there are two 75-minute multiple-choice sections—one Quantitative (Math) and one Verbal. The Quantitative section contains 37 questions in two formats—Problem Solving and Data Sufficiency—which are mixed together throughout the section. The Verbal section contains 41 questions in three formats—Reading Comprehension, Sentence Correction, and Critical Reasoning—which are also mixed throughout the section. Within each section, question types appear in random order, so you never know what's coming next.

This is how the sections break down:

- AWA: 60 minutes, 2 essay assignments
  - Analysis of an Argument topic (30 minutes)
  - Analysis of an Issue topic (30 minutes)
- Quantitative (Math) Section: 75 minutes, 37 questions
  - Data Sufficiency questions
  - Problem Solving questions
- Verbal Section: 75 minutes, 41 questions
  - Reading Comprehension questions
  - Sentence Correction questions
  - Critical Reasoning questions

Some important things to note:

- After you have completed the second essay, you'll get an 8-minute break. Then, between the two multiple-choice sections, you will get another break.
- So-called "experimental" questions will be scattered throughout the test. They will look just like the other multiple-choice questions but won't contribute to your score.

We'll talk more about each of the Verbal question types in later chapters. For now, note the following. You'll be answering 78 multiple-choice questions in 2½ hours. That's less than 2 minutes per question, not counting the time it takes to read the passages. Clearly, you'll have to move fast. But you can't let yourself get careless. Taking control of the GMAT means increasing the speed of your work without sacrificing accuracy.

GMAT SCORING

You'll receive four scores for the GMAT:

- Overall scaled score, from 200 to 800
- Quantitative scaled subscore, from 0 to 60
- Verbal scaled subscore, from 0 to 60
- AWA score, from 0 to 6. This score is separate from your overall score for Quantitative and Verbal.

Because the test is graded on a preset curve, the scaled score will correspond to a certain percentile, which will also be given on your score report. A 650 overall score, for instance, corresponds to the

80th percentile, meaning that 80 percent of test takers score at or below this level. The percentile figure is important because it allows admissions officers at business schools to get a sense quickly of where you fall in the pool of applicants.

Percentile	Approximate Score
99th percentile	760
95th percentile	720
90th percentile	700
80th percentile	650
75th percentile	630
50th percentile	550

Though many factors play a role in admissions decisions, the GMAT score is usually an important one. And, generally speaking, being average just won't cut it. While the median GMAT score is around 550, you need a score of at least 650 to be considered competitive by the top B-schools. According to the latest Kaplan/*Newsweek* careers guide, the average GMAT scores at the best business schools in the country—such as Stanford, Sloan (MIT), Kellogg (Northwestern), and Wharton (Penn)—are above 700. That translates to a percentile figure of 90 and up!

Fortunately, there are strategies that can give you an advantage on the computer-adaptive GMAT. You can learn to exploit the way that the computer-adaptive test (CAT) generates a score. We'll explain how in the next section.

Score Reports

About 20 days after your test date, your official score report will be available online. You'll receive an email when yours is ready. Reports will only be mailed to candidates who request that service. The official score report includes your scores for the Analytical Writing Assessment (AWA), Verbal, and Quantitative sections, as well as your total score and percentile ranking. Test takers who skip the AWA do not receive score reports.

Your report also includes the results of all the exams you've taken in the previous five years, including cancellations. Any additional reports are US$28 each. All score report requests are final and cannot be canceled.

GMAT ATTITUDE

In the chapters that follow, we'll cover techniques for answering the GMAT Verbal questions. But you'll also need to go into the test with a certain attitude and approach. Here are some strategies.

The Art of Using Noteboards

Test takers are given noteboards, which are spiral-bound booklets of laminated paper, and a black wet-erase pen. Here are the specs so you know what to expect on test day.

Noteboard

- 5 sheets, 10 numbered pages
- Spiral-bound at top
- Legal-sized paper (8.5″ × 14″) in United States, Canada, and Mexico; A4 paper elsewhere
- First page has test administration and chair operation instructions and is not suitable for scratchwork. Pages 2–10 consist of a gridded work surface.
- Pale yellow paper in United States, Canada, and Mexico; a different color possible elsewhere

Pen

- Black fine-print Staedtler wet-erase pen

You will not be given an eraser, and you are not supposed to reuse the noteboard. Each time you fill up your noteboard during the test, the administrator will replace your used noteboard with a clean one. You can also request a new pen, if necessary. The noteboards cannot be removed from the test room during or after the exam, and you must return your noteboard to the administrator when your exam is complete.

We know how important it is for test takers to be as prepared as possible for the actual testing experience. That's why we have always recommended that students use scratch material with this book. Since the noteboards will be your only option on test day, we suggest that you use an eraser board (or anything with a similar surface) and a nonpermanent marker while doing the practice tests. Although using them won't mimic the test day experience exactly, at least you'll get the feel of working in a comparable medium. And at the very least, using the noteboard and pen on test day won't be jarring or unfamiliar, as it might be otherwise. In fact, students who take a Kaplan classroom course receive a noteboard that mimics the writing surface that GMAT test takers use, as well as the same type of pen.

Most test takers have not had any difficulties using the noteboards and pens on test day. Plus, practicing with the eraser board and marker will help you feel even more comfortable and in control. However, nothing is perfect, so based on all the feedback we've received from test takers, here are two snags that you just can't prepare for… and how to tackle them:

1. **Erasable ink you're not supposed to erase:** Say you smudge your work with your hand.

   The noteboard's surface probably won't lend itself to quick-and-easy erasing (not surprisingly, since you are not meant to reuse it). And you can't write on top of the smudge or error because you'll just be left with a blob of ink that you can't read. So what should you do? Just start over. Seriously. Think of it this way—you won't waste precious time in a futile attempt to save what is essentially a sinking ship. Left-handed test takers (and some right-handed ones, too) might find that their writing styles make them particularly susceptible to smudging. If this sounds like you, practicing with the eraser board will help you work out any such problems before test day.

2. **A problematic pen:** Difficulties with pens are not common at all. The test administrators are careful to provide good writing utensils so test takers don't have any extra anxieties. Also, keep in mind that you should recap your pen when you are not using it so that it doesn't dry out.

However, you could get a pen that's simply dry from the get-go or dries out quickly no matter how careful you are. Don't sweat it. The best thing to do is just get a new pen. And should you be saddled with a pen that leaves wayward blobs of ink, don't waste time with it either. Ask the administrator for a new pen as soon as it starts to act up.

More Noteboard Strategies

Using one booklet for an entire section, and requesting a replacement during breaks, is perhaps the most efficient method for using the noteboards. Since you are given nine pages to write on, this technique can be used without difficulty, especially with planning and practice. However, should you need a new noteboard (or pen) during a section, hold the used one in the air to clarify immediately the nature of the request (rather than just raising your hand).

Draw a Grid

If you find crossing off answer choices on paper tests particularly helpful (as a process of elimination), consider doing the same thing here. It's an obvious challenge, since you're working on computer, but it can be done with your noteboard.

Your noteboard is already gridded, so reserve five lines at the top of one of the pages and label them A through E before you begin the exam. Use the grid to mark off answer choices that you have eliminated, as shown below. That way, you can tell at a glance which answer choices are still in the running. If you end up using it often, it'll be worth the 10 seconds it takes to draw it up.

A	✗	✗		✗		✗			✗		✗		
B		✗	✗	✗			✗	✗	✗	✗		✗	
C					✗				✗				✗
D	✗		✗		✗			✗		✗		✗	
E	✗	✗		✗			✗			✗			

Be Systematic

Because it's so important to get to the hard questions as early as possible, work systematically. Use your noteboard to organize your thinking. If you eliminate choices, cross them off on your noteboard using the grid just described and then guess intelligently. Make sure to leave enough time to answer every question in the section. You'll be penalized for questions you don't reach.

Pace Yourself

Of course, the last thing you want to happen is to run out of time before you've done all the questions. Pace yourself so that this doesn't happen. We're not saying you have to spend exactly 90 seconds, for instance, on every Critical Reasoning question. But you should have a sense of how much time to spend on each question.

Before you go in to take the exam, you must get a sense of how long is too long to spend on a question. This is something you can do only with practice, so while working on the practice questions in this book, time yourself. (If you're using your watch, take off your watch and set it on the table in front of you.)

Stop the Clock

The timer in the corner of the GMAT screen can work to your advantage, but if you find yourself looking at it so often that it becomes a distraction, turn it off for 10 or 15 minutes and try to refocus. Even if you lose track a bit without the clock, there is no replacement for focus and accuracy. No matter what your preference is for the clock, when there are five minutes left, the clock turns on permanently, counts down the seconds, turns red, and flashes.

Don't Waste Time on Questions You Can't Do

Yes, forgoing a tough question is easier said than done. It's natural to want to plow through a test and answer every question as it appears. But that doesn't pay off here. If you dig in your heels on a tough question, refusing to move on until you've cracked it, you're letting your test macho get in the way of your test score. Like life itself, a test section is too short to waste on lost causes.

Remain Calm

It's imperative that you remain calm and composed during the test. You can't let yourself get rattled by one hard question or a Reading Comprehension passage to the degree that it throws off your performance on the rest of the Verbal section. When you face a tough question, remember that you're surely not the only one finding it difficult. The test is designed to challenge everyone who takes it. Having trouble with a difficult question isn't going to ruin your score, but getting upset and letting it throw you off track will. When you understand that part of the test maker's goal is to reward those who keep their composure, you'll recognize the importance of not panicking when you run into challenging material.

GMAT CHECKLIST

The GMAT is offered by appointment, at your convenience, almost every day of the year. You will be required to register online before making an appointment.

Choose a Test Center

Before you register to take the exam, search for a test center that's convenient for you and determine whether that site has available seats. Each test center operates on its own schedule and can accommodate varying numbers of test takers throughout the day. To locate a test center near you, go to **mba.com**.

Register and Schedule Your Appointment

Available time slots change continuously as people register for the test. You will find out what times are available at your chosen test center when you register. You may be able to schedule an appointment within a few days of your desired test date, but popular dates (especially weekends) fill up quickly.

Admissions deadlines for business schools vary. Check with the schools and make your test appointment early enough to allow your scores to be reported before the schools' application deadlines.

You may register and schedule your appointment online, by phone, by mail, or by fax:

- Online: Go to **mba.com.**
- Phone: Use one of the following numbers, based on your location:
- The Americas: Call toll-free (within the United States and Canada only) 800-717-GMAT (4628) or call the customer service line (952) 681-3680. The lines are operational from 7:00 a.m. to 7:00 p.m. Central Time.
- Asia Pacific: 160 38318-9961, 8:30 a.m. to 6:00 p.m. AEST
- China: 186 10 62798877, 8:30 a.m. to 5:00 p.m. Beijing Time
- India: 191 120 439-7830, 9:00 a.m. to 6:00 p.m. Indian Standard Time
- Europe/Middle East/Africa: 144 (0) 161 855 7219, 8:00 a.m. to 6:00 p.m. BST
- Mail or fax (slowest options):
  - Download the Test Center List, Country Code List, and GMAT Appointment Scheduling form, available at **mba.com**.
  - Fill out the GMAT Appointment Scheduling form.
  - If you wish to fax your form, use one of the following fax numbers, based on your location:
    - The Americas: (952) 681-3681
    - Asia Pacific and India: 160 38319 1092
    - China: 186 10 82520243
    - Europe/Middle East/Africa: 144 (0) 161 855 7301
- If you wish to mail your form, send your completed form to the address that follows. Keep in mind that mail from some countries can take as long as eight weeks to arrive in the United States.

Pearson VUE
Attention: GMAT Program
5601 Green Valley Drive, Suite 300
Bloomington, MN 55437-1186
USA

The fee to take the GMAT is US$250 worldwide (at the time of printing). It is payable online by credit card or by mailing in a check. If you have questions about GMAT registration, visit **mba.com** or call 800-717-GMAT (4628).

The Day of the Test

You should arrive at your testing center 30 minutes before the time of your scheduled appointment. A late arrival (15 minutes or more) may result in you being turned away from the test center and the forfeiture of your test fee. Plus, you must complete a number of security measures before you will be allowed to take the exam. Visit **mba.com** for the current requirements.

Noteboards

To make notes during the exam, you will be provided with a spiral-bound booklet that is comprised essentially of five pieces of laminated, legal-size paper, as well as a black pen.

Breaks

The length of your appointment is approximately four hours. Two breaks are scheduled into the exam—one after the second essay is complete and another between the two multiple-choice sections. Each time you leave and return to the testing room, you will be digitally fingerprinted or palm scanned. If you exceed the allotted time for your break, the excess time will be deducted from the next section of your exam. For more information on administrative regulations and testing procedures, visit **mba.com**.

Bring the Names of Five Business Schools You Wish to Receive Your Scores

You may select up to five schools to receive your scores before you take the test. Your registration fee will cover that cost. Before test day, decide which schools you want to get your GMAT scores and bring that list with you. You will not be able to change the list once you have made your selection.

THE CAT EXPLAINED

The computer-adaptive format of the GMAT takes some getting used to—in fact, it's pretty unusual at first. Here's how it works.

There's a large pool of potential questions ranging from moderately easy to very difficult. To start, you're given a question of moderate difficulty. If you get it right, the computer will give you a harder question next. But if you get it wrong, the computer will give you an easier question next. In other words, the computer scores each question and then uses that information—along with your previous responses and the requirements of the test design—to determine which question to present next. The process continues throughout, and the computer will have an accurate assessment of your ability level.

If you keep getting questions right, the test will get harder and harder; if you slip up and make some mistakes, it will adjust and start giving you easier problems. But if you begin to answer those easier problems correctly, the test will go back to the hard ones.

The GMAT is trying to find a level of difficulty at which you get the right answer half the time. Ideally, that's your "score level." The practical consequence for you, the test taker, is that you shouldn't be surprised to see a number of questions that you can narrow down to two answer choices but then struggle to figure out which is right. That would give you a 50 percent chance of getting the question right—exactly what the test is trying to achieve. You're not failing; the test is just doing its job.

You will see only one question at a time. The computer must score a question before providing you a new one, so you'll be required to answer every question. For this reason, too, once you have confirmed your response and moved on to the next question, you will not be able to return to a question. The computer has already scored your response and has selected a new question for you.

Because a string of wrong answers can significantly lower your score, making several random guesses at the end of a section is very dangerous. So whenever you don't know how to answer a question, eliminate whatever answer choices you can and then select the answer you think is best. Otherwise, you'll run out of time at the end of the section and be forced into a lower score.

Another major consequence of the GMAT format is that hard questions are worth more than easy ones. It has to be this way, because the very purpose of this adaptive format is to find out at what level you reliably get about half the questions right; that's your scoring level.

Imagine two students—one who does 10 basic questions, only half of which she gets right, and one who does 10 very hard questions, only half of which she gets right. The same number of questions has been answered correctly, but this does not reflect an equal ability.

In fact, the student who got 5 out of 10 hard questions wrong could still get a very high score on the GMAT. But to get to these tough questions, she first had to get medium-difficulty questions right.

So no matter how much you want to start practicing those tough questions now, first make sure that you can get most of the intermediate questions right. You can struggle with some tough questions and still earn a high score because if you dip back into the intermediate range, you'll get a bunch right and bounce right back up. But if you struggle at the intermediate questions, you'll never reach the high-scoring tough ones in the first place. GMAT success is built from the bottom up, not from the top down.

NAVIGATING THE GMAT: COMPUTER BASICS

Let's preview the primary computer functions that you will use to move around on the GMAT. This screen is typical for an adaptive test.

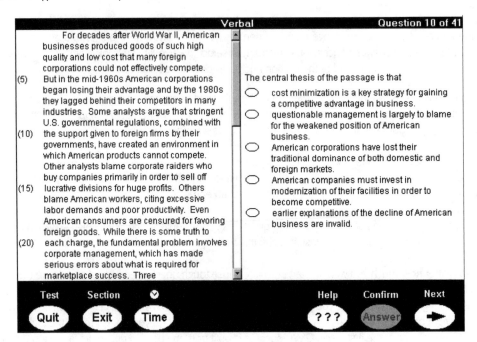

As you can see, there are empty bubbles for the answer choices—no letters (A), (B), (C), (D), (E). This is different from most multiple-choice tests.

To make the questions in this book appear as test-like as possible, the five answer choices in practice questions are not identified by letters. You will see blank ovals, just as you will on test day. However, for the purposes of discussion, we identify each answer choice using the corresponding letter in the answer explanation.

Here's what the various buttons do.

The Scroll Bar

Similar to the scroll bar on a Windows-style computer display, this scroll bar is a thin, vertical column with up and down arrows at the top and bottom. Clicking on the arrows moves you up or down the page you're reading.

The Next Button

Hit this when you want to move on to the next question. After you press Next, you must hit Confirm.

The Confirm Button

This button appears in a pop-up window after you click the Next button. The Confirm button tells the computer you are happy with your answer and are really ready to move to the next question. You cannot proceed until you have hit this button.

The Time Button

Clicking on this button turns the time display at the top of the screen on and off. When you have five minutes left in a section, the clock flashes, and the display changes from hours/minutes to hours/minutes/seconds.

The Help Button

This one leads to directions and other stuff from the tutorial. You should know all this already, and besides, the test clock won't pause just because you click on Help.

The Exit Button

This allows you to exit the section before the time is up. If you budget your time wisely, you should never have to use this button—time will run out just as you are finishing the section.

The Quit Button

Hitting this button ends the test.

PROS AND CONS OF THE COMPUTER-ADAPTIVE FORMAT

There are both good and annoying things about the GMAT's computer-adaptive format. The following are a few things you should be thankful for—or watch out for—as you prepare to try your luck on the test.

7 Good Things about the CAT

1. There's a timer at the top of the computer screen to help you pace yourself. (You can hide it if it distracts you.)
2. There will be only a few other test takers in the room with you—it won't be like taking an exam in one of those massive lecture halls with distractions everywhere.
3. You get an eight-minute pause between each section. The pause is optional, but you should always use it to relax and stretch.
4. You'll find the CAT much more convenient for your schedule than the pencil-and-paper exam. It's offered at hundreds of centers almost every day of the year.

5. Registering to take the exam is very easy, and sometimes you can sign up just a few days before you'd like to go. However, depending upon the time of the year and the availability of testing centers in your area, you may have to register several weeks in advance for a desired test date.

6. The CAT format gives you more time to spend on each question than you had on the paper-based test.

7. Perhaps the CAT's best feature is that it gives you an immediate score and your chosen schools will receive it just 20 days later.

7 Annoying Things about the CAT

1. You cannot skip around. You must answer the questions one at a time in the order the computer gives them to you. There is only one question on the screen at a time.

2. If you realize later that you answered a question incorrectly, you cannot go back and change your answer.

3. If the person next to you is noisy or distracting, the proctor cannot move you or the person, since your test is on the computer.

4. You cannot cross off an answer choice and banish it from your sight (it's on a computer screen, after all), so you have to be disciplined about not reconsidering choices you've already eliminated.

5. You have to scroll through Reading Comprehension passages, which means you won't be able to see the whole thing on the screen at once.

6. You can't write on your computer screen the way you can on the paper test, so you have to use the scratch paper they give you, which will be inconveniently located away from the computer screen.

7. Lastly, many people find that computer screens tire them and cause eyestrain—especially after four hours.

KAPLAN'S CAT STRATEGIES

Using certain CAT-specific strategies will have a direct, positive impact on your score:

- At the start of the section, each question you get right or wrong will rapidly move the computer's estimate of your score up or down. Your goal is to get the computer's estimate of your score up to where you're handling the hard questions. That's because getting a hard question right will help your score a lot but getting a hard question wrong will hurt your score only slightly.

- It's great to get as many of the first 10 questions right as you can, because this moves you very quickly into the high-value questions. But you can't afford to take much extra time to do so, because doing so will force you (1) not to answer several questions at the end, (2) to make many random guesses at the end, or (3) to rush your way into many careless errors at the end. Needless to say, each of those options would hurt your score. At Kaplan, we've run countless experiments on the GMAT scoring engine, and the best approach is always to move at a steady pace at the beginning, not taking much extra time.

- As you progress through the middle part of the section, try your best not to get several questions in a row wrong, as this will sink your score on the CAT. If you know that the previous question you answered was a blind guess, spend a little extra time trying to get the next one right.

- The CAT will switch from one question type to another within a section (going from Reading Comprehension to Sentence Correction, for example) without automatically showing the directions for each new question type. Knowing the format and directions of each GMAT question type beforehand will save you a lot of time—and aggravation—during the exam.

- Because the level of difficulty of questions on the CAT is not predictable, always be on the lookout for answer-choice traps.

- Because each right or wrong answer directly affects the next question you get, the CAT does not allow you to go back to questions you've already answered. In other words, you cannot go back to double-check your work. So be sure about your answers before moving on.

- If you're given a question you cannot answer, you'll have to guess. Guess intelligently and strategically by eliminating any answer choices that you know are wrong and guessing among those remaining.

- Don't get rattled if you keep seeing really tough questions. It just means you're doing very well! Keep it up!

PART TWO

Verbal Strategies

Chapter 2: **GMAT Sentence Correction**

Many people are surprised to discover that Sentence Correction questions are the most common question type on the Verbal Section of the GMAT. You'll probably see about 15 or 16 Sentence Correction questions out of the 41 questions on the Verbal Section of your GMAT, so they account for almost 40 percent of the entire section.

So why is grammar such a big deal on the GMAT? The GMAC and the schools it represents believe that the best managers are those who can communicate effectively, and knowing the rules of standard written English is part of being an effective communicator. The bad news about Sentence Correction questions is that they cover a range of grammar and style errors, some of which are so obscure that even good writers commit them.

The good news about Sentence Correction is that you don't need to be a grammar maven to do well on this question type. While there are lots of rules of standard written English, the GMAT most commonly concentrates on the following five:

1. Verb usage (proper agreement and correct tense)
2. Reference (proper use of pronouns and modifiers)
3. Parallel structure (consistency among items in a list or comparison)
4. Idioms (proper use of idiomatic expressions)
5. Style (avoiding excess verbiage, using active verbs, etc.)

Having a method for attacking Sentence Correction questions and reviewing the five rules of GMAT English will help you to maximize your performance on this question type.

ANATOMY OF A SENTENCE CORRECTION QUESTION

The first step towards doing your best on GMAT Sentence Corrections is to get familiar with the format. Let's take a look at the various parts of a typical Sentence Correction question.

The Directions

The directions for these questions look something like this:

Directions: The following question presents a sentence, part or all of which is underlined. Below each sentence you will find five ways to phrase the underlined portion. Choice (A) repeats the original version, while the other four choices are different. If the original seems best, choose choice (A). If not, choose one of the revisions.

This question tests correctness and effectiveness of expression. Choose an answer that follows the norms of standard written English: grammar, word choice, and sentence construction.

Choose the answer that produces the most effective sentence, aiming to eliminate awkwardness, ambiguity, redundancy, and grammatical error.

First, note that the first answer choice repeats what's underlined in the original sentence. Since the first thing you should do on a Sentence Correction question is to read the entire original sentence, this means you should *never bother reading the first answer choice*.

Second, always remember that you are looking for the best answer given, not the right answer. The test makers are skilled at finding sentences that obey the rules of standard written English without sounding particularly appealing. If the original sentence doesn't sound great, but you can't find anything specifically wrong with it and none of the other choices sound better, stick with the first choice.

Finally, note the wording the test makers use in distinguishing what makes one answer best. It should be "clear and exact, without awkwardness, redundancy, or ambiguity." Basically, this boils down to following the five basic rules of GMAT grammar (which we'll discuss later in the chapter), but if you're still struggling between two answer choices, go for the shortest answer that doesn't sound awkward and doesn't leave anything in doubt.

The Question and Answer Choices

1. A recent spate of news reports questioning the long-term health benefits of high-fat diets <u>have done little to convince its practitioners that they should follow more traditional weight-loss plans.</u>

Here's what a typical Sentence Correction sentence looks like. The first thing you should do on a Sentence Correction question is to *read the sentence in its entirety* and try to spot an error. If you spot an error, eliminate choice (A). Can you spot you spot any errors in this sentence? If you can't, there's another way to get to the correct answer . . .

- ⬭ have done little to convince its practitioners that they should follow more traditional weight-loss plans
- ⬭ have done little to convince their practitioners to follow more traditional weight-loss plans
- ⬭ has done little to convince its practitioners to follow more traditional weight-loss plans
- ⬭ has done little to convince practitioners of these diets to follow more traditional weight-loss plans
- ⬭ has done little to convince practitioners of these diets they should follow more traditional weight-loss plans

Go to the answer choices! Here's where you can isolate any error being tested, even if you couldn't spot it in the original sentence. The key is to scan the answer choices, looking for differences. Try reading vertically. What's the first difference you can spot among the answer choices? If you spotted *have* versus *has*, then you simply have to figure out which is correct, and eliminate answers with the wrong verb. You'll be left with either two or three choices.

Time to read vertically again and spot any other differences in the remaining choices. Eliminate choices as soon as you find a mistake, until only one choice remains. Then read your selected choice back into your sentence just to confirm that it makes sense. This is the gist of the Kaplan Three-Step Method for Sentence Corrections.

THE KAPLAN METHOD FOR SENTENCE CORRECTION

Now we come to the Kaplan Method for tackling a Sentence Correction.

Step 1: Read the Original Sentence Carefully, Looking for Errors

Read the sentence. Look for things that sound wrong but also keep your eyes peeled for signs of the classic errors that the GMAT loves to repeat. If you spot an error, eliminate (A) immediately. If you don't spot an error the first time through, don't bother rereading. You're no more likely to spot a problem the second time around—especially because there may not be an error at all! Instead, move straight to Step 2.

Step 2: Scan and Group the Answer Choices

Instead of wasting time reading each answer choice individually, quickly scan and compare the answers with one other. If you spotted an error in Step 1, sort the answer choices into two groups: those that do not fix the error (which you can eliminate) and those that correct it.

If you *didn't* spot an error, try to zero in on a grammatical or stylistic difference that splits the answer choices into distinct groups. This will let you identify one of the issues that the question is testing. Once you know what is being tested, you can apply your knowledge of English grammar to determine which group is correct—thereby eliminating multiple answers at once.

Step 3: Eliminate Choices Until Only One Remains

If more than one choice remains, go back to Step 2 and scan again to find another difference. Then eliminate accordingly. Repeat this process until only one answer remains.

Important Pacing Tip: If more than one choice remains after you have eliminated all of the answers that you are sure are wrong, just go with your best guess. If you don't know the rule by test day, you probably won't successfully teach it to yourself while taking the exam. You'll get a much higher score by investing that time in other questions.

If you are working on a quiz or a practice test, of course, reading the answer explanation closely will help you to learn the important rules so you can use them successfully on test day.

Now let's apply the Kaplan Method to the following Sentence Correction question:

> Several consumer protection agencies have filed suit, seeking to bar distributors from advertising treatments for baldness <u>that brings no discernible improvement and may even result in potential harm.</u>

- ⬭ that brings no discernible improvement and may even result in potential harm
- ⬭ that bring no discernible improvement and may even prove harmful
- ⬭ bringing no discernible improvement and even being harmful
- ⬭ that brings no discernible improvement and may even potentially result in harm being done
- ⬭ that bring no discernible improvement, maybe even resulting in harm

Step 1: Read the Original Sentence Carefully, Looking for Errors

The underlined phrase is a clause that is describing something in the first part of the sentence. (The use of the word *that* is a good clue.) What in the first part of the sentence "brings no discernible improvement" and may cause harm? *Treatments.* But you can't say *treatments brings*.

We've found a problem with this sentence (subject-verb agreement), so (A), the original structure, can't be correct.

Step 2: Scan and Group the Answer Choices

Now quickly scan among the choices, looking for any that repeat the error. That's (D).

If you didn't spot the error at first, you'd look for the main differences among the choices: two say *brings*, two say *bring*, and one says *bringing*. Which is correct?

Step 3: Eliminate Choices Until Only One Remains

If you spotted the error, you eliminated (A) and (D) as wrong, which leaves *bring* and *bringing*.

If you didn't spot the error, you'd now say to yourself, "Hmm...two answer choices say *brings*, two say *bring*—one is plural, the other singular. This is very likely about the subject-verb agreement. So what *brings* no improvement? Is it *baldness*? There's an *of* before *baldness*, so *baldness* can't be the subject. Plus "baldness brings no discernable improvement," just doesn't make sense. It has to be *treatments*. Now that makes sense! Sneaky, GMAT, but I figured it out!" Now you'd eliminate (A) and (D) and turn your attention to *bring/bringing*.

You'd eliminate *bringing*, either because you recognize that the continuous tense is awkward and unnecessary here or because you know that on the GMAT, *–ing* forms are almost always wrong in verb questions. Plus, only one answer choice uses *bringing*, so eliminate it and move on.

Scanning between (B) and (E), you spot a difference at the end: *and may even prove harmful* versus *maybe even resulting in harm*. *Prove* is parallel with *bring*, while *resulting* is not. Eliminate (E). That leaves only one answer, (B).

THE FIVE FUNDAMENTAL RULES OF GMAT ENGLISH

It's time for a quick grammar review. Fortunately, as noted earlier, GMAT Sentence Corrections do not test every variety of grammatical error. In fact, the test makers tend to recycle the same classic errors over and over again. Get to know the five fundamental rules of GMAT English and you'll do well on this question type. Let's take a look.

Rule 1: Verb Usage (agreement, correct tense)

Just about everyone knows that a verb should agree with the subject (singular or plural) of the sentence. So how do the GMAT writers manage to catch so many test takers with this rule? By finding ways to confuse the issue by separating the verb from the subject or by putting it before the subject, that's how. Take a look. Choose the best response in each of the following sentences:

 RULE

Make sure that each verb matches its subject, and that its tense fits the rest of the sentence.

1. Each of the entertainers involved in the festivities (was, were) paid in advance.
2. A series of sightings of UFOs (has, have) turned the sleepy town into a tourist mecca.
3. Neither the prosecutor's eloquent closing argument nor the mountains of incriminating evidence (was, were) able to convince the jury to find the defendant guilty.
4. There (is, are) a number of delicious ways to prepare artichokes.

You also have to make sure that the verb tense agrees with the sequence of events in the rest of the sentence. Depending on the sentence, the appropriate verb tense may be past, present, future, or something a bit more complicated. As a rule, you should keep the verb tense as simple as possible while still allowing for the sequence of events to make sense. Choose the right verb tenses in the following sentences:

5. The criminal escaped from custody and is believed (to flee, to have fled) the country.

6. I (did not see, had not seen, have not seen) him since last Saturday.

7. She already (closed, has closed, had closed) the door behind her when she realized that she (wasn't, won't be, wouldn't be) able to get back in later.

Answers and Explanations

1. *Each . . . was* paid in advance. "Each" is always singular. Ignore the prepositional phrases containing plurals that follow the subject. They're there to confuse you.

2. A *series . . . has* turned the sleepy town . . . . The subject is *series*, which is always singular. Watch out for subjects like *series*, *string*, *spate*, and *succession*, which are often followed by prepositional phrases containing lots of plurals, but are still singular subjects.

3. Neither the prosecutor's eloquent closing argument nor the *mountains* of incriminating evidence *were* able to convince the jury to find the defendant guilty. In *neither . . . nor* sentences, the verb has to agree with the subject following *nor*—in this case *mountains*, which is plural. Likewise in *either . . . or* sentences, the verb must agree with the subject following *or*.

4. There *are a number* of delicious ways . . . . In "There is . . . " and "There are . . . " sentences, the subject follows the verb; here the subject "a number of delicious ways" is plural ("a number of"—meaning "several"—will always signal a plural subject on the GMAT).

5. The criminal escaped from custody and is believed *to have fled* the country. The criminal has already *escaped*, and so the logical belief is that he has already *fled* the country.

6. I *have not seen* him since last Saturday. The "since last Saturday" in the sentence tells you that the (non)activity under discussion began in the past and continues into the present; thus you should use the present perfect tense, *have not seen*.

7. She already *had closed* the door behind her when she realized that she *wouldn't be* able to get back in later. When the rest of the sentence is in the past tense (as in "she realized") and the verb in question refers to an action that occurred *before* that, you should use the past perfect tense (here, it's *had closed*). And when the verb in question refers to the future as contemplated in the past, you should use the past tense of *will, would*, as in *wouldn't be*.

For a more exhaustive review of verb tenses and agreement, check out the Grammar Reference Guide in appendix 1 of this book.

 RULE

Make sure that each pronoun clearly and correctly refers to one and only one thing (or group), and that each modifying phrase is placed as close as possible to what it modifies and clearly and correctly refers to what it modifies.

Rule 2: Reference (proper use of pronouns and modifiers)

To break down this rule a bit, there are two things to look for when you see a pronoun underlined (especially *it, its, they, them, their, that, those,* and *which*). First, does the pronoun agree with the noun it is replacing (singular with singular and plural with plural)? Second, is it absolutely clear what noun the pronoun is replacing? If there's any doubt or ambiguity, the pronoun use is wrong. Choose the best response in each of the following sentences:

1. Although the company had promised to maintain operational factories within the city limits, (it, they) later reneged on the agreement.

2. If the partners cannot resolve their differences, the courts may have to do (it, so).

3. After Orson Welles created an unflattering portrait of newspaper mogul William Randolph Hearst in the movie *Citizen Kane*, (he, Hearst) set about to destroy (his, Welles's) career and reputation.

Modifying phrases must also clearly and correctly refer to what they modify, which means they should be placed as close as possible to what they modify. On the GMAT, these phrases most often begin the sentence and are followed by a comma; what follows the comma should be the subject of the phrase. For instance, if a sentence begins "Born in a log cabin," you should expect that "Abraham Lincoln" will follow that comma.

Misplaced modifiers can occur anywhere in a sentence, however, so the best rule once again is to avoid any possibility of ambiguity. And if a phrase seems to occur in different parts of the sentence as you examine the answer choices, ask yourself: What does that phrase modify? Where does it belong? Finally, you may have to choose between an adverb (which usually ends in *-ly*) and an adjective; if so, ask yourself whether the word modifies a noun (in which case it should be an adjective) or a verb or another adjective (in which case it should be an adverb). Try your hand at the following:

4. While eating spaghetti, (a meatball rolled, I let a meatball roll) off my plate.

5. He laid the trousers (flat, flatly) upon the table.

Answers and Explanations

1. Although the *company* had promised . . . , *it* later reneged . . . .Watch out for collective nouns like *company*, *committee*, *group*, *gang*, etc., which require singular pronouns.

2. . . . the courts may have to do *so*. Using *it* would make no sense here. What does *it* refer to? Since we're not referring to an antecedent noun here, the proper choice is *so*.

3. After Orson Welles created an unflattering portrait of newspaper mogul William Randolph Hearst in the movie *Citizen Kane*, *Hearst* set about to destroy *Welles's* career and reputation. Using pronouns would have led to ambiguity in this sentence as either man could have set out to destroy the other's (or even his own) reputation.

4. While eating spaghetti, *I let a meatball roll* off my plate. Unless the meatball was in fact eating spaghetti as it rolled off the plate, it should be assumed that the subject of the modifying phrase "While eating spaghetti" is "I."

5. He laid the trousers *flat* upon the table. The modifier here refers to the *trousers*, and not the verb *laid*, and so adjective form *flat* is correct.

Rule 3: Parallel Structure (consistency among items in a list or comparison)

The basic idea behind parallel structure is pretty simple. Ideas with the same importance and function in a sentence should be expressed in the same grammatical form—all nouns, all verbs, or all whatever. Any time you recognize items being listed, be on the lookout for parallel structure. Try to pick the correct responses to the following:

 RULE

Make sure that similar elements in a list or series have similar constructions, and that comparisons are made only between the same sorts of elements.

1. The city's decay stems from governmental mismanagement, increasing unemployment, and (downtown businesses are relocating, the relocation of businesses) outside the city.

2. I remember my aunt making her own dandelion wine and (playing, that she played) the fiddle.

3. To visualize success is not the same as (to achieve, achieving) it.

Likewise, comparisons must also exhibit parallel structure—and more than that. Most faulty comparisons relate to the notion that you can't compare apples and oranges. You don't merely want comparisons to be grammatically similar; they must be logically similar as well. You have to compare one individual to another, one quality to another, one verb to another, etc. Be on the lookout for faulty comparisons, and try the following:

4. Even though our stands stood side by side, I sold more lemonade than (the girl next door, the girl next door did).

5. The article questioned the popularity of jazz compared to (classical music, that of classical music).

6. The challenger weighed 20 pounds less than (the defender, that of the defender).

Answers and Explanations

1. The city's decay stems from governmental *mismanagement*, increasing *unemployment*, and *the relocation of downtown businesses* outside the city. The list here is of nouns: mismanagement . . . unemployment . . . relocation.

2. I remember my aunt *making* her own dandelion wine and *playing* the fiddle.

3. *To visualize* success is not the same as *to achieve* it.

4. Even though our stands were side by side, *I sold more* lemonade *than the girl next door did*. When you are comparing actions as here (how much *I sold* to how much *the girl next door sold*), you need to include that second verb "did" to make the comparison clear.

5. The article questioned *the popularity of jazz* compared to *that of classical music*. Otherwise, the article would be comparing *popularity* to *music*.

6. The *challenger* weighed 20 pounds less than *the defender*. Here, you're comparing people.

Rule 4: Idioms (proper use of idiomatic expressions)

 RULE

Use correct idioms. There really is no rule for idiom usage, just a "right" way of saying things. Certain expressions, often involving prepositions, have established themselves as correct in standard English.

As anyone who's ever studied a foreign language can attest, learning proper idioms can be extremely annoying because there is no general rule, only lists to memorize. When it comes to GMAT English, either your ear will recognize the correct idiom, or you should take the time to learn the idioms that appear over and over again on the GMAT. Try out your ear for idioms on the following:

1. Matthew Brady is regarded (as, to be) one of the greatest nineteenth-century American photographers.

2. The destruction of the tropical rainforest is generally (considered, considered as, considered to be) a major threat to the environment.

3. It took me four times as long to write the report collaboratively (as, than) it would have taken by myself.

4. Her client didn't tell her (if, whether) he had sent his payment yet.

5. The movie's ending was different (than, from) that of the book.

Also note that many idioms also set up comparisons, and thus must be followed by parallel constructions (e.g., "both A and B"). Try the following.

6. Jewel is not only a great singer, (and also, but also, but is also) a talented poet.
7. I (either must read, must either read, must read either) the newspaper or listen to the radio before I go to work.

Answers and Explanations

1. Matthew Brady is *regarded as* one of the greatest nineteenth-century American photographers.
2. The destruction of the tropical rainforest is generally *considered* a major threat to the environment. (While "considered to be" is also technically correct, it will never be correct on the GMAT.)
3. It took me four times *as long* to write the report collaboratively *as* it would have taken by myself. (Use *than* when preceded by an -er word and *as* when preceded by as or so, e.g., *longer than, as long as*.)
4. Her client didn't tell her *whether* he had sent his payment yet. (On the GMAT, *whether* will always beat *if*.)
5. The movie's ending was different *from* that of the book.
6. Jewel is *not only* a great singer, *but also* a talented poet. (not only A but also B)
7. I *must either read* the newspaper or listen to the radio before I go to work. (either A or B)

For a more exhaustive list of idioms that commonly appear on the GMAT, be sure to check out the Common GMAT Idioms in appendix 3 of this book.

Rule 5: Style (effective expression)

Some errors are best classified as problems of "style"—that is, as problems of ineffective expression. The most common of these on the GMAT is using too many words to get an idea across. Sometimes the problem is outright redundancy, but more often the wording is just needlessly verbose. Another common style error is using a passive verb when the sentence could easily be written using an active verb.

 RULE

Eliminate unnecessary wording and redundancy. Avoid passive verbs wherever possible.

Try rewriting the following sentences to correct for errors of style, and then compare your final versions to ours:

1. There are many children who believe in Santa Claus but there are few adults who do.

_____

2. The country's procedures for the processing of visas are extremely inefficient.

_____

3. The shrine is at least 2,000 years old or older.

_____

4. Because I have studied the five rules of GMAT grammar, therefore I will do well on Sentence Correction.

_____

5. *A Confederacy of Dunces* has been bought and enjoyed by millions of readers since it was first published in 1974.

_____

Answers and Explanations

1. Many children believe in Santa Claus but few adults do. "There is/are" sentences are often needlessly wordy and therefore wrong on GMAT Sentence Correction.

2. The country's procedures for processing visas are extremely inefficient.

3. The shrine is at least 2,000 years old. The redundant phrase *or older* is already implied by *at least*.

4. Because I have studied the five rules of GMAT grammar, I will do well on Sentence Correction. *Because* implies that the second part of the sentence is the conclusion, so *therefore* here is redundant and wrong.

5. Millions of readers have bought and enjoyed *A Confederacy of Dunces* since it was first published in 1974.

PRACTICE QUESTIONS

Now that you know the five big rules of GMAT English, it's time to try out your knowledge on some practice Sentence Correction questions. Although the five big rules explain the great majority of Sentence Correction errors, the Grammar Reference Guide in appendix 1 of this book offers a more thorough treatment of these rules, as well as all the possible grammatical rules and errors that could appear in these questions. Make sure to apply the Kaplan Method as you answer the following questions. Answers and explanations follow.

1. Nineteenth-century authors often included encyclopedic information in their novels; Melville's famous chapter of the physiology on whales, <u>contained as it is in</u> his masterwork *Moby-Dick*, serves as a perfect example of this phenomenon.

    ⬭ contained as it is in

    ⬭ contained as it is within

    ⬭ contained in

    ⬭ found contained in

    ⬭ being found contained in

2. Due to the limitations imposed by the speed of light, the visible universe <u>is estimated as</u> a mere fraction of the total universe.

    ⬭ is estimated as

    ⬭ is estimated to be

    ⬭ is estimated at

    ⬭ estimated to be

    ⬭ estimated at

3. For over thirty years, Dr. Jane Goodall has conducted field studies of large primate species and <u>shares her findings with the general public in an effort</u> to promote conservation of these species and their habitats.

    ⬭ shares her findings with the general public in an effort

    ⬭ has shared her findings with the general public so as

    ⬭ shared her findings with the general public in an effort

    ⬭ will share her findings with the general public so as

    ⬭ would share her findings with the general public in an effort

4. Cattle were domesticated both for the uses made of the animal—food and leather—<u>but also for</u> the labor the animal could provide.

    ⬭ but also for

    ⬭ and for

    ⬭ or for

    ⬭ but also

    ⬭ and also

5. Recent surveys indicate that, contrary to popular belief, total abstinence from alcohol does not correlate <u>as strongly with good health as does moderate drinking</u>.

    ◯ as strongly with good health as does moderate drinking
    ◯ strongly with good health, like moderate drinking does
    ◯ as strongly with good health as does moderately drinking
    ◯ as strongly with good health as with moderate drinking
    ◯ as strongly with good health as moderate drinking

6. Despite <u>the platform of the Republican Party supporting the measure, they keep voting</u> against campaign finance reform in Congress.

    ◯ the platform of the Republican Party supporting the measure, they keep voting
    ◯ the Republican Party's platform supporting the measure, they keep voting
    ◯ the Republicans' platform supporting the measure, it keeps voting
    ◯ the Republican Party's platform supporting the measure, party members keep voting
    ◯ the supporting measure of the platform of the Republican Party, they keep voting

7. <u>The creation of an independent treasury, establishing lower tariffs, and purchasing</u> the Oregon Territory, all credited to the presidency of James Knox Polk, are among the significant accomplishments that persuade historians to rank this former governor of Tennessee well as a U.S. president.

    ◯ The creation of an independent treasury, establishing lower tariffs, and purchasing
    ◯ The creation of an independent treasury, securing lower tariffs as well as purchasing
    ◯ The creation of an independent treasury, the establishment of lower tariffs, and the purchase of
    ◯ Creating an independent treasury, securing lower tariffs, and purchasing
    ◯ Creating an independent treasury, the securing of lower tariffs, and the purchasing of

8. In many coastal New England towns, <u>the fisherman still operates as they have</u> for generations, displaying and selling their catch dockside at the end of each day.

    ◯ the fisherman still operates as they have
    ◯ the fisherman still operates as was done
    ◯ fishermen still operate as they have done
    ◯ the fisherman still operates as he has
    ◯ fishermen still operate as they had

9. The average salary of new jobs <u>is expected to rise in the near future as jobs become available in high-paying industries</u>.

   ○ is expected to rise in the near future as jobs become available in high-paying industries

   ○ are expected to rise in the near future as jobs become available in high-paying industries

   ○ are expected to rise in the near future through jobs becoming available in high-paying industries

   ○ would be expected to rise in the near future through jobs becoming available in high-paying industries

   ○ will rise in the near future because jobs in high-paying industries are expected to become available

10. Pablo Picasso's genius is fully revealed only when one considers the various facets of his work as they developed through many artistic phases, <u>beginning with his Red period, continuing through his Blue period, and finishing with his period of Cubism</u>.

    ○ beginning with his Red period, continuing through his Blue period, and finishing with his period of Cubism

    ○ beginning with his Red period, continuing through his Blue period, and finishing with his Cubist period

    ○ beginning with his Red period, and continuing through his Blue period and his Cubist period

    ○ beginning with his Red period phase, his Blue period phase, and his phase of Cubism

    ○ beginning with his Red period, his Blue period, and his period of Cubism

11. Many climatologists now suspect that the effects of global warming will include unusual temperature fluctuations throughout the northern and southern hemispheres that <u>far exceeds what scientists were predicting only a few years ago</u>.

    ○ far exceeds what scientists were predicting only a few years ago

    ○ far exceeds those predicted by scientists only a few years ago

    ○ exceeds by far that which scientists had predicted only a few years ago

    ○ exceed by far those that scientists had predicted only a few years ago

    ○ far exceed what scientists were predicting only a few years ago

12. The ancient Sumerians are credited <u>as having</u> created the first phonetic writing system as long ago as 3100 B.C.

    ○ as having

    ○ to have

    ○ for having

    ○ with having

    ○ as being the ones who

13. Several stock market analysts now report that the plummeting <u>values of many high-tech stocks have fallen so as to make</u> them once again attractive to investors.

   ⬭ values of many high-tech stocks have fallen so as to make

   ⬭ high-tech stock values have fallen, making

   ⬭ descent of many high-tech stock values have made

   ⬭ values of many high-tech stocks are making

   ⬭ values of many high-tech stocks have fallen, which has made

14. Unlike <u>its fellow Baltic nations, Latvia and Lithuania, the economy of Estonia grew at an astonishing rate in the late 1990s, and at the end of the decade it was placed on the fast track to join</u> the European Union.

   ⬭ its fellow Baltic nations, Latvia and Lithuania, the economy of Estonia grew at an astonishing rate in the late 1990s, and at the end of the decade it was placed on the fast track to join

   ⬭ its fellow Baltic nations, Latvia and Lithuania, Estonia's economy grew at an astonishing rate in the late 1990s, and at the end of the decade was placed on the fast track to join

   ⬭ its fellow Baltic nations, Latvia and Lithuania, Estonia's economy grew at an astonishing rate in the late 1990s, and at the end of the decade they were placed on the fast track to join

   ⬭ Latvia and Lithuania, its fellow Baltic nations, the economy of Estonia grew at an astonishing rate in the late 1990s, and at the end of the decade was placed on the fast track to join

   ⬭ Latvia and Lithuania, its fellow Baltic nations, Estonia possessed an economy that grew at an astonishing rate in the late 1990s, and at the end of the decade the country was placed on the fast track to join

15. <u>By the number of carbons in the compound's longest chain, a hydrocarbon's standard name is partly determined.</u>

   ⬭ By the number of carbons in the compound's longest chain, a hydrocarbon's standard name is partly determined

   ⬭ The number of carbons in the compound's longest continuous chain enables partial determination of the standard name of a hydrocarbon

   ⬭ The standard name of a hydrocarbon is partly determined by the number of carbons in the compound's longest continuous chain

   ⬭ Counting the number of carbons in the compound's longest continuous chain enables partially determining a hydrocarbon's standard name

   ⬭ As the carbons on a hydrocarbon's longest continuous chain are counted, so that partially determines the compound's standard name

ANSWERS AND EXPLANATIONS

1. C	6. D	11. E
2. B	7. C	12. D
3. C	8. C	13. D
4. B	9. A	14. E
5. A	10. B	15. C

1.

When you suspect that excess verbiage may be at issue, check to see whether the shortest choice makes sense. In this case, it does.

2.

The correct idiom is "estimate(d) to be" (and of course you need "is estimated to be" because it's not the universe that's doing the estimating).

3.

Sometimes determining the proper verb tense is simply a matter of maintaining the same tense as the other verbs in the sentence (parallel structure), as in "Dr. Jane Goodall has *conducted* . . . and *shared* . . . ." Choice (B), with "has shared," would also work, but it contains that awkward construction "so as," which is never correct on the GMAT (although "so . . . as to be . . . " often is correct).

4.

The key here is to recognize that the "both" in the sentence sets up the parallel-structure idiom "both *A* and *B*," so we can anticipate the correct answer here to be "*both* for the uses . . . *and* for the labor," which is exactly what (B) gives us. By the way, "and also" is considered redundant on the GMAT. Moreover, phrases between dashes, as in "—food and leather—" here, are usually thrown into Sentence Correction sentences just to confuse the issue. They should always be ignored on your first reading of the sentence.

5.

The first thing to recognize is that there's a comparison going on here, so we need to make sure that it's an appropriate comparison. The comparison here is between how strongly total abstinence from alcohol correlates with good health and how strongly moderate drinking correlates with good health. Choices (B) and (D) mangle the sense of that comparison. Choice (C) is out because "drinking" here is being used as a noun, so it should be modified by the adjective "moderate," not the adverb "moderately." Finally, (E) is out because that second verb, "does," is necessary to convey the sense that the comparison is between how one "correlates" and how the other "correlates."

6.

Be suspicious anytime you see *they* or *it* in the underlined portion of the sentence or among the answer choices. For starters, (A) is out because there is no antecedent plural noun that "they" could be referring to. (B) and (E) are out for the same reason. And (C) is out because the "it" here makes it sound as if the platform is doing the voting in Congress. Only (D) avoids these pronoun pitfalls.

7.

Look for consistency among items in a list. (A) and (B) are out, "The creation . . . securing . . . purchasing,"
as is (E), "Creating . . . the securing of . . . the purchasing of . . . ." Both (C) and (D) are internally
consistent, but since the list is supposed to refer to accomplishments, (C), a list of nouns, "The creation . . .
the establishment . . . the purchase," makes more sense than (D), a list of gerunds, "Creating . . .
establishing . . . purchasing." (Standard noun forms are generally considered preferable to gerunds on the
GMAT.)

8.

You have to read the entire sentence to know whether to go singular or plural here. Because the
sentence refers to "their catch," you need plural "fishermen" and plural "they." That eliminates
everything but (C) and (E). And (E) is out because under discussion is a practice that has continued
from the past into the present, so the proper verb tense is present perfect, as in "fishermen still
operate as they *have done* . . . ."

9.

The subject is "salary," so the verb should be singular, which eliminates (B) and (C). As written, "is
expected to rise in the near future" makes good sense; there's no need to complicate the verb tense,
as (D) does. (E) scrambles the meaning of the sentence, turning an expectation into a fact.

10.

Again, we're looking for consistency throughout this sequence. (A) is out because after "Red
period" and "Blue period," why change it to "period of Cubism"? Choices (D) and (E) have similar
inconsistencies. Choice (B) makes the fix we want: "Red period . . . Blue period . . . Cubist period."
Choice (C) also has this fix, but loses the sequential sense contained in the original sentence of
"beginning with . . . continuing with . . . and finishing with . . . ."

11.

A vertical scan reveals a choice between *exceeds* and *exceed*, so ask yourself, what is the subject
of the verb? The answer is *fluctuations*, which is plural, so the proper verb form is *exceed*—(A), (B),
and (C) are out. And (D) is not only wordier than (E), but it also makes inappropriate use of the past
perfect verb tense *had predicted* (which should be used only when you're discussing something that
occurred before something else you're also discussing that occurred in the past).

12.

The idiom is "credit(ed) with"—learn it.

13.

In this sentence, there's an out-and-out redundancy; "plummeting" means falling, so get rid of any
answer choices that discuss falling, including (A), (B), and (E). Choice (C) is also a bit off, with its
"plummeting descent." Choice (D) is the only choice that avoids redundancy and makes sense.

14.

Be on the lookout for modifying phrases followed by commas at the beginning of a sentence. In this
case, all the sentences begin with variations of "Unlike its fellow Baltic nations, Latvia and Lithuania," so
what follows this introduction should in fact be a Baltic nation—that is, Estonia, not Estonia's economy.
Only (E) corrects this misplaced modifier error.

15.

When the entire sentence is underlined, style problems are often found in many of the answer choices, so read and eliminate aggressively. Here choice (A) needlessly complicates the sentence by sticking the long and confusing prepositional phrase "By the number . . . ") at the beginning of the sentence (it's also a misplaced modifier, as the phrase should be next to "determined"). In choice (B), does the wording "enables partial determination of the standard name" strike you as a bit off? Surely there must be a better way of phrasing this sentence. Choice (C) is the first version that makes sense. Choice (D) is off: "Counting . . . enables . . . partially determining . . . ." And (E) not only mangles the sense of the sentence, but is not even a complete sentence. Moral of the story: You don't have to know what stylistic error a sentence is committing, so long as your ear can distinguish effective expression from ineffective expression. (Also, note that the passive voice is not *always* wrong. In this case, the clearest way to express the idea was to use the passive "*is . . . determined.*")

Chapter 3: **The Basic Principles of GMAT Reading**

Usually we read to learn something or to pass the time pleasantly. Neither of these goals has much to do with the GMAT. On test day, we have a very specific goal—to get as many right answers as we can. So our reading needs to be tailored to that goal.

Here are the four basic things you need to do to accomplish this.

LOOK FOR THE TOPIC AND SCOPE OF THE PASSAGE

Think of the Topic as the first big idea that comes along. Almost always, it will be right there in the first sentence. It will be something broad, far too big to discuss in the 150–450 words that most GMAT passages provide. Here's an example of how a passage might begin:

> The great migration of European intellectuals to the United States in the second quarter of the 20th century prompted a transmutation in the character of Western social thought.

What's the Topic? The migration of European intellectuals to the United States in the second quarter of the 20th century. It would also be okay to say that the Topic is the effects of that migration on Western social thought. Topic is a very broad concept, so you really don't need to worry about how exactly you word it. You just need to get a good idea of what the passage is talking about so you feel more comfortable reading.

Now, as to Scope. Think of Scope as a narrowing of the Topic. You're looking for an idea that the author might reasonably focus on for the length of a GMAT passage. If the topic is "the migration of European intellectuals to the United States in the second quarter of the 20th century," then perhaps the Scope will be "some of the effects of that migration upon Western social thought." More likely it will be more specific: "one aspect of Western social thought affected by the migration." But perhaps something unexpected will come along. Might the passage compare two different migrations? Or contrast two different effects? We need to think critically about what's coming and look for clues in the text that let us know on what specific subject(s) the author intends to focus.

Finding the Scope is critically important to doing well on Reading Comprehension. As in Critical Reasoning, most Reading Comprehension wrong answers are wrong because they are outside the

Scope of the passage. It's highly unlikely that there will be a "topic sentence" in the traditional sense—but the first paragraph probably will have some indication of what the author intends to focus on.

Note: Some passages are only one paragraph long. In these cases, the Topic will still be in the first sentence. The passage will probably (but not necessarily) narrow down to Scope somewhere in the first third of the paragraph, as the author doesn't have much text to work with and needs to get down to business quickly.

GET THE GIST OF EACH PARAGRAPH AND NOTE ITS STRUCTURAL ROLE IN THE PASSAGE

The paragraph is the main structural unit of any passage. At first, you don't know Topic or Scope, so you have to read the first paragraph pretty closely. But once you get a sense of where the passage is going, all you need to do is understand what role each new paragraph plays. Ask yourself the following:

- Why did the author include this paragraph?
- What's discussed here that's different from the content of the paragraph before?
- What bearing does this paragraph have on the author's main idea?
- What role do the details play?

Notice that last question—don't ask yourself, "What does this mean?" but rather, "Why is it here?" Many GMAT passages try to swamp you with boring, dense, and sometimes confusing details. Consider this paragraph, which might show up on a difficult science-based passage:

The Burgess Shale yielded a surprisingly varied array of fossils. Early chordates were very rare, but there were prodigious numbers of complex forms not seen since. *Hallucigenia*, so named for a structure so bizarre that scientists did not know which was the dorsal and which the ventral side, had fourteen legs. *Opabinia* had five eyes and a long proboscis. This amazing diversity led Gould to believe that it was highly unlikely that the eventual success of chordates was a predictable outcome.

Wow. Pretty dense stuff. But if we don't worry about understanding all of the science jargon and focus on the gist of the paragraph and *why* the details are there, things get easier. The first sentence isn't that bad:

The Burgess Shale yielded a surprisingly varied array of fossils.

Okay, the "Burgess Shale," whatever that is, had a lot of different kinds of fossils.

Early chordates were very rare, but there were prodigious numbers of complex forms not seen since. *Hallucigenia*, so named for a structure so bizarre that scientists did not know which was the dorsal and which the ventral side, had fourteen legs. *Opabinia* had five eyes and a long proboscis.

Oh, this is just a list of the different kinds of fossils and some facts about them. Not a lot of "chordates," whatever they are, but lots of other stuff.

This amazing diversity led Gould to believe that it was highly unlikely that the eventual success of chordates was a predictable outcome.

Notice how the beginning of this sentence tells us *why* those annoyingly dense details are there; they are the facts that led Gould to a belief—namely that the rise of "chordates" couldn't have been predicted. So, on our noteboard, we'd jot down something like this:

Evidence for Gould's belief—chordate success not predictable.

Doing this for every paragraph allows you to create a map of the passage's overall structure. We'll call this a "Passage Map" from here on. This map will help you keep a clear understanding of the "big picture." And making it will give you a sense of mastery over the passage, even when it deals with a subject you don't know much about.

LOOK FOR OPINIONS, THEORIES, AND POINTS OF VIEW—ESPECIALLY THE AUTHOR'S

An important part of critical reading is distinguishing between factual assertions and opinions/interpretations. Reading Comprehension passages are built on the opinions/interpretations, and you should pay the most attention to them.

Consider how the critical reader would react to this:

Abraham Lincoln is traditionally viewed as an advocate of freedom because he issued the Emancipation Proclamation and championed the Thirteenth Amendment, which ended legal slavery in the United States. And indeed this achievement cannot be denied. But he also set uncomfortable precedents for the curtailing of civil liberties.

"Ah," the critical reader says, "that phrase *traditionally viewed* lets me know how people usually think about Lincoln. But the author might not completely agree. Sure enough, I see that she brings up the fact that he restricted civil liberties. And the word *uncomfortable* is a pretty big sign that the author is not at all pleased with Lincoln because of it! I should note, though, that the phrase *this achievement cannot be denied* means that she won't go so far as to say that Lincoln was an enemy of freedom."

"In fact," the reader continues, "I bet I know what the author is going to do structurally. She'll have to have at least one paragraph describing these *precedents* and how they restricted civil liberties. It might even be possible, since she uses the word *precedents*, that she goes on to describe how later presidents used Lincoln's actions as justification for their own restrictions. Holy smokes! Three sentences in, and I bet I've got the passage already!"

Put together, the passage's structure and its opinions/theories (especially the author's) will lead you to understand the author's primary purpose in writing the passage. This is critical, as most GMAT passages have a question that directly asks for that purpose. For the Lincoln passage, you might get a question like this:

Which of the following best represents the main idea of the passage?

○ The Emancipation Proclamation had both positive and negative effects.

○ Lincoln's presidency laid the groundwork for future restrictions of personal freedoms.

○ The traditional image of Lincoln as a national hero must be overturned.

○ Lincoln used military pressure to influence state legislatures.

○ Abraham Lincoln was an advocate of freedom.

Just from a critical reading of the first few sentences, you could eliminate (A) as being a distortion of the first and third sentences, (C) as being too extreme because of the *cannot be denied* phrase in the passage, (D) as out of scope—either too narrow or just not there at all, and (E) as missing the author's big point—that Lincoln helped restrict civil liberties. That leaves (B) as the correct answer. And just like that, you've gotten a right answer and increased your score!

DON'T OBSESS OVER DETAILS

On the GMAT, you'll need to read only for short-term—as opposed to long-term—retention. When you finish the questions on a certain passage, that passage is over, gone, done with. You're promptly free to forget everything about it.

What's more, there's certainly no need to memorize—or even fully comprehend—details. Furthermore, you can hurt your score by reading the details too closely. Here's how:

- **Wasted time.** Remember, there will only be three or four questions per passage. They can't possibly ask you about all the little details. So don't waste your valuable time by reading what you don't need to know! If you do, you won't have nearly enough time to deal with the questions.

- **Extra-tempting wrong answers.** There just isn't time to read and understand fully every last little detail, so trying to do so inevitably causes us to jumble all the details together in a confusing blob. Since most of the wrong answers in GMAT Reading Comprehension come from irrelevant or distorted bits of the passage, uncritical readers find almost every answer choice tempting! The critical reader who doesn't read the details too closely doesn't recognize those answers as familiar and thus isn't tempted by them. Instead, she takes advantage of the open-book nature of the test to find the answer when asked.

- **Losing the big picture.** It's very easy to miss the forest for the trees. If you get too drawn into the details, you can pass right by the emphasis and opinion signals that you'll need to understand the author's main purpose.

Here's a great trick for cutting through confusing, detail-laden sentences: Focus on the subjects and verbs first, throwing away modifying phrases, and don't worry about confusing terminology. Consider the following detail-laden passage:

The coral polyps secrete calceous exoskeletons, which cement themselves into an underlayer of rock, while the algae deposit still more calcium carbonate, which reacts with sea salt to create an even tougher limestone layer. All of this accounts for the amazing renewability of the coral reefs despite the endless erosion caused by wave activity.

Yuck. But look at what happens if we distill this to main subjects and verbs, ignore modifiers, and don't worry about words we don't understand:

Coral polyps (whatever they are) secrete something . . . and algae deposit something. This accounts for the amazing renewability of the coral reefs.

Not too bad! And now the bulkiness of that first sentence isn't slowing us down, so we can understand its role in the big picture.

GETTING THE GIST EXERCISE

Here's an exercise designed to give you some additional practice at "getting the gist" of GMAT text. When tackling GMAT prose in this way becomes second nature, your timing improves—you get through the passages much faster—and your ability to answer questions improves as well, because getting the gist is all about thinking about difficult prose and interpreting it.

> The "Robber Baron" industrialists of the late 19th and early 20th centuries are often portrayed as having no interest in the well-being of society as a whole in their ruthless pursuit of power and personal fortunes. Quite apart from the incidental benefits they provided to society through industrial development, this view ignores the philanthropic endeavors with which most of the Robber Barons were associated. Admittedly a good deal of their philanthropy took the form of bequests; still, these industrialists are responsible for many of our best museums and symphony halls, and the foundations they established continue to rank among the most important sources of charity to this day.

Keeping in mind the issues of topic, scope, and purpose, sum up the gist of this paragraph in one sentence, using your own words as much as possible. Then read on to compare your version with ours.

What this author is basically saying is:

_____

_____

Here's one way to sum up that paragraph:

> Contrary to popular belief, turn-of-the-century "fat cats" did a lot of things (like donating money) to make society better.

This version has hit on the right topic ("Robber Baron" industrialists) and scope (their concern, or lack of same, for society during the late 19th and early 20th centuries). Just as importantly, it's got the author's purpose right. It would be a distortion, for instance, to say that this author is out to whitewash the Robber Barons, to argue that they were totally selfless. There's no attempt here to deny that these guys were out to make money for themselves. What the author wants to do is acknowledge that they also score some points on the "Helping Society" side of the ledger, in contrast to the prevailing view. "They weren't all bad" is the bottom line.

What's important to note is that this paragraph, like so many other GMAT passages (in both Reading Comprehension and Critical Reasoning), is contrasting a common view with the author's own view; and as long as you get the gist of each of those viewpoints, you'll be okay. You don't have to underline or memorize all the details—all the specific examples of Robber Baron largesse—unless and until questions demand it. As long as you've gotten the gist of the text, you're armed well enough to move on.

Try the same process with the following paragraphs, reading and distilling them one at a time. Remember:

- Look for the Topic and Scope of the passage.
- Get the gist of each paragraph and its structural role in the passage.
- Look for opinions, theories, and points of view—especially the author's.
- Don't obsess over details.

1. It is a commonplace observation that people have become much more sophisticated about evaluating media-delivered messages than used to be the case. But take a closer look. Media celebrities still act as spokespeople to persuade the public to buy every kind of product from automotive parts to cell phones. Political campaigns are waged entirely on the basis of 30-second television spots. People can be stirred to favor foreign intervention in response to television images. How sophisticated is that?

What this author is basically saying is:

_____

_____

_____

2. Observers moved by the plight of a country in the throes of famine will sometimes call for the international community to act. Unfortunately, the solution is often more complicated than first appears; if it weren't, the country would be able to solve the problem itself. Famines are usually caused by civil strife. In order to alleviate the famine, the international community must send in a "peacekeeping force" to resolve the dispute. That means they must either come down in favor of one side, often without understanding the issues at stake, or try to keep either side from winning, and as a result, artificially prolong the war.

What this author is basically saying is:

_____

_____

_____

3. When people get older, their memories of "the good old days" are not always accurate. They may remember that a movie cost a quarter and a trolley ride cost a nickel, but they forget that those amounts represented an appreciable part of the average person's hourly wage. They remember living in close-knit communities, but they forget the depressions and wars that sometimes struck those communities.

What this author is basically saying is:

_____

_____

_____

4. Last week I got a letter from Leon saying that he has finally found the perfect house, and he'll never move again. I've gotten similar letters from him on at least two other occasions. He began praising the house, the neighborhood, and the town to the skies. But there always turned out to be something wrong. Once he moved because the winters were too harsh where he was living; another time, the house was too small after he got married. So I'll wait and see.

What this author is basically saying is:

_____

_____

_____

ANSWERS AND EXPLANATIONS

Here are some possible statements of the gist of each of the previous paragraphs. Your versions will surely differ from these, probably in major ways. But see how many of the key issues you picked up on.

1. People probably are no better at resisting sales pitches than they used to be.

Once again, the "commonplace" view is contrasted to the author's view. She uses several examples of how the media sells us products or ideas in quick, unsophisticated snippets, and ends with a rhetorical question, "How sophisticated is that?" to evoke the response: Not very. It's easy to overlook the implied comparison in the first sentence ("much more sophisticated . . . *than used to be the case*" [emphasis ours]), but that comparison is important to the scope.

2. Would-be international rescuers of countries suffering famine and civil wars inevitably get caught up in those wars.

The "inevitably" is justified by the painful choice offered in the last sentence: Countries trying to relieve famine, the author says, "must" send in peacekeepers and "must" either favor one side or prolong the war through their efforts at neutrality. Other issues raised in the paragraph—the motives for international relief efforts; the deceptive complexity of the situations; the causes of famine—are secondary to, or supportive of, the key point made.

3. Older people sometimes remember only the "good parts" of their youth.

That the gist of this paragraph is merely a paraphrase of the first sentence is no surprise: The second and third sentences are simply acting as evidence for the opening assertion. This happens a lot on the test, especially in Critical Reasoning. These last two examples were written in much more casual language, but that doesn't mean that you shouldn't continue to use your own casual language to paraphrase them.

4. Despite his claim, Leon may very well move again.

This paragraph shouldn't be read as "Leon will move again" or even "he will probably move again." It would be a mistake to infer that the author would take any kind of a bet on Leon's relocation. The gist of the paragraph is simply that there has been a historical disjunction between Leon's previous expressions of homeowner satisfaction and his subsequent behavior. With Leon's claim to love his current home, the pattern may be on its way to repeating itself.

KEYWORDS

The best GMAT test takers are anticipatory readers. They know that every passage is more than the sum of its parts—that the parts must fit together to create a unified whole. To better understand the function of each part within the passage, they keep asking themselves, "Where is this going?" In other words, they try to sense how each piece of information helps the author set up the next. These readers know that because GMAT prose is extremely logical, the passage will almost always go where logic dictates. Occasionally, the author may surprise you—but if you know what to expect, his taking a different tack will be all the more striking. And all this means you can stay on top of the author instead of several steps behind.

The best GMAT readers also think structurally. They do so by picking up the clues left by the author, structural clues that we at Kaplan call keywords. Keywords are the structural signals that every author uses: the words and phrases whose only purpose is to organize and shape the text. For example . . . hey wait a second, that's a keyword phrase right there! The moment you see the phrase "for example," you know that it signals an illustration of whatever was just said. And that's what we mean by thinking structurally.

We generally respond to keywords unconsciously. But that's not good enough. Those who are best at GMAT Verbal locate, interpret, and use keywords knowingly. Keyword signals exist only because they have a function: to help the author structure the prose. By concentrating more on the function of words than on their information content, the GMAT Verbal champs save themselves an awesome amount of time and are rewarded with faster and better answers. Check out how meaningful these important categories of keywords are to you. Jot down as many examples as you can think of for each category, and then compare your responses to what we've provided.

Contrast Keywords
On the other hand

_____   _____   _____   _____

_____   _____   _____   _____

Continuation Keywords
And

_____   _____   _____   _____

_____   _____

Evidence Keywords
Because

_____   _____

Conclusion Keywords
Therefore

_____   _____   _____   _____

Illustration Keywords
For example

_____   _____

Sequence Keywords
First of all

_____   _____

Emphasis Keywords
Most of all

_____   _____

Opinion/Idea Keywords
believe

_____   _____

(Now read on.)

KAPLAN

Contrast keywords signal an opposition or shift. There are lots of these besides the one we provided:

Although	*By contrast*	*However*	*Conversely*	*Still*	*Yet*	*Whereas*
But	*Despite*	*Nevertheless*	*Otherwise*	*Though*	*Notwithstanding*	

Contrast keywords are among the most significant in both Reading Comprehension and Critical Reasoning, because so many passages are based on contrast or opposition. Almost certainly, something important is happening when a Contrast keyword shows up.

Continuation keywords announce that more of the same is about to come up. *And* is the most common one in English; others include:

Also	*Likewise*	*In addition*	*At the same time*
As well as	*Furthermore*	*Moreover*	

Also (there's a signal for you!), the colon usually does the same job: it tells you that what follows expands upon, or continues, what came before. Note that some Continuation keywords can also function as Sequence keywords.

Evidence keywords, which tell you that the author is about to provide support for a point. Here are the most important Evidence keywords:

Because	*Since*	*For*	*Given that*

Conclusion keywords signal that the author is about to sum up or announce her thesis. The most common one is *therefore*, to which we can add:

Consequently	*Thus*	*It can be seen that*	*We can conclude that*
As a result	*Hence*	*So*	*In conclusion*

Since these keywords have to do with the author's logic, it's small wonder that they're especially crucial for Critical Reasoning. No less important are:

Illustration keywords signal that an example is about to arrive. *For example* and *for instance* are the most obvious. But think about these:

> *In the words of Jean-Paul Sartre*
> *As Maya Angelou says*

In each case, what's about to follow is an example of that person's thinking.

Sequence keywords are the author's way of telling you, "Hey, there's some sort of order at work here." They announce that a logical arrangement of the author's reasoning is taking place. These are the most common:

Second (third, fourth, etc.)	*Next*	*Finally*

When all is said and done, **Emphasis keywords** may be the most welcome. If we're supposed to read for author point of view, and we are, what better than to stumble across words and phrases whose sole purpose is to announce "I, the author, find this important"? Note these well:

Above all   *Most of all*   *Essentially*
Primarily   *Indeed*

Opinion/Idea keywords reveal the author's or others' opinions. The easiest to spot is something like *I disagree*, but here are others:

believe   *hypothesis*   *unsupported*
theory   *valid*

Keywords will come up again in this book, so be sure you understand their purpose on the GMAT.

KEYWORDS EXERCISE

Each of the following pieces of text—any of which might be found in a Reading Comprehension passage or Critical Reasoning argument—ends with a familiar keyword or phrase. After you read it, try to formulate an idea of what ought to follow the keyword; then look at the three possibilities listed. Choose the one that would be the most logical completion of the sentence: Which one (if any) comes the closest to your expectation?

1. The latest research seems to suggest that people who consume alcohol in moderation may be healthier, on average, than either teetotalers or heavy drinkers. Hence,

    ○ people who enjoy a single glass of wine with dinner need not fear that they are endangering their health

    ○ at least one clinical study rates both nondrinkers and heavy drinkers as less psychologically stable compared with moderate drinkers

    ○ without more data, it would be premature to change one's lifestyle on the basis of these findings

2. The photograph being copied must be in good condition; otherwise,

    ○ it should be examined with a magnifying glass under strong white light

    ○ its dimensions must be identical to those of the desired duplicate

    ○ the duplicate will exhibit the same scratches or smears as the original

3. After Giotto's death, the fresco was completed by an apprentice whose skills were not quite up to the task, and

    ○ he clearly attempted to imitate the master's strokes

    ○ neither the perspective nor the colors are convincing

    ○ he had studied with the master for only a short time

KAPLAN

4. The evidence suggesting that the two species of felines may have existed simultaneously on the African veldt is purely circumstantial. For example,

  ⬭ with no direct proof to the contrary, many experts still believe that the giant cats died out long before their smaller relatives appeared

  ⬭ fossil traces of both species have been found in separate areas in sediments that are thought to have been laid down by the same floodwaters

  ⬭ since all of the giant fossils found so far have been male, some scientists suspect that the smaller ones represent the females and young of the same sexually dimorphic species

5. Only one day-care facility in this city bases its fees on a sliding scale according to family income, and there are over three hundred children on its waiting list. Consequently,

  ⬭ it is nearly impossible for most low-income mothers to work outside the home while providing care for their children

  ⬭ the blame for the lack of affordable childcare alternatives must be placed on state legislators, who have stymied every attempt to redress the situation

  ⬭ the number of high- and middle-income families who place their preschool children in day care primarily to give them an educational advantage continues to rise

6. The purpose of the proposed advertising campaign is, first, to increase public awareness of the company's new logo. For instance,

  ⬭ it is hoped that the new commercial will reinforce brand loyalty among consumers

  ⬭ a major portion of the budget has been allocated to create a striking and memorable design

  ⬭ television viewers should be able to identify the design correctly after seeing the commercial only once

7. That Nabokov's novels found a mass audience in the United States, a country in which relatively few people study foreign languages, is mystifying, especially given

  ⬭ his appeal to academics and literary critics

  ⬭ his penchant for multilingual puns

  ⬭ the ribald adult content of his books

ANSWERS AND EXPLANATIONS

1. A	4. B	7. B
2. C	5. A	
3. B	6. C	

1.

Hence is a Conclusion keyword, and (A) is the only one of the choices that can reasonably be deduced from the previous sentence. (B) provides additional evidence along the same lines, and would more logically follow a Continuation keyword like *moreover*. (C), which takes a different view, would probably start off with a Contrast keyword like *however*.

2.

The Contrast keyword *otherwise* warns of some undesired consequence to follow if the photo is in bad shape; (C) fits the bill. (A) is a precondition to ensure that the original photo is okay; it should take a Conclusion keyword like *therefore*. (B) describes a second requirement that's distinct from the photo's condition; it needs a Continuation keyword like *also* to set it up.

3.

And expresses continuation, another piece of evidence that points in the same direction. Replacing *and* with a wordier Evidence keyword, such as *as evidenced by the fact that*, would make (B) even more clearly correct. Contrast keyword *although* would more appropriately introduce (A), which expresses a subtle contrast (the apprentice didn't succeed, though he tried). (C) attempts to explain why the apprentice wasn't up to snuff; an Evidence keyword like *since* should set up this choice.

4.

For example, one of the most common Illustration keywords, sets the stage for (B), a specific piece of the circumstantial evidence mentioned in the first part of the sentence. (A) suggests an opposing conclusion—that the two species did not coexist—and would probably be introduced by a Conclusion keyword like *thus*. (C) reinforces the main clause's statement that only circumstantial evidence supports the conclusion that the two species coexisted; this choice raises additional evidence pointing to an alternative conclusion and would be more effectively set up by the Continuation keyword *in addition*.

5.

The Conclusion keyword *consequently* leads nicely to (A), a natural result of the first sentence. Placing blame, (B), is not a result but a conclusion and can't be introduced by this Conclusion keyword because it's buttressed by new evidence (the legislators have stymied every attempt to redress the situation). Emphasis keywords like *in large measure* would serve better. (C) discusses a simultaneous but different trend. *At the same time*, a Continuation keyword with subtle overtones of contrast, would set it up better.

6.

Illustration keywords *for instance* should lead to an example of how the campaign would increase public awareness; (C) would be a reasonable result to hope for. A Sequence keyword like *second* would more effectively indicate that (A) raises a new issue, brand loyalty, that is an additional purpose of the campaign, unrelated to public awareness. (B) requires a Conclusion keyword like *hence* to show that the previously stated objective mandates a hefty design budget for the new logo.

7.

Especially is another Emphasis keyword. (B) is the only choice that would make Nabokov's mass appeal in a linguistically provincial country even more mystifying. His appeal to academic and literary critics might explain his mass readership, or at least render it less mystifying; (A) should thus be introduced by a Contrast keyword like *despite*. (C) would tend to work in favor of Nabokov's mass appeal, rather than against it; a combination of Contrast and Evidence keywords—something like *though perhaps understandable, given*—would make for a better transition.

IN CONCLUSION

We've shown you the basic tools that will allow you to read GMAT passages more quickly and with a better grasp of the essentials. What we've basically been advocating is a different approach to reading, one specifically tailored to the demands of GMAT Verbal. This approach involves reading for the "why" and the "how" of the passage and giving less attention to the "what"—in particular, the details that weigh down the passage and aren't worth the time it takes to digest them.

The bad news about GMAT reading passages is that they tend to be dense with information and, for most test takers, deadly dull. The good news about these passages is that they are logically constructed, and the reader who reads for the gist and structure of the passage, who takes note of the Keywords that the author provides to facilitate this process, who mentally paraphrases the big ideas found within each paragraph, and who skips quickly over the details and filler until and unless they're needed to answer a question, is bound to do well on the GMAT Verbal Section.

Learning to read this way takes practice. You'll have plenty of opportunities to hone this approach to reading the GMAT way throughout this book, but you needn't stop there. In fact, if you're serious about really doing well on GMAT Verbal, you should also apply these principles to your general reading for a while and challenge yourself with some of the denser journals and magazines found on the newsstand.

If you don't do so already, get into the habit of reading *The Economist* or another serious business journal for practice reading business passages (this has the added benefit of giving you ideas and stories to use in your AWA essays). Reading literary journals such as the *New York Review of Books* can help you to sharpen your reading skills for just about any type of passage. And if science passages are your worst nightmare, try reading a serious science journal such as *Scientific American* or *Astronomy* (those GMAT writers just love astronomy passages). With practice, you'll find that you don't have to "get" the science to understand the author's main idea when you read an article in one of these journals—and the same is true of GMAT Science passages.

And after you've aced the GMAT, we promise you can go back to reading for fun.

Chapter 4: **GMAT Reading Comprehension**

Reading Comprehension tests critical reading skills. Among other things, it tests whether you can do the following:

- Summarize the main idea of a passage.
- Understand logical relationships between facts and concepts.
- Make inferences based on information in a text.
- Analyze the logical structure of a passage.
- Deduce the author's tone and attitude about a topic from the text.

In Reading Comprehension, you are presented with a reading passage (in an area of business, social science, biological science, or physical science) and then asked three or four questions about that text. You are not expected to be familiar with any topic beforehand—all the information is contained in the text in front of you. In fact, if you happen to have some previous knowledge about a given topic, it is important that you not let that knowledge affect your answers. Naturally, some passages will be easier than others, though all will present a challenge. The passages will have the tone and content that one might expect from a scholarly journal.

You will see four Reading Comprehension passages—two shorter passages with 3 questions each and two longer passages with 4 questions each, for a total of 14 questions. You will see only one question at a time on the monitor, however, and you will have to answer each question before you can see the next question.

The passage will be visible on one side of the monitor as long as you have a question on that passage. If the text is longer than the available space, you'll be given a scroll bar to move through it.

ANATOMY OF A READING COMPREHENSION QUESTION

Doing well on Reading Comprehension begins with understanding the format. Let's examine the various parts of a typical Reading Comprehension question.

The Directions

The directions for this question type look something like this:

Directions: The questions in this group are based on the content of the passage. After reading the passage, choose the best answer to each question. Base your answers only according to what is stated or implied in the text.

There are two important facts to be gleaned from these directions. First, recall that here and throughout the Verbal Section, you are looking for the *best* answer to each question, not the *right* answer. In fact, the correct answer to a Reading Comprehension question tends to be fairly inconspicuous, while each of the four wrong answer choices contains something that makes it *wrong*. Therefore, using the process of elimination is essential on this question type. Second, you must answer each question based solely on what's stated or implied in the passage; applying outside knowledge can often get you into trouble.

The Question and Answer Choices

Here's an example of a typical question:

Which of the following does the author suggest about the importance of the emigration of Southerners to Brazil?

- ◯ Without the Southern presence, Brazil would never have been settled.
- ◯ The Southerners' sole purpose in immigrating was to introduce new inventions to the Brazilians.
- ◯ If the Southerners had not emigrated, they would have gone to prison for war crimes.
- ◯ Dom Pedro II feared the condition Brazil would be in without the presence of the Americans.
- ◯ The Southerners' arrival had a great impact on the development of education and agriculture in Brazil.

READING COMPREHENSION QUESTION TYPES

Though you might want to break down the Reading Comprehension section according to the kinds of passages that appear—business, natural science, and social science—we at Kaplan feel that it's more effective to do so by question type. While passages differ in their content, you should read them in essentially the same way, employing the same critical reading techniques for each.

The four main question types on GMAT Reading Comprehension are **Global**, **Detail**, **Inference**, and **Logic**.

Global Questions

Any question that explicitly asks you to consider the passage as a whole is a Global question. Here are some examples:

- Which one of the following best expresses the main idea of the passage?
- The author's primary purpose is to . . . ?
- Which of the following best describes the organization of the passage?
- Which of the following would be an appropriate title for this passage?

The correct answer will be consistent with the passage's Topic, Scope, Purpose, and Structure. If you've jotted them down on your noteboard—and you should!—then you will only need a few seconds to select the right answer. Most wrong answers will either get the Scope wrong (either too narrow or too broad) or misrepresent the author's point of view.

The GMAT will probably word the answer choices rather formally, so by "few seconds," we mean closer to 45 than to 10. But that's still significantly under your average time per question, meaning that you can spend more time dealing with the more time-consuming Inference questions.

Detail Questions

Detail questions ask you to identify what the passage explicitly says. Here are some sample Detail question stems:

- According to the passage, which of the following is true of X?
- The author states that . . . ?
- The author mentions which of the following in support of X?

"Wait a minute, Kaplan," you might be saying. "Didn't you just tell me not to read the details too closely? What's the deal?"

Good question! Reading carefully through all the details at once would be a big waste of time because you're likely to get only one, possibly two, Detail questions per passage. Plus, most Detail questions point you straight to the detail, anyway. That is, they reference a specific word or phrase that's easily located or give you line numbers to specify the detail's location. Occasionally, the screen even highlights the referenced phrase both in the question stem and in the passage.

So between highlighting, line references, and your Passage Map, finding the detail that the GMAT is asking about is usually not much of a challenge. What, then, could they possibly be testing? They are testing whether you understand that detail *in the context of the passage*. The best strategic approach, then, is to read not only the sentence that the question stem sends you to but also the sentence before and after it. Usually the context you need comes before the detail from the question stem. Consider this question:

According to the passage, which of the following is true of the guinea pigs discussed in line 17?

Let's say that line 17 goes like this:

> ...a greater percentage of the guinea pigs that lived in the crowded, indoor, heated area survived than did the guinea pigs in the outdoor cages.

If we don't read for context, we might think that the right answer might be this:

> Guinea pigs survive better indoors.

But what if we read the full context, starting one sentence before?

> Until recently, scientists had no evidence to support the hypothesis that low temperature alone, and not other factors such as people crowding indoors, is responsible for the greater incidence and severity of influenza in the late fall and early winter. Last year, however, researchers uncovered a journal from a Yellowstone Park camp that suffered an influenza outbreak in October of 1945; this journal documented that a greater percentage of the guinea pigs that lived in the indoor, heated area survived than did the guinea pigs in the outdoor cages.

Now we know that the right answer will be this:

> Researchers discovered that some guinea pigs survived better indoors than outdoors during a flu outbreak.

By reading not just line 17 but the information before it, we realize that not all guinea pigs survive better outdoors; only a specific subset did. If we had picked an answer that matched our first prediction, we would be distorting the facts—we need to understand the information in context.

Inference Questions

Reading Comprehension Inference questions, like Critical Reasoning Inference questions, ask you to find something that must be true based on the passage but is not mentioned *explicitly* in the passage. In other words, you need to read "between the lines."

Inference questions come in two types. The first type is Inference questions with a specific reference. Like Detail questions, these prompts will use key phrases and line numbers to point you directly to a part of the passage—and like Detail questions, they are best solved by reviewing the context of that detail and then making a prediction about what the answer will be.

Consider the following Inference question, once again asking about the guinea pigs we discussed earlier:

> Which of the following is implied about the guinea pigs mentioned in line 17?

Just like last time, we want to review the context around the line reference. Doing so, we'll find that "until recently," there was "no evidence" that temperature affected the virulence of the flu; "however," last year these guinea pig records appeared. The logical inference is not explicitly stated, but we can easily put two and two together. The answer will be something like this:

> Their deaths provided new evidence that influenza may be more dangerous in lower temperatures.

Other Inference questions make no specific references, instead asking what can be inferred from the passage as a whole or what opinion the author might hold. Valid inferences can be drawn from anything in the passage, from big-picture issues like author opinion to any of the little details. But you will probably be able to eliminate a few answers quickly because they violate the big picture.

Then you'll investigate the remaining answers choice by choice, looking to put each answer in one of three categories—(1) proved right, (2) proved wrong, or (3) not proved right but not proved wrong either. It's distinguishing between the second and third categories that will give you success on Inference questions.

Here are some sample Inference question stems:

- Which of the following can be most reasonably inferred from the passage?
- The author would most likely agree that . . . ?
- Which of the following is suggested about X?

Logic Questions

Logic questions ask why the author does something—why he cites a source, why he includes a certain detail, why he puts one paragraph before another, and so forth. Another way of thinking of this is that a Logic question asks not for the purpose of the passage as a whole but for the purpose of a part of the passage. As a result, any answer choice that focuses on the actual content of a detail will be wrong.

Here are some sample Logic question stems:

- The author mentions X most probably to . . . ?
- Which of the following best describes the relationship of the second paragraph to the rest of the passage?
- What is the primary purpose of the third paragraph?

Most Logic questions can be answered right from your Passage Map—the written summary of each paragraph and the passage's overall Topic, Scope, and Purpose. If the question references a detail, as does the first sample question stem above, then you should read the context of that detail as well—just as you should for any Detail or Inference question that references a specific detail.

THE KAPLAN METHOD FOR READING COMPREHENSION

As noted in the previous chapter, reading for the GMAT means reading with different goals and employing different techniques than you do in the course of everyday life. This is in part because Reading Comprehension passages are designed not to be easily digestible reading matter for the average test taker. And furthermore, there's just no time under strict test conditions to understand everything that's being said in the passage. Time management is a critical issue in Reading Comprehension. How you approach reading the passage may vary depending upon time issues, where you are in the test, and the type of passage you have before you. Because most test takers spend far too much time reading the passage—and not enough time researching the answer to the question in the passage, scrutinizing the answer choices, and choosing the best response—Kaplan has developed the following method for handling Reading Comprehension questions:

Step 1: Read the passage strategically.

Step 2: Analyze the question stem.

Step 3: Research the relevant text in the passage.

Step 4: Make a prediction.

Step 5: Evaluate the answer choices.

Step 1: Read the Passage Strategically

To read strategically, be on the lookout for structural keywords and phrases. They will help you to distinguish important things (like opinions) from unimportant (like supporting examples) and to understand why the author wrote each sentence.

- **Contrast** keywords such as *but, however, nevertheless*, and *on the other hand* tell you that a change or disagreement is coming.

- **Continuation** keywords such as *moreover, also*, and *furthermore* tell you that the author is continuing on the same track or general idea.

- **Evidence** keywords let you know that something is being offered in support of a particular idea. The specifics of the support are usually unimportant for the first big-picture read, but you do want to know what the idea is! Examples of evidence keywords are *since, because*, and *as*.

- **Conclusion** keywords such as *therefore* and *hence* are usually not associated with the author's main point in Reading Comprehension. Rather, they indicate that the next phrase is a logical consequence of the sentence(s) that came before.

- **Illustration** keywords let you know that what follows is an example of a broader point. Examples include, of course, *example*. *For instance* is another favorite.

- **Sequence** is a broader category of keywords. These are any words that create lists or groupings. *First, second*, and *third* are obvious examples. But you could also get a chronological sequence (*17th century, 18th century*, and *today*). Science passages may also group complicated phenomena together using simpler sequence keywords (*at a high temperature* and *at a low temperature*, for example).

- **Emphasis** keywords are used when the author wants to call attention to a specific point. These come in two varieties: generic emphasis, such as *very* and *critical*, and charged emphasis, such as *beneficial* or *dead end*.

- **Opinion/Idea** keywords are perhaps the most important of all. The GMAT cares much more about the ideas in a passage and how details support or attack those ideas than about the details themselves. Be sure to distinguish between the author's opinion and that of others. Others' opinions are easier to spot and will be triggered by words like *believe*, *theory*, or *hypothesis*. The author's opinion is more likely to reveal itself in words that imply a value judgment, such as *valid* or *unsupported*. (If the passage gives you something in the first person, like *I disagree*, that's also a pretty clear sign.)

With this strategic analysis as a guide, you should construct a Passage Map—a brief summary of each paragraph and its function in the passage's structure—and note the author's Topic, Scope, and Purpose. Start by identifying the Topic and then hunt for Scope, trying to get a sense of where the passage is going, what the author's going to focus on, and what role the first paragraph is playing. Then jot down the gist of the paragraph, noting the structure and the role it plays in the passage. Finish by double-checking to make sure that you got the Topic and Scope right (sometimes passages can take unexpected turns) and note the author's overall Purpose.

Remember to ask yourself the following questions:

- Why did the author include this paragraph?
- What shift did the author have in mind when moving on to this paragraph?
- What's discussed here that's different from the paragraph before?
- What bearing does this paragraph have on the author's main idea?
- What role do the details play?

Topic will be the first big, broad idea that comes along. Almost always, it will be right there in the first sentence. There's no need to obsess over the exact wording of the Topic; you just want to get a general idea of what the author is writing about so the passage gets easier to understand.

Scope is the narrow part of the Topic that the author focuses on. If the author expresses her own opinion, then the thing she has an opinion about is the Scope. Identifying Scope is crucial because most wrong answers are wrong because they are outside the Scope of the passage. Remember that even though the first paragraph usually narrows the Topic down to the Scope, there won't be a "topic sentence" in the traditional sense.

Purpose is what the author is doing. You'll serve yourself well by picking an active verb for the Purpose. This helps not only to set you up to find right answers—many Global and Logic answer choices use active verbs—but also to force you to consider the author's opinion. Here are some "neutral" verbs: *describe, explain, compare.* Here are some "opinionated" verbs: *advocate, argue, rebut, analyze.*

Like most sophisticated writing, the prose you will see on the GMAT doesn't explicitly reveal its secrets. Baldly laying out the why and how of a passage up front isn't a hallmark of GMAT Reading Comprehension passages. And even more important (as far as the test makers are concerned), if ideas were blatantly laid out, the test makers couldn't ask probing questions about them. So to set up the questions—to test how we think about the prose we read—the GMAT uses passages in which authors hide or disguise their statement of purpose and challenge you to extract it. After you finish reading, your Passage Map would look something like this example:

¶1 Critics: current election system unfair, suggest alternatives

¶2 Alternative—approval voting; pros & cons

¶3 Alternative—rank voting; pros & cons

¶4 Change unlikely

Topic: U.S. Presidential Election System ◄———┐

Scope: Alternatives to ___↑   │

Purpose: Describe two alternatives to ———┘

You don't want to take more than four minutes to write the Passage Map. In fact, as long as you get the Topic, Scope, and Purpose right, you want to spend as little time as possible reading. After all, you get points for answering questions, not for nicely detailed Maps. So the more time you can spend working on the questions, the better your score will be!

And your Map can be as complete or as cryptic as you need it to be. Don't waste time trying to write out entire sentences if fragments and abbreviations will do. And notice in the previous example how effective arrows can be. There's no sense writing out "Describe the advantages and disadvantages of two possible, if unlikely, alternatives to the current American presidential election system."

Step 2: Analyze the Question Stem

The next step is to identify the question type: Global, Detail, Inference, or Logic. Ask yourself, "What should I do on this question? What is being asked?" Here are some guidelines:

If you see "purpose of the passage" or "main idea" = Global question
If you see direct language like "according to" or "states" = Detail question
If you see indirect language like "agree" or "suggest" = Inference question
If you are asked for the purpose of a detail or paragraph = Logic question

Also, be sure to focus on exactly what the question is asking about. Let's say you see this question:

The passage states which of the following about the uses of fixed nitrogen?

Don't look for what the passage says about "nitrogen" in general. Don't even look for "fixed nitrogen" alone. Look for the uses of fixed nitrogen. (And be aware that the GMAT may ask you to recognize that *application* is a synonym of *use*.)

Finally, the GMAT occasionally asks questions that do not fall into one of the four major categories. Don't obsess over these outliers. They make up less than 10 percent of GMAT Reading

Comprehension questions, so chances are you won't even see one. But if you do, don't worry. These unusual questions usually involve paraphrasing or analyzing specific points of reasoning in the passage. Because you can use your Passage Map, you will be prepared to crack even these rare problems.

Step 3: Research the Relevant Text in the Passage

Since there just isn't enough time to memorize the whole passage, you shouldn't rely on your memory to answer questions.

Step 4: Make a Prediction

As you've already seen, it really helps to know what you're looking for before you consider the answer choices. Doing so will help the right answer jump off the screen at you. Here are how you should form your predictions for each question type:

- **Global:** Use your notes on the Passage Map and the Topic, Scope, and Purpose as the basis of your prediction.
- **Detail:** Predict an answer based on what the context tells you about the detail.
- **Inference:** The right answer must be true based on the passage. (Since many valid inferences could be drawn from even one detail, it's often best not to make your prediction more specific than that.)
- **Logic:** Predict an answer that focuses on why the paragraph or detail was used, not on what it says.

Some answers are very tempting because they have the correct details and the right scope, but they have a *not*, *doesn't*, or other twist that flips their meanings to the opposite of what the text provides. Watch out for these "180s."

Step 5: Evaluate the Answer Choices

Hunt for the answer choice that matches your prediction. If only one answer does, it's the right answer!

If you can't find a match for your prediction, if more than one seems to fit your prediction, or if you weren't able to form a prediction at all (this happens for some Inference questions), then you'll need to evaluate each answer choice, looking for errors. Eliminating four wrong answers is the same as finding the one right answer!

Here are some common wrong answer traps to look out for:

- **Global:** Answers that misrepresent the Scope or Purpose of the passage and answers that focus too heavily on details from the beginning or end of the passage
- **Detail:** Answers that distort the context or focus on the wrong details entirely
- **Inference:** Extreme language or exaggerations of the author's statements, distortions of the passage's meaning, and the exact opposite of what might be inferred
- **Logic:** Answers that get the specifics right but the purpose wrong

Always be on the lookout for Scope shifts and for "half-right/half-wrong" answers, which are mostly okay except for one or two words.

Now let's try the Kaplan Method on an actual GMAT-length passage and some of its questions. On test day, you won't be able to take notes on the passage or skip forward or backward between questions. So challenge yourself to take notes on a separate paper and to answer the questions in order.

Line   Since 1980, the notion that mass extinctions at the end of the Cretaceous period
        65 million years ago resulted from a sudden event has slowly gathered support,
        although even today there is no scientific consensus. In the Alvarez scenario, an
        asteroid struck the earth, creating a gigantic crater. Beyond the immediate effects
  (5)   of fire, flood, and storm, dust darkened the atmosphere, cutting off plant life.
        Many animal species disappeared as the food chain was snapped at its base.

        Alvarez's main evidence is an abundance of iridium in the KT boundary, a
        thin stratum dividing Cretaceous rocks from rocks of the Tertiary period. Iridium
        normally accompanies the slow fall of interplanetary debris, but in KT boundary
 (10)   strata, iridium is 10–100 times more abundant, suggesting a rapid, massive
        deposition. Coincident with the boundary, whole species of small organisms
        vanish from the fossil record. Boundary samples also yield osmium isotopes,
        basaltic sphericles, and deformed quartz grains, all of which could have resulted
        from high-velocity impact.

 (15)   Paleontologists initially dismissed the theory, arguing that existing dinosaur
        records showed a decline lasting millions of years. But recent studies in North
        America, aimed at a comprehensive collection of fossil remnants rather than
        rare or well-preserved specimens, indicate large dinosaur populations existing
        immediately prior to the KT boundary. Since these discoveries, doubts about
 (20)   theories of mass extinction have lessened significantly.

        Given the lack of a known impact crater of the necessary age and size to fit the
        Alvarez scenario, some scientists have proposed alternatives. Courtillot, citing huge
        volcanic flows in India coincident with the KT boundary, speculates that eruptions
        lasting many thousands of years produced enough atmospheric debris to cause
 (25)   global devastation. His analyses also conclude that iridium in the KT boundary
        was deposited over a period of 10,000–100,000 years. Alvarez and Asaro reply
        that the shock of an asteroidal impact could conceivably have triggered extensive
        volcanic activity. Meanwhile, exploration at a large geologic formation in Yucatan,
        found in 1978 but unstudied until 1990, has shown a composition consistent with
 (30)   extraterrestrial impact. But evidence that the formation is indeed the
        hypothesized impact site remains inconclusive.

1. It can be inferred from the passage that supporters of the Alvarez and Courtillot theories would hold which of the following views in common?

   ◯ The KT boundary was formed over many thousands of years.

   ◯ Large animals such as the dinosaurs died out gradually over millions of years.

   ◯ Mass extinction occurred as an indirect result of debris saturating the atmosphere.

   ◯ It is unlikely that the specific cause of the Cretaceous extinctions will ever be determined.

   ◯ Volcanic activity may have been triggered by shock waves from the impact of an asteroid.

2. The author mentions "recent studies in North America" (lines 16–17) primarily in order to

   ◯ point out the benefits of using field research to validate scientific theories

   ◯ suggest that the asteroid impact theory is not consistent with fossil evidence

   ◯ describe alternative methods of collecting and interpreting fossils

   ◯ summarize the evidence that led to wider acceptance of catastrophic scenarios of mass extinction

   ◯ show that dinosaurs survived until the end of the Cretaceous period

Step 1: Read the Passage Strategically

Take a couple of minutes to read the passage. Aim at the Topic, Scope, and author's Purpose or point of view. Where is the text going?

Here's an example of how the passage should be analyzed. We've reprinted the passage through the lens of critical reading. On the left is the passage as you might read it, with keywords in bold. On the right is what you might be thinking as you read.

PASSAGE	ANALYSIS
. . . **the notion** that mass extinctions at the end of the Cretaceous period 65 million years ago resulted from a sudden event **has slowly gathered support, although** even today there is **no** scientific **consensus**. In the **Alvarez scenario**, [bunch of details about an asteroid].	Wow, what a rich first sentence. Not only do we get Topic (*mass extinctions at the end of the Cretaceous period*—whatever that is), but we also get an idea (*the notion that [the mass extinction] resulted from a sudden event*), the fact that some people agree with it (*slowly gathered support*), and the fact that not everyone does (*no scientific consensus*). Wow! I'll bet the passage goes on to talk not only about the support but also about why not everyone agrees. We also get one specific theory (*the Alvarez scenario*) and an elaborate description of what that is—seems to involve an asteroid.

Alvarez's main evidence is [lots of detail].	The keywords are pretty clear—here's some evidence in support of one "sudden event" theory. Don't care what the evidence is until there's a question about it.
Paleontologists initially dismissed the theory, arguing that [something] last[ed] **millions of years. But** recent studies . . . **doubts** about theories of mass extinction **have lessened significantly.**	With *dismissed the theory*, it's clear that this paragraph opposes the "sudden event" idea (just what we predicted!). Note how *millions of years*, not normally a keyword, creates contrast with "sudden event." But what's this? *But* announces a change. Are we going to more support for "sudden event"? Yep! *Doubts...have lessened significantly.*
Given the **lack** of [evidence] to **fit the Alvarez scenario, some scientists have proposed alternatives. Courtillot, citing** [evidence], **speculates** that eruptions . . . cause[d] global devastation. **His analyses also conclude** [something about iridium]. **Alvarez and Asaro reply.** . . . **But evidence** . . . **remains inconclusive.**	Alvarez lacks some evidence still, so there are some other theories. This Coutillot guy says something about volcanoes and iridium. Looks like Alvarez has something to say about Courtillot, too. And there isn't enough evidence either way, so the author doesn't pick a "winner."

Your Passage Map would look something like this:

Topic: Mass extinctions at end of Cret. period

Scope: Theories about ⌐↑

Purpose: Describe two "sudden event" theories.

Step 2: Analyze the Question Stem

Now identify the question type. Question 1 is clearly an Inference question: It uses the phrase *can be inferred*. Luckily, this Inference question contains referents that will point us to a specific part of the passage. This will save us a lot of time. Question 2 is a Logic question. The phrase *in order to* shows us that we're asked to identify *why* the detail was used.

Step 3: Research the Relevant Text in the Passage

Question 1 asks us to find something that must be true according to both the Alvarez and the Courtillot theories. Our Passage Map shows us that the Alvarez theory takes all of Paragraph 2 and some of Paragraph 4. That's too much to read through closely. But the Courtillot theory is mentioned only once, in Paragraph 4 lines 22–26. Probably the most efficient way to research this question is to read through those two sentences and then deal with Paragraph 2 answer by answer so we can do focused research.

Question 2 references lines 16–17, which are in Paragraph 3. Since this is a Logic question, it's best to begin our research with the Passage Map. Here's what our Map has to say about Paragraph 3:

¶ 3 Initial disagreement, now less doubt

Okay, so the "recent studies in North America" are either part of the initial disagreement or a reason that theories of mass extinction are less doubted now. Already, the word *recent* suggests the latter. But if we weren't confident about that, we could read the context of lines 16–17. The keywords *initially dismissed the theory* [of mass extinction] from the sentence before and from the sentence after (*Since those discoveries, doubts about theories of mass extinctions have lessened significantly.*) seal the deal.

Step 4: Make a Prediction

Question 1, we know, must be consistent with both theories. Since we researched Courtillot's theory, we can quickly eliminate any answer that disagrees with it.

Question 2 asks *why* the "recent studies in North America" were mentioned. Our research shows us that they provide the evidence that reduces doubt about theories of mass extinction. So an easy prediction would be something like "reasons why theories of mass extinction are doubted less than they used to be."

Step 5: Evaluate the Answer Choices

Question 1—(A) says that the KT boundary was formed over thousands of years, and that's consistent with Courtillot (line 26). What about Alvarez? Scanning through Paragraph 2 for anything about "KT boundary" and time, we read in lines 9–11 "KT Boundary . . . rapid, massive deposition." The word *rapid* is the only time signal at all, and it hardly fits with *many thousands of years*. Eliminate (A). Perhaps you could eliminate (B) right away if you remembered that both theories are in the "sudden event" camp. But if not, your Passage Map saves the day—*dinosaurs died out gradually over millions of years* fits with *dinosaur records showed a decline lasting millions of years* in Paragraph 3. But your Map shows that to be evidence *against* Alvarez, not in support. So (B) is gone.

Debris saturating the atmosphere is consistent with Cortillot (line 24). What about Alvarez? Well, line 9 says *slow fall of interplanetary debris*. So the debris issue is settled. Does it saturate the atmosphere? Not explicitly. But this is an Inference question, and we don't expect to see things explicitly. We do see that there was a *massive deposition* . . . and *massive* would suggest that there's a lot of this stuff, so it's plausible that it saturated the atmosphere. Hmm. Let's leave (C) alone.

(D) is the opposite of what Courtillot (as well as Alvarez) is trying to do, so this is a quick big-picture elimination. (E) is consistent with Alvarez's reply (lines 26–28). But this is a reply to Courtillot's theory—not his theory itself. So we can't claim that Courtillot would agree, and (E) is eliminated. Since (C) is left standing, it must be right.

Note that we can prove (C) to be the right answer without proving *why* it's right. To do so, we'd not only have to connect all the dots in Paragraph 2, we'd have to tie it all to *mass extinctions* by going back to the details from Paragraph 1. It's much more efficient to throw away (A), (B), (D), and (E).

Question 2—Our predicted answer ("reasons why theories of mass extinction are doubted less than they used to be") leads directly to (D), the correct answer.

(A) sounds nice on its own, but the context has nothing to do with the benefits of field research in a specific way. (B) is the opposite of why those studies are introduced—it is in fact the old belief that these studies dispel. (C) and (E) focus on the details on lines 16–17 themselves—(C) in a distorted way—but not on *why* those details are there.

PRACTICE QUESTIONS

Make sure to apply the Kaplan Method for Reading Comprehension to the following questions. Also, try timing yourself and see if you can finish this practice set of 14 questions about four passages in less than 25 minutes (this may require you to alter the way you read some of the passages, as discussed earlier in this chapter). Remember that on the CAT you have to answer the questions in the order they're given. Keep this in mind and try to answer the questions in order as you go through this and other practice sets in this book.

Questions 1-3 refer to the following passage.

Line The search for an explanation of the historically weak status of U.S. third-party movements is illuminated by examining the conditions that have favored the growth of a
  strong two-party system. Different interests and voting blocs predominate in different
  regions, creating a geographically fragmented electorate. This heterogeneity is comple
(5) mented by a federal political structure that forces the major parties to find voter support
  at state and local levels in separate regions. For example, the Democratic Party long
  sought and drew support simultaneously from northern black urban voters and from
  segregationists. Such pressures encourage the major parties to avoid political programs
  that are too narrowly or sharply defined. The nondoctrinal character of U.S. politics
(10) means that important new issues and voting blocs tend to be initially ignored by the
  major parties. Such issues—opposition to immigration and the abolition of slavery are
  two historic examples—tend to gain political prominence through third parties.

   Ironically, the same factors that lead to the emergence of third parties contribute
  to the explanation of their failure to gain national political power. Parties based on
(15) narrow or ephemeral issues remain isolated or fade rapidly. At the same time, those
  that raise increasingly urgent social issues also face inherent limits to growth. Long
  before a third party can begin to broaden substantially its base of voter support, the
  major parties are able to move to attract the minority of voters that it represents.
  The Democratic Party, for instance, appropriated the agrarian platform of the
(20) Populist Party in 1896, and enacted Socialist welfare proposals in the 1930s, in both
  cases winning much of the popular bases of these parties. Except for the Republican
  Party, which gained national prominence as the Whigs were declining in the 1850s,
  no third party has ever achieved national major-party status. Only at state and local
  levels have a handful of third parties been sustained by a stable voting bloc that
  remains unrepresented by a major party.

1. The primary purpose of this passage is to

    ◯ examine the appeal of U.S. national third parties to the electorate at state and local levels

    ◯ trace the historical rise and decline of third-party movements in the United States

    ◯ explain why most U.S. third-party movements have failed to gain major-party status

    ◯ demonstrate that U.S. politics has traditionally been non-ideological in character

    ◯ suggest a model to explain why certain U.S. third-party movements have succeeded while others have failed

2. Which of the following does the author suggest was an important factor in the establishment of the Republican Party as a major national party?

    ◯ the polarization of national opinion at the time of a major social crisis

    ◯ the unique appeal of its program to significant sectional interests

    ◯ the acceptance of its program by a large bloc of voters unrepresented by a major party

    ◯ the simultaneous decline of an established major party

    ◯ the inability of the major parties of the era to appeal to all sectional interests

3. According to the author, the major factor responsible for the rise of third parties in the United States has been the

    ◯ domination of major parties by powerful economic interests

    ◯ inability of major parties to bring about broad consensus among a variety of voters and interest groups

    ◯ slow response of major parties to new issues and voting groups

    ◯ exclusion of immigrants and minorities from the mainstream of U.S. politics

    ◯ variety of motivations held by voting blocs in different regions

Questions 3-7 refer to the following passage.

Line   Despite increasing enrollments of women in medical schools, feelings of isolation among women medical students persist. Women students still have to contend with the social stereotype of a male doctor. In addition, institutions themselves may unintentionally foster feelings of separateness. Comparatively few women are hired for faculty
(5)   positions, thus offering women students few role models. The pervasive sexual humor of male doctors and students further intensifies the women students' alienation. Alienation, in turn, negatively affects individual self-perception.

       As women enter medical study in increasing numbers, they may feel less at odds with their peers and the teaching establishment. Institutional bias will, no doubt,
(10)   also change in response to changing societal values. However, we should not wait passively for gradual social processes to bring changes; schools must provide current students with support services designed to meet women's needs. In a recent study, 48 percent of the women questioned rated a student support group as the most important support service a school can provide.

4. The passage cites all of the following as causing psychological problems for women medical students EXCEPT

    ◯ feelings of alienation from teachers and fellow students

    ◯ prevailing societal conceptions about doctors

    ◯ declining enrollments of women to medical schools

    ◯ expressions of sexism by peers and superiors

    ◯ absence of positive female models for women students

5. The author of the passage would be most likely to agree with which of the following?

    ◯ Medical schools practice widespread discrimination on the basis of sex.

    ◯ Gender-based stereotyping encourages feelings of isolation among women medical students.

    ◯ Some medical school policies are deliberately designed to make women students feel isolated.

    ◯ Social norms must change before institutional bias can decline.

    ◯ The majority of women medical students have a negative self-image.

6. The passage suggests that which of the following would be likely to reduce the isolation felt by women medical students?

    I.   An increased proportion of women in medical schools

    II. An increase in the number of women filling faculty positions in medical schools

    III. An increase in support services available to women students

    ◯ I only

    ◯ II only

    ◯ I and II only

    ◯ I and III only

    ◯ I, II, and III

7. In terms of its tone and content, the passage is most appropriately described as

    ◯ an impassioned polemic

    ◯ an indignant protest

    ◯ a reasoned appeal

    ◯ a detached summary

    ◯ a biased speculation

Questions 8-10 refer to the following passage.

Line   Shopping mall developers seek to attract large department stores that will act as "anchors"—high-traffic stores that will bring many customers into their complex. However, when a department store chain seeks to site a new store, it must take into consideration that the high level of customer traffic generated by the new store may be
(5) exploited by nearby smaller retailers. It will decline to build if it is judged that the large store's "positive externality" will serve primarily to increase sales at nearby small competitors. Mall developers can circumvent this problem and retain a mixture of large and small retailers by internalizing the department store's externality—that is, by bringing some of the benefits associated with the department store back to the store itself.

(10)   The ability of malls to do so lies in the fact that their developers own the entire complex. They can charge rents that reflect not only the contribution that each store makes to the mall's overall revenues, but also the business that a store brings to the mall's other tenants. Recent studies of malls in the American Midwest show that in a mall with two or three department stores, a small shoe store or restaurant might pay rent per square
(15) foot that is five times the rate charged to department stores in the complex, while a jeweler in a mall with four or five department stores could pay twenty times the rate paid by the mall's anchors.

    The partiality shown department stores increases with mall size, even though the study shows that department stores in different-sized complexes usually generate about
(20) the same sales per square foot. The disparity in the rents charged between department stores and small retailers cannot be explained simply by the fact that small stores make greater sales per square foot of floor space; rather, the smaller stores are willing to subsidize the department stores for the sales that department stores generate for them, and the greater the traffic, the more they are willing to pay.

8. The author's primary purpose in writing this passage is to

    ◯ indicate the competitive advantages that malls have over traditional shopping districts

    ◯ introduce the concept of positive externality and explain its relevance to shopping malls located in the American Midwest

    ◯ argue that mall owners exploit small stores by manipulating their rents so that large store owners benefit

    ◯ explain how mall developers attempt to increase customer traffic for a mall by varying rental rates for different kinds of stores

    ◯ demonstrate how mall developers maximize the number of retailers in their malls by internalizing the benefits of positive externality

9. Which of the following can be inferred from the passage?

   ⬭ Jewelers in small malls pay more rent per square foot than do shoe stores in large malls.

   ⬭ Department store chains consider more than potential sales per square foot when determining where to locate stores.

   ⬭ If mall developers were to charge the same rent per square foot for every store, malls would likely experience a surplus of department stores and a shortage of smaller retailers.

   ⬭ Positive externality is a greater problem for small stores than for larger department stores.

   ⬭ If not for the phenomenon of positive externality, malls would not be able to attract large department stores as tenants.

10. Which of the following statements about large malls and small malls can be logically inferred from the passage?

   ⬭ Department stores in large malls generate more sales per square foot than do department stores in small malls.

   ⬭ Small malls tend to attract more specialized stores than large malls, and therefore do not need as many anchor stores.

   ⬭ The disparity in rent per square foot between small retailers and anchor stores is greater in larger malls than smaller malls.

   ⬭ Small retailers in large malls often resent paying higher rent than anchor stores, and eventually move to smaller malls where the disparity is less pronounced.

   ⬭ Because larger malls are normally assumed to attract an upscale clientele, they can charge small retailers more rent per square foot than smaller malls can.

Questions 11-14 refer to the following passage.

Line   For many years, the observation that certain intensely bright young stars are concentrated along the spiral arms of disk-shaped galaxies remained unexplained. But recent research suggests both a solution to the puzzle of these "O-stars," which are a million times brighter than the sun, and a mechanism that may partially explain the process of
(5) star formation in general.

    Astronomers have long been aware that stars are made up of interstellar gas and dust, but until recently the specific sequence of events that signaled their birth was a mystery. Today, however, the stars in spiral arms of disk-shaped galaxies are thought to result from density waves induced by gravitational fluctuations at the galactic center. These
(10) waves appear to function as the lines along which scattered clouds of interstellar gas and dust collect into much larger clouds, which then coalesce into clumps of high concentration, out of which different types of stars, including O-stars, eventually emerge. Extensive mapping of these cloud complexes, or nebulas, has established a correlation between these complexes and O-stars—a coincidence too striking, in view of the expanse
(15) of empty space within galaxies, to be the result of chance.

Since they produce a red florescence, O-stars are usually found in glowing nebulas that astronomers have labeled H II regions. O-stars cannot migrate out of these regions because their lifespans are too short. Therefore, astronomers have studied H II regions to determine how clouds and O-stars interact.

(20) These observations suggest that the interaction between clouds and O-stars is a self-perpetuating cycle in which stars will be produced until the cloud material is used up. O-stars consume their fuel rapidly and release huge amounts of energy. Moreover, O-star radiation contributes to driving a shock wave into these clouds, compressing gas and dust there. Out of this tremendous compression of gas and dust arises a second
(25) generation of young stars, among them new O-stars.

11. Which of the following best describes the organization of the passage?

   ◯ A puzzle is presented and then two possible scientific solutions are discussed.

   ◯ A new phenomenon is described and then the scientific methods used to study it are discussed.

   ◯ Recent scientific research is described and then applied to solve an existing problem.

   ◯ A previously known phenomenon is described and then explained by scientific observations.

   ◯ A number of scientific hypotheses are discussed and then observations concerning their validity are described.

12. The passage states all of the following about O-stars EXCEPT:

   ◯ They consume their fuel quickly.

   ◯ They are found in glowing nebulas.

   ◯ They are much bigger than the sun.

   ◯ They emit large amounts of radiation.

   ◯ They cannot migrate out of H II regions.

13. According to the passage, interstellar gas and dust coalesce into "clumps of high concentration" (lines 11–12)

   ◯ only in H II regions of space

   ◯ because of gravitational fluctuations in galactic arms

   ◯ when O-stars migrate out of H II regions

   ◯ after releasing huge amounts of energy

   ◯ before new stars are formed

14. The author mentions "O-star radiation" (lines 22–23) in order to

   ◯ explain why O-stars have short lifespans

   ◯ outline the role of O-stars in star formation

   ◯ emphasize the reddish glow of certain nebulas

   ◯ prove that O-stars interact with cloud complexes

   ◯ predict the rate at which nebulas use up their gas and dust

ANSWERS AND EXPLANATIONS

1.	C	6.	E	11.	D
2.	D	7.	C	12.	C
3.	C	8.	D	13.	E
4.	C	9.	B	14.	B
5.	B	10.	C		

1.

Here the "primary purpose" is fairly clearly articulated in the very first sentence of the passage. "The search for an explanation of the historically weak status of U.S. third-party movements is illuminated by examining the conditions that have favored the growth of a strong two-party system." In other words, the purpose of the passage is to explain why most U.S. third party movements have failed to gain major party status (C).

A quick vertical scan of the verbs knocks out a few answer choices. GMAT passages are never comprehensive enough to "trace the historical rise and decline" (B) or "demonstrate" (D) anything exhaustively—(D) is also out because it doesn't mention third-party movements, clearly the topic of this passage. (A) is out because the passage is primarily concerned with the failure of third parties to rise above the state and local levels, not their success there. Finally, (E) is out because no "model" is given to explain the success of some third-party movements; again, the passage is about the general failure of third-party movements nationally.

2.

This is a Detail question, so you just have to scan the passage to find where the Republican Party is mentioned, near the end of the passage. The exact line states: "Except for the Republican Party, which gained national prominence as the Whigs were declining in the 1850s, no third party has ever achieved national major-party status." Clearly, it doesn't take much to infer that the party's establishment was facilitated by the "simultaneous decline of an established major party."

Because this is a Detail question, answers from the wrong part of the passage can be counted out, including (C), an irrelevant detail from the second paragraph. (A) is nowhere mentioned, nor is (B) or (E). *Note*: Just because the question uses the word *suggest*, don't overthink it; just locate the information in the passage—the correct answer will still very often be almost a paraphrase of what you locate.

3.

You're looking for factors to explain the rise of third parties, not their ultimate failure, so you want to research the first paragraph. There it states: "important new issues and voting blocs tend to be initially ignored by the major parties. Such issues . . . tend to gain political prominence through third parties." (C) represents a close paraphrase of this thought.

(A) is out; "powerful economic interests" are not mentioned. (B) is off base; as a general rule major parties are able to bring about broad consensus. And (D) is out; if minorities were excluded from the mainstream of U.S. politics, black urban voters would not have been a significant voting bloc of the Democratic Party. Finally, (E) is out; major parties generally deal successfully with the variety of motivations held by voting blocs in different regions by avoiding narrowly defined political programs.

4.

We're looking for the one answer not cited by the passage. According to sentence 1, enrollments of women in medical schools are increasing, not declining.

Choice (A) is the major problem mentioned in the passage, described variously as feelings of "isolation," "separateness," and "alienation" (sentences 1, 3, and 5) from "peers and the teaching establishment" (paragraph 2). Choices (B), (D), and (E) all contribute to this major problem.

5.

This is one form of Inference question, but as we know, on the GMAT, you aren't expected to infer too much. Sentence 3 mentions "the social stereotype of a male doctor." Since this comes right after the reference to "feelings of isolation" in sentence 1, we can infer that the author thinks gender-based stereotypes are one cause of such feelings (B).

Of the wrong answers, (A) is not supported; enrollments of women are increasing, though there are still few women faculty members—at worst there's a mixed picture, and nothing in the passage supports the idea of "widespread discrimination." (C) contradicts sentence 4, which says institutional policies may "unintentionally" foster feelings of separateness. (D) distorts sentence 2 in the second paragraph; to say changing values will cause institutional bias to decline is not to say that social norms *must* change before bias will decline. (E) exaggerates the last sentence in paragraph 1; we can infer that some women medical students have a negative self-perception, but not that they are the majority.

6.

This is a fairly easy question. Option I is supported by the first sentence of paragraph 2. As women increasingly enter medical schools, they "may feel less at odds with their peers and the teaching establishment." Option II is supported by paragraph 1, which states that the lack of women in faculty positions results in a lack of role models, inferably a source of feelings of isolation. Finally, the author argues that schools should "provide . . . support services designed to meet women's needs." Their "needs" inferably relate to their feelings of isolation. Thus, option III is correct as well.

7.

The question asks about both tone and content. The *tone* of the passage is quiet; the author summarizes facts, cites a statistic, and does not yell or scream. The *content*, however, is not disinterested; the author definitely advocates changes—medical schools should not "wait passively" for society to change but should do more to address the problems of "current students." (C) is the choice that best fits this combination of a quiet, persuasive tone and clear-cut advocacy. "Impassioned" and "indignant" in (A) and (B) are both too shrill; and the passage is not really a "polemic" (a sharply phrased argument directed against some person or position) or a "protest" (the author is *for* certain changes, but that's not the same thing). "Detached" (D) misses the author's involvement in the subject—this author *cares*—and "summary" misses her advocacy. In (E), some persons might feel the author is "biased," but the passage is not primarily a "speculation," but a plea for changes, or an "appeal," as in correct choice (C).

8.

The primary purpose is set up in the first paragraph: mall developers seek department stores because they bring a lot of customers to the malls; however, in order to get those department stores, they have to make it worthwhile for them. The next two paragraphs explain how developers solve this problem by varying rents to compensate the department stores. So, the primary purpose is concisely stated in choice (D), to explain how mall developers attempt to increase customer traffic by varying rental rates for different kinds of stores. Choices (A) and (E) state ideas that are not present in the passage: a comparison with other shopping districts is not made; and maximizing the number of retailers is not discussed. Choice (C) is way too strongly worded and contrary to the tone of the passage; it is never suggested that small stores are exploited, and in any event hiking rents on small stores is not the main point of the passage. Choice (B) may be tempting, because the concept of positive externality clearly is important to the passage, but it's too specific, referring only to the American Midwest. The studies of Midwestern malls are brought up only to support the author's argument.

9.

The question provides no clues as to where to look in the passage for the answer, so we have to work from the answer choices. Choice (B) is correct because the passage states that department store chains will decline to build in a mall if their presence will "primarily" benefit other stores. Therefore, it can't be just their own sales that concern them: They also consider the benefit they provide to other stores. (B) is also a fairly softly worded answer choice, which we love to see as the answer to an inference question. (A) goes too far; while we are given examples of jewelers in malls with more department stores paying more rent than shoe stores in malls with fewer anchors, there is no way to infer a generalization for the opposite cases of jewelers in small malls and shoe stores in large malls. (C) states the opposite of what the passage implies. Department stores demand lower rents per square foot to compensate for their "positive externalities," so a developer offering the same rates to all stores would have a dearth of department stores. (D) likewise contradicts the passage; smaller stores are never said to have "positive externalities," only department stores. Even if smaller stores have that "problem," nothing in the passage implies that smaller stores suffer more from that problem than do larger ones. Finally, (E) gets it wrong because the passage never suggests that positive externality is what attracts department stores to malls. The developers want the department stores for their "positive externalities," not vice versa.

10.

(A) is contradicted by the passage, which says that sales per square foot for department stores are about the same for large and small malls. (B) is nowhere suggested by the passage; differences between the mix of stores in large and small malls are never discussed. (C) is a winner. The passage states that "the partiality in rent shown department stores increases with mall size," which is equivalent to saying that the disparity in rent between anchor (department) stores and small stores is greater for larger malls than smaller malls. (D) is way off base. Resentment never comes up in the passage, nor does the feelings of developers or store owners. (E) makes a claim about "upscale clientele," which is not supported by the passage; the passage explains rental rates based on only customer traffic, not on how chic the store is. Remember to stick closely to the text on inference questions.

11.

The good news about "hard" science passages is that you don't actually have to understand the science to get the correct answer. This Global question asks about the organization of the passage, so after quickly reading through the passage, attack the answer choices aggressively. Paragraph 1 mentions a previously known phenomenon: the location of O-stars in the spiral arms of disk-shaped galaxies. The rest of the passage explains the why and the what of this phenomenon: why O-stars form there and what function they serve there.

The first part of (A) is okay: a "puzzle" is presented; but this choice hops the tracks when it mentions two solutions. This is one of those "half-right, half-wrong" choices that you should watch out for. No new phenomenon is described (B), nor are scientific methods ever discussed. This choice violates the scope of the passage. (C) has things backwards: in the passage, the problem comes before the research. Like (B), (E) violates the scope: the author doesn't discuss a "number of scientific hypotheses."

12.

The only comparison made between O-stars and the sun appears in lines 3–4, which say that O-stars are brighter than the sun, not that they're bigger. Line 22 says that O-stars "consume their fuel rapidly" (A) and "release huge amounts of energy" (D); lines 16–17 indicate that they're "usually found in glowing nebulas" (B) and "cannot migrate out of" H II regions (E). Note that in EXCEPT questions you're looking for the choice that is not true. Use process of elimination to throw out true choices.

13.

Since the question stem sends you back to lines 11–12, the answer is to be found in the middle of the second paragraph. The third sentence of this paragraph explicitly states that gas and dust are concentrated into dense clumps prior to the birth of stars, which is what (E) says. (A) and (C) refer to the wrong part of the passage: the third paragraph; moreover, (C) flatly contradicts information in that paragraph. (D) also refers to the wrong part of the passage, the fourth paragraph, and, besides, pertains to O-stars, not interstellar gas and dust. Finally, (B) gets the paragraph right, but, like (C), flatly contradicts the passage.

14.

Lines 22–23 say that O-star radiation "contributes to driving a shock wave" that compresses gas and dust in clouds. The following lines go on to say that new stars emerge out of this compressed gas and dust.

The short lifespans of O-stars (A) and the reddish glow of "certain nebulas" (C) are brought up in paragraph 3, but aren't linked to O-star radiation. (D) misrepresents the author's purpose: he's not out to "prove that O-stars interact with cloud complexes," he's out to explain how the two interact. (E) also misrepresents the author's purpose: he doesn't "predict" anything. Note that most questions to "hard" science passages tend to be very specific detail questions, in which either a line reference will be provided or the wording in the question will help you to locate the relevant information in the passage. Even if you don't fully understand the passage, you can often get these questions right.

Chapter 5: **GMAT Critical Reasoning**

We hope you're in a contentious mood, because people who love to argue are likely to do well in Critical Reasoning, our last Verbal question type. This is because Critical Reasoning is all about arguments, and your ability to break them apart, identify their weak spots, attack them, defend them—do what you will with them.

"Why are arguments so darn important?" you may well ask. Good question: This means you're not taking things lying down. This means you're getting in a mood to argue! The answer is that the ability to argue persuasively—to understand the logic of an argument, evaluate its merits, and be able to respond to its strengths and weaknesses—requires the critical thinking skills that any good business manager should have. Business managers need to be able to evaluate arguments and proposals with a critical eye. After all, not all business proposals are created equal!

The 41-question Verbal Section contains about 12 or 13 Critical Reasoning questions, so Critical Reasoning will account for about 30 percent of your Verbal score. Critical Reasoning tests reasoning skills involved in making arguments, evaluating arguments, and formulating or evaluating a plan of action. These questions are based on materials from a variety of sources, though you will not need to be familiar with any subject matter beforehand.

Specifically, you are measured on your ability to reason in the following areas:

- **Argument construction:** Recognizing the basic structure of an argument, properly drawn conclusions, underlying assumptions, explanatory hypotheses, or parallels between structurally similar arguments
- **Argument evaluation:** Analyzing an argument, recognizing elements that would strengthen or weaken it, identifying reasoning errors committed in the argument or aspects of the argument's development
- **Formulating and evaluating a plan of action:** Recognizing the relative appropriateness, effectiveness, and efficiency of different plans of action, as well as factors that would strengthen or weaken a proposed plan of action

ANATOMY OF A CRITICAL REASONING QUESTION

Let's start by looking at the various parts of a typical Critical Reasoning question.

The Directions

The directions for this question type are short and sweet:

> **Directions**: Select the best of the answer choices given.

The directions are straightforward, but note once again that they ask you for the best answer—not the perfect answer.

The Stimulus

Above every question you'll find what we at Kaplan call the *stimulus*:

> A study of 20 overweight men revealed that each man experienced significant weight loss after adding SlimDown, an artificial food supplement, to his daily diet. For three months, each man consumed one SlimDown portion every morning after exercising and then followed his normal diet for the rest of the day. Clearly, anyone who consumes one portion of SlimDown every day for at least three months will lose weight and will look and feel his best.

This is a short passage, typically in the form of an argument, which may be drawn from many possible areas, including the natural sciences, the humanities, business, and even casual conversation. Even if the subject matter seems strange, relax. All the information you need to answer the question is on the screen. You don't need to bring in any outside knowledge.

The Question and Answer Choices

Here's the question:

> Which one of the following is an assumption upon which the argument depends?

Read this first! Here's where you find out your task. You may need to identify an argument's assumption or flaw; you may need to determine what would strengthen or weaken the argument; or you may be asked to make a deduction. Pay close attention here: if you misinterpret the question, all your other work will go to waste.

- ⬭ The men in the study will gain back the weight if they discontinue the SlimDown program.
- ⬭ No other dietary supplement will have the same effect on overweight men.
- ⬭ The daily exercise regimen was not responsible for the effects noted in the study.

◯ Women won't experience similar weight reductions if they adhere to the SlimDown program for three months.

◯ Overweight men will achieve only partial weight loss if they don't remain on the SlimDown program for a full three months.

And these are the answer choices. As you no doubt know by now, the test makers have set up one (and only one) of these choices to be correct. If you understand the question and are able to follow the argument, you should be able to zero in on the correct answer quickly. Wrong answer choices usually distort the text, misrepresent its scope, or are the opposite of what you're looking for.

BREAKING DOWN AN ARGUMENT

As noted, the typical Critical Reasoning stimulus is in the form of an argument, and the typical Critical Reasoning question will require you to understand the argument, which involves being able to identify its component parts. But just what do we mean by "argument" on the GMAT?

On the GMAT, an argument is an attempt at a reasoned appeal—it's a piece of text in which an author puts forth a claim and tries to support it. Thus, every GMAT argument contains the following parts:

- The conclusion (the author's claim; the point he or she is trying to make)
- The evidence (the support the author offers for the conclusion)

Identifying the Conclusion and Evidence

For starters, you don't want to make the mistake of thinking that the *conclusion* must come at the *end* of the stimulus. A conclusion could be the first sentence, followed by the evidence, or it could be the last sentence, with the evidence preceding it. Since doing well on Critical Reasoning requires being able to identify an argument's component parts, we must have a way to distinguish the argument's conclusion from its evidence. Fortunately, there are several.

Keywords

In chapter 3 and in the Kaplan Method in chapter 4, we discussed the concept of keywords, the structural clues that authors use to signal logical connections between ideas. Luckily, there are distinct Conclusion keywords and distinct Evidence keywords, and even luckier still, the GMAT writers use these keywords frequently. Here are the most important ones to watch out for:

Conclusion keywords: *Therefore   Thus   As a result   Hence   Clearly   So   Consequently*

Evidence keywords: *because   since   for*

Note: If a sentence contains an Evidence keyword, the part with the Evidence keyword contains evidence; the rest of the sentence contains the conclusion.

But what if the structure of the argument isn't handed to you on a platter? Sometimes, there are no explicit keyword signals in the argument. Fortunately, there are other ways to determine the argument.

The One Sentence Test

As already noted, an argument's conclusion is the author's main point. It's the belief the author wants the reader to adopt, or the actions she wants him to take. Evidence, on the other hand, is just there to support the conclusion; a piece of evidence tends to sound like an undisputed fact rather than a strongly held view.

Therefore, if no obvious keyword points the way to the conclusion, give the stimulus the One Sentence Test: ask yourself what statement the author would make if limited to a single sentence. The statement you come up with (which may sound like a recommendation or an order) should be the conclusion.

The "What" versus "Why" Test

There's one last technique that can help you to distinguish between evidence and conclusion. It's based on the fact that the evidence and the conclusion answer two different types of questions, as you can see:

This part:	Answers the question:
Conclusion	What does the author believe (should be done)?
Evidence	Why does the author believe this?

So if you're unsure whether a particular statement is evidence or a conclusion, ask yourself: Does this sentence express what the author believes? Or, does it explain why the author believes it?

Identify the conclusions in the following arguments:

1. *Get Going* magazine surveyed its readers and found that three out of every four people who want to visit the Andaman Islands wish to do so on a package tour provided by a tour operator. Since tour operators currently in business can provide tours for only 60 percent of those who wish to visit the Andaman Islands, setting up a travel company that offers tours to the Andaman Islands is a relatively risk-free way to make money.

2. In a recently published study, researchers concluded that steady chromium intake, even in small doses, can significantly lower the life expectancy of some primates. In the study, 250 chimpanzees were reared in a laboratory and given small but constant doses of chromium. Within 17 years, all of the chimps had died. Moreover, their average life span was just over 11 years, whereas the average life span for untreated chimps in the wild is approximately 40 years.

Once you locate the conclusion, the rest of the stimulus should be evidence that supports the conclusion. We'll see whether you've properly identified the conclusions in a bit. But there's a third crucial component to every GMAT argument. Did you find the evidence in these arguments strong enough to convince you of the conclusions? Or, did you find that additional evidence would be necessary for the argument to be convincing? This additional evidence—facts that need to be, but haven't been, established or mentioned—has a special name.

Assumptions

There are very few vocabulary words you need to know for the GMAT, but here's one of them:

Assumptions act as additional, unstated evidence. They are statements that must be true for the argument to be valid.

To find assumptions, compare the terms in the conclusion with the terms in the evidence. Then ask yourself: "What's missing?" Almost every GMAT argument contains a logical gap between the evidence and the conclusion. The author's assumptions are what fills that gap. With practice, as you read a GMAT argument, the author's assumptions should start to jump right out at you. This is because the same types of assumptions appear over and over again on GMAT arguments.

ASSUMPTIONS EXERCISE

Let's see how well you do at spotting assumptions. Take another look at the two arguments you just analyzed. Weigh the conclusions you identified against the evidence, and ask yourself what's missing. Remember to read critically. Put the author's assumptions in your own words and then see whether you identified the same assumptions (and conclusions) that we did.

1. The Andaman Islands Argument
   The author assumes that _____

   _____

   _____

2. The Chromium Chimps Argument
   The author assumes that _____

   _____

   _____

ANSWERS AND EXPLANATIONS

1. *The Andaman Islands Argument*: We hope you located the conclusion in the last sentence, namely: "[S]etting up a travel company that offers tours to the Andaman Islands is a relatively risk-free way to make money." This conclusion is based on a survey by *Get Going* magazine, which found that 75 percent of those who want to visit Andaman Islands would like to do so on a package tour, whereas package tour providers at present can provide such tours for only 60 percent of those wishing to visit the islands. Here are some assumptions we found:

   - The author assumes that everyone who *wishes* to visit the Andaman Islands will in fact *do* so. If some of the people who wish to visit the islands won't actually do so, then the present tour providers may be more than sufficient to handle the numbers wanting package tours who actually will visit the islands.

- The author also assumes that the survey is not biased. What if *Get Going* magazine specializes in reviewing package tours and its readership is much more likely to prefer package tours than your average tourist? If the survey is not representative, then the conclusion is not valid.

2. *The Chromium Chimps Argument*: Here the conclusion was found in the first sentence: "[S]teady chromium intake, even in small doses, can significantly lower the life expectancy of some primates." This conclusion was based on the study in which chimps given small but constant doses of chromium in a laboratory had average life spans of 11 years, compared with average life spans of chimps in the wild of about 40 years. This is a classic causal argument, and here are some assumptions we found:

- The author assumes that chimps raised in a lab and chimps in the wild would normally have similar life expectancies.
- Even more important, the author assumes that there wasn't something else that caused the chimps in the study to die prematurely. Who knows? Maybe most of the chimps succumbed to a sudden outbreak of Ebola virus. The point is that in a causal argument, it's always assumed that there's not another plausible explanation for what happened.

Let's recap what we've learned about the structure of arguments.

Evidence + (*Assumption*) → Conclusion

These are the components of an argument. When you break down an argument on the GMAT, you should begin by identifying the author's conclusion (what the author wants you to believe) and the evidence (why the author thinks you should accept the conclusion). From there you should be able to identify the missing steps or gaps between the evidence and the conclusion. These are the author's assumptions.

Spotting the author's assumptions will obviously help you to answer questions that ask about assumptions. But uncovering an argument's assumptions is also key to handling many other types of questions. It's time to examine the types of questions that commonly appear on Critical Reasoning.

CRITICAL REASONING QUESTION TYPES

Certain question types crop up again and again on the GMAT, and it pays to understand them beforehand.

Assumption Questions

As we just discussed, an assumption is a piece of support that isn't explicitly stated but is necessary for the argument to remain valid. When a question asks you for what's missing from the argument or what the argument depends on, then it's asking you to find the assumption.

Strategies for Solving Assumption Questions

You can often predict an answer to an Assumption question. By previewing the question stem, you'll know what to look for. Once you understand the argument's structure, you may well see a missing piece. Consider this simple stimulus:

Allyson plays volleyball for Central High School. Therefore, Allyson must be over 6 feet tall.

The conclusion is pretty clearly the second sentence, and the evidence is the first. Where's the problem? Well, who's to say that all high school volleyball players have to be over 6 feet tall? So we can pretty confidently predict that an answer would say something like this:

All volleyball players at Central High School are over 6 feet tall.

But what if the assumption doesn't just jump out at you like this? Can you track it down? Of course you can! One of the most common ways the GMAT uses assumptions is to cover over a scope shift in the argument. Notice how the argument starts by talking about playing volleyball and then all of a sudden is talking about being over 6 feet tall. Look closely at the terms in each part of the argument. Could the scope be slightly different?

Consider this seemingly solid argument:

Candidate A won the presidential election, carrying 40 out of 50 states. Clearly, Candidate A has a strong mandate to push for her legislative agenda.

Sounds pretty good. But take a close look at the terms of the argument. The evidence is a win representing a sizeable majority of states. The conclusion is about a strong mandate for an agenda. Even if you don't immediately see why those two things don't have to be the same, you could still make a prediction like this: "Candidate A's big victory means she has a mandate for her agenda." You'd be much more likely to recognize the right answer between these two possibilities:

⬭ No other candidate in the last 24 years has won as many states as did Candidate A.
⬭ Most of the people who voted for Candidate A support her legislative agenda.

The first answer choice doesn't deal with Candidate A's agenda at all. The second one shows a connection between her victory and her agenda, so it must be the right answer.

But what if you still aren't sure that your answer choice is correct? Or what if the assumption is so subtle that you can't predict the answer at all? You can use the Denial Test.

The Denial Test

Because an assumption must be true for the conclusion to be valid, we can test each answer by seeing whether the conclusion could still be valid even the answer were negated (e.g., rewritten to say the opposite). If the argument falls apart, then that answer choice is a necessary assumption. If the argument is unaffected, then the choice is wrong. Let's look at the volleyball answer choice:

All volleyball players at Central High School are over 6 feet tall.

Now let's negate it:

Some volleyball players at Central High School are not over 6 feet tall.

Would Allyson still have to be over 6 feet tall? Of course not! That's why that answer choice would be a necessary assumption. And now look at the Candidate A answer choices:

○ No other candidate in the last 24 years has won as many states as did Candidate A.
○ Most of the people who voted for Candidate A support her legislative agenda.

And now we'll negate them:

○ Some candidates in the last 24 years have won as many states as did Candidate A.

Could Candidate A still enjoy a strong mandate? Of course. Just because others in the past were as popular doesn't mean that she doesn't enjoy support for her agenda as well.

○ Most of the people who voted for Candidate A do not support her legislative agenda.

Now can Candidate A claim a mandate for her agenda? Of course not. That's why the second choice would be credited as correct.

Sample Question Stems

Assumption questions are worded in some of the following ways:

- Which one of the following is assumed by the author?
- Upon which one of the following assumptions does the author rely?
- The argument depends on the assumption that . . .
- Which one of the following, if added to the passage, would make the conclusion logical?
- The validity of the argument depends on which one of the following?
- The argument presupposes which one of the following?

Strengthen and Weaken Questions

Determining an argument's necessary assumption, as we've just seen, is required to answer an Assumption question. But it also is required to answer another common type of question: Strengthen or Weaken.

In the real world, we can weaken someone's argument by attacking her evidence. But the GMAT is not testing your ability simply to find evidence but rather your ability to analyze how that evidence is used. The right answer to a Weaken question on the GMAT will always weaken the connection between the evidence and the conclusion—in other words, the assumption.

The answer to many Weaken questions is the one that reveals an author's assumption to be unreasonable; conversely, the answer to many Strengthen questions provides additional support by affirming the truth of an assumption.

Let's use the same stimulus as before but in the context of these other question types:

Allyson plays volleyball for Central High School. Therefore, Allyson must be over 6 feet tall.

Remember the assumption holding this argument together? It was that all volleyball players for Central High are over 6 feet tall. That's the assumption that makes or breaks the argument. So if you're asked to weaken the argument, you'd want to attack that assumption:

Which one of the following, if true, would most weaken the argument?

Prediction: Not all volleyball players at Central High School are over 6 feet tall.

Answer:

⬭ Some volleyball players at Central High School are under 6 feet tall.

We've called into doubt the author's basic assumption, thus damaging the argument. But what about strengthening the argument? Again, the key is the necessary assumption:

Which one of the following, if true, would most strengthen the argument?

Prediction: All volleyball players at Central High School are over 6 feet tall.

Answer:

⬭ No member of the Central High School volleyball team is under 6'2".

Here, by confirming the author's assumption, we've in effect bolstered the argument.

Sample Stems

The stems associated with these two question types are usually self-explanatory. Here's a list of what you can expect to see on test day:

Weaken:

- Which one of the following, if true, would most weaken the argument above?
- Which one of the following, if true, would most seriously damage the argument above?
- Which one of the following, if true, casts the most doubt on the argument above?
- Which of the following, if true, would most seriously call into question the plan outlined above?

Strengthen:

- Which one of the following, if true, would most strengthen the argument?
- Which one of the following, if true, would provide the most support for the conclusion in the argument above?
- The argument above would be more persuasive if which one of the following was found to be true?

It's also common for the question stem to refer explicitly to part of the argument. You might, for example, see the following:

Which of the following, if true, casts the most doubt on the author's conclusion that the Brookdale Public Library does not meet the requirements of the new building code?

By reading the question stem first, we are told outright what the author's conclusion is, making our reading of the stimulus much easier to manage.

INFERENCE QUESTIONS

The process of inferring is a matter of considering one or more statements as evidence and then drawing a conclusion from them. A valid inference is something that must be true if the statements in the stimulus are true. Not *might* be true, not *probably* is true, but *must* be true.

Think of an inference as a conclusion that requires no assumption whatsoever. But the answer to an Inference question is just as likely to be drawn from only one or two details as it is to take into account the stimulus as a whole. For this reason, it can be very difficult to predict an exact answer. Nevertheless, you can make a general prediction: The answer is the one that *must* be true based on the facts in the stimulus. You can use this prediction to help eliminate choices answer by answer, ruling out options that clearly don't match the facts as you paraphrased them. This is the beauty of a multiple-choice test—find four wrong answers, and you've also found the right one!

Let's examine a somewhat expanded version of the volleyball team argument:

Allyson plays volleyball for Central High School, despite the team's rule against participation by nonstudents. Therefore, Allyson must be over 6 feet tall.

Wrong answer: Allyson is the best player on the Central High School volleyball team.

Certainly Allyson *might* be the best player on the team. It's tempting to think that this would *probably* be true—otherwise the team would not risk whatever penalties violating the rule might entail. But *must* it be true? No. Allyson could be the second best. Or the third best. Or perhaps the coach owed Allyson's dad a favor. We have no support for the idea that she's the best on the team.

Valid inference: Allyson is not a student at Central High School.

Clearly, if Allyson plays volleyball *despite* the team's rule against participation by nonstudents, she must not be a student. Otherwise, she wouldn't be playing despite the rule; she'd be playing in accordance with the rule. But note that this inference is not an essential assumption of the argument because the conclusion about Allyson's height doesn't depend on it.

So be careful: Unlike an assumption, an inference need not have anything to do with the author's conclusion. In fact, many Inference questions don't have conclusions at all—they consist solely of individual facts. Make sure you are prepared for Inference questions, as they require a different approach than do other Critical Reasoning questions. Remember, everything that you'll need will be contained in the stimulus, so focus on the information as it's presented and avoid answers that twist the facts (or make up new ones).

Sample Stems

Inference questions probably have the most varied wording of all the Critical Reasoning question stems. Some question stems denote inference fairly obviously. Others are more subtle, and still others may even look like other question types entirely. The bottom line is that if a question asks you to take the stimulus as fact and find something based on it, then you're looking at an Inference question. Here's a quick rundown of various Inference question stems that you may see on your test:

- Which one of the following is inferable from the argument above?
- Which one of the following is implied by the argument above?
- The author suggests that . . .
- If all the statements above are true, which one of the following must also be true on the basis of them?
- The statements above, if true, support which of the following?
- Which of the following is best supported by the statements above?
- Which of the following is the conclusion toward which the author is probably moving?
- The statements above best support which of the following conclusions?

Other Question Types

Assumption, Strengthen, Weaken, and Inference make up about 85 percent of all Critical Reasoning questions, but you might run into other question types as well.

Explain Questions

These ask you to find an explanation for a seeming discrepancy in the question stem. Your paraphrasing skills are the key to this problem type—in your own words, restate not only the details in the stimulus but also the nature of the apparent inconsistency. Then, look for an answer that explains how the apparently contradictory facts in the stimulus could both be true.

Here are some example question stems:

- Which of the following would best explain the discrepancy above?
- Which of the following would best resolve the paradox described above?

Flaw Questions

These are similar to Weaken questions, but instead of asking you for some new fact that, if true, would make the argument questionable, Flaw questions ask what's already wrong. So your prediction should focus on reasoning errors made in the argument.

Here are some example question stems:

- Which of the following is a flaw in the reasoning above?
- The argument above is vulnerable to which of the following criticisms?

Boldface Questions

Boldface questions ask for the role that specific sentences play in relation to an author's argument. The relevant sentences are, as the name implies, written in bold font. The answers to these questions will be abstract, using language such as "The first provides a counterexample to an opinion, while the second reaffirms that opinion by dismissing the counterexample." This technical language may make these problems seem intimidating.

Fortunately, these questions are rare, appearing only occasionally on the tests of high-scoring test takers. Moreover, if you do see one of these questions on test day, it shouldn't be nearly as scary as it looks. Remind yourself that Boldface questions test the same core skill as the rest of the Critical Reasoning section: the ability to identify the evidence and the conclusion of an argument.

One caution: Unlike most GMAT stimuli, Boldface questions often contain multiple arguments. Make sure that you note not only which parts of the argument are evidence and which are conclusions but also which evidence is connected to which conclusion. In addition, use keywords in the stimulus to identify which conclusion (if any) the author agrees with. Once you've done so, you should be able to make a prediction about the role of the boldface statements. Then you can turn these difficult questions into points.

Here is an example question:

- The portions of the argument in **boldface** play which of the following roles?

THE KAPLAN METHOD FOR CRITICAL REASONING

We've developed a method that you can use to attack each and every Critical Reasoning question.

Step 1: Identify the Question Type

Reading the question stem is a great way to focus your reading of the stimulus. Determine the question type, and you'll know exactly what you're looking for. There may be other important information in the question stem as well—possibly even the conclusion itself.

Step 2: Untangle the Stimulus

With the question stem in mind, read the stimulus. Read actively, paraphrasing to make sure you understand the argument's construction and hunting for any potential problems.

Step 3: Predict the Answer

Form an idea of what the right answer choice should say or do.

Step 4: Evaluate the Choices

Attack each answer choice critically. Keep your prediction in mind and see whether the answer choices match it. If you don't find a "clear winner," start looking through the answers that you haven't eliminated. You know what you *like* about each; now focus on what might be *wrong*.

Here's how your Prediction and Evaluation steps will work for the major question types:

- **Assumption:** Predict what the central assumption should say and hunt for the answer that matches your prediction. If that fails, use the Denial Test.
- **Strengthen/Weaken:** Identify the central assumption and predict an answer explaining why that assumption is more (for a Strengthen question) or less (for a Weaken question) likely to come true.
- **Inference:** It's often difficult to form a prediction beyond "the right answer must be true." Work through the answers one by one, eliminating choices that are clearly wrong. Don't eliminate an answer that you're unsure of—it may be right.
- **Explain:** Predict the answer that explains how seemingly discrepant facts can both be true.
- **Flaw:** Predict the reasoning error committed by the argument.
- **Boldface:** Predict an answer based on your understanding of the author's use of logic.

Now let's apply the Kaplan Method to the Critical Reasoning item we saw earlier:

A study of 20 overweight men revealed that each man experienced significant weight loss after adding SlimDown, an artificial food supplement, to his daily diet. For three months, each man consumed one SlimDown portion every morning after exercising and then followed his normal diet for the rest of the day. Clearly, anyone who consumes one portion of SlimDown every day for at least three months will lose weight and will look and feel his best.

Which one of the following is an assumption on which the argument depends?

- ○ The men in the study will gain back the weight if they discontinue the SlimDown program.
- ○ No other dietary supplement will have the same effect on overweight men.
- ○ The daily exercise regimen was not responsible for the effects noted in the study.
- ○ Women won't experience similar weight reductions if they adhere to the SlimDown program for three months.
- ○ Overweight men will achieve only partial weight loss if they don't remain on the SlimDown program for a full three months.

Step 1: Identify the Question Type

We see, quite clearly, that we're dealing with an Assumption question. So we can immediately adopt an "assumption mindset," which means we know before we even read the stimulus that there will be some missing link in the chain of reasoning—a missing piece of support without which the conclusion wouldn't be valid. Now we turn to the stimulus, ready to find that link.

Step 2: Untangle the Stimulus

Sentence 1 introduces a study of 20 men using a food supplement product, resulting in weight loss for all 20. Sentence 2 describes how they used it: once a day, for three months, after morning exercise. So far so good; it feels as if we're building up to something. The keyword *clearly* usually indicates that some sort of conclusion follows, and in fact it does: Sentence 3 says that anyone who has one portion of the product daily for three months will lose weight, too.

We might paraphrase the argument like this:

> Each of 20 overweight men lost weight by consuming some SlimDown every morning after exercise, then eating normally. So anyone who consumes SlimDown will lose weight.

Reading critically, do we see any scope shifts or other potential problems? Sure—what happened to the exercise? It's in the evidence as part of the study regimen but is totally dropped from the conclusion. That's a pretty significant change in scope, and we can use that as the basis of our prediction in Step 3.

We could, if we were so inclined, look at the argument even more abstractly:

> A bunch of guys did A and B and had X result. So if someone does A, they'll get X result too.

Sounds pretty fishy—who says A (SlimDown) caused X (weight loss)? Why couldn't it have been B (exercise)? We can use this insight to make a prediction in Step 3, too. Notice that no matter how abstractly or concretely we analyze the question stem, we arrive at the same basic issue—that the author isn't accounting for the exercise.

Step 3: Predict the Answer

We've realized that the argument forgot to consider the exercise. So we might predict something like "The author assumes exercise doesn't matter." That's it. There's no need to paraphrase with something fancy and glamorous. A vague paraphrase, as long as it's focused on the right scope, is enough to find the right answer.

Step 4: Evaluate the Choices

Judge the answer choices based on how well they fulfill the requirements of your prediction. And sure enough, only (C) even mentions the exercise regimen! Reading it closely, we see it fits our prediction perfectly, clearing up the question of whether the exercise caused the weight loss.

Since the difficulty of Critical Reasoning is often in the answer choices (rather than the stimulus), you can't let them make you indecisive. Pick (C) with confidence and move on.

We also could have used the Denial Test. Let's look at what the answer choices would look like when negated:

- Answer choice (A): The men in the study will not gain back the weight if they discontinue the SlimDown program. There's no reason to think that just because the weight loss is permanent, it wasn't caused by SlimDown. Wrong answer.

- Answer choice (B): Other dietary supplements would have the same effect. That's no reason to think that SlimDown wouldn't work. (The conclusion says that SlimDown will work, not that *only* SlimDown could work.) Wrong answer.

- Answer choice (C): The daily exercise regimen was responsible for the effects noted in the study. If it was the exercise, it wasn't the SlimDown. Now the conclusion isn't possible . . . so this is definitely the right answer!

- Answer choice (D): Women will experience similar weight reductions if they adhere to the SlimDown program for three months. That's no reason to think that it didn't work for the men. Wrong answer.

- Answer choice (E): Overweight men could achieve total weight loss if they don't remain on the program for a full three months. If anything, this makes the conclusion even stronger. Wrong answer.

PRACTICE QUESTIONS

Now that we've examined the Kaplan Method and all the most common Critical Reasoning question types, you should be ready to try out what you've learned on the following practice questions. If you encounter a question type you haven't seen before, fear not. Identifying the conclusion, evidence, and underlying assumptions of the argument will most likely be the key to solving the question. If you can't ascertain the correct answer, eliminate as many wrong answer choices as you can, make your best guess, and move on.

1. Enrollment in graduate and professional programs tends to be high in a strong economy and much lower during recessions. The perceived likelihood of future job availability, therefore, affects people's willingness to pass up immediate earning potential in order to invest in career-related training.

   The argument above assumes that

   ○ the perceived likelihood of job availability has decreased in recent years

   ○ all those who avoid graduate and professional school during an economic slump do so because of the perceived lack of future jobs

   ○ perceptions of the likelihood of job availability are related to the state of the economy

   ○ those who enroll in graduate and professional schools during a strong economy help increase the economy's strength

   ○ graduate and professional programs admit fewer students during recessions

2. **The university's decision to scale back significantly its teaching of the literary and philosophical classics of the Western Tradition is misguided.** Proponents of the move argue that today's students are not interested in these works and desire more practical business-related courses that will help them in their future careers. But any student lacking a sufficient grounding in the thought and tradition that underlie the present civilization cannot be said to be fully educated. **The classics are the primary vehicle for instilling such knowledge.**

    Which of the following best expresses the relationship between the two bolded statements above?

    ◯ The first statement offers a hypothesis, and the second statement offers conflicting evidence.

    ◯ The first statement suggests an alternative explanation for the phenomenon described in the second statement.

    ◯ The second statement provides evidence for a conclusion drawn in the first statement.

    ◯ The second statement must be true for the first statement to be true.

    ◯ The second statement is an inference drawn from the first statement.

3. Due to a string of dismal performances, a touring band has begun to lose its audience. News of the disappointing concerts has traveled quickly via the Internet and has negatively influenced ticket sales for future performances. Due to the poor ticket sales, a number of promoters have canceled the band's upcoming shows, forcing the band to attempt to recoup its touring and recording expenses from fewer total performances.

    Which of the following, if true, taken together with the information above, best supports the prediction that more of the band's shows will be canceled?

    ◯ The promoters who canceled shows did so with the promise that they would monitor the band's reception in other cities before deciding whether or not to reschedule the canceled shows.

    ◯ The pressure to restore its diminishing fan base and recoup its overall expenses from a decreased number of performing opportunities is likely to cause the band to perform poorly in future concerts.

    ◯ Because of the canceled shows, it will be impossible for the band to earn a profit on the current tour.

    ◯ If the band cannot salvage the tour, its next album will likely fail economically unless the band can restore its image through online videos.

    ◯ It is impossible for the management of a rock band to predict accurately the success of a tour because fans of rock bands are notoriously fickle in their tastes.

4. Over the past several years, Running River Water Park has experienced a serious decline in attendance and sales despite the addition of several state-of-the-art water slides. This year, the Board of Directors lowered the park's weekday admission prices in order to attract more customers. Attendance during the first two months of this year's season has been 30 percent higher than the attendance during the same two months last year. Clearly, the price cut has had the desired effect.

Each of the following, if true, weakens the conclusion above EXCEPT:

○ Nationwide, the number of people attending amusement parks has increased by 30 percent this year over last year.

○ Grand Excursions Amusement Park, located ten miles from Running River, has been closed during most of this year's season due to unexpected equipment problems.

○ The most popular movie released this summer, *The Big Chase*, features a long action sequence that was filmed at Running River.

○ Several large businesses relocated near Running River during the past year bringing with them many employees and their families.

○ Most amusement park visitors are aware of the admission prices before they arrive at an amusement park.

5. Staff members at the Willard Detention Center typically oversee students' schedules and make all final decisions regarding the required activities in which students participate. Students are permitted, however, to make their own decisions regarding how they spend their free time. Therefore, students should be permitted to make their own decisions regarding the elective courses that they wish to take.

The conclusion above would be more reasonably drawn if which of the following were inserted into the argument as an additional premise?

○ Decisions regarding required activities are more important than decisions regarding the elective courses that students take.

○ Students are more willing to take elective courses than to participate in required Center activities.

○ Required activities contribute more to the students' rehabilitation than do their free-time activities.

○ Staff members at Willard have found that elective courses are more beneficial for students than the available free-time activities.

○ When compared for decision-making purposes, elective courses are more like free-time activities than required activities.

6. The average math score on a state-wide proficiency exam for students attending Middlebury High School last year was 20 points higher than the average math score for students attending nearby Ellingsford High School. Therefore, any student at Ellingsford High School wishing to achieve a better math score on next September's proficiency exam should transfer to Middlebury High School over the summer.

    Which of the following statements, if true, would most significantly strengthen the conclusion drawn in the passage?

    ○ Middlebury High School offers its students a unique, week-long course just before they take the proficiency exam that has consistently proven effective in raising student scores.

    ○ One-third of all the students who have transferred to Middlebury High School the summer before taking the test got scores that are at least 20 points higher than the average score at Ellingsford High School.

    ○ Middlebury High School students who transfer to Ellingsford High School in the summer before they take the proficiency exam get average scores that are comparable to the average scores of students who remain at Middlebury.

    ○ In the past five years, the average score at Ellingsford High School has been rising at a faster rate than has the average score at Middlebury High School.

    ○ Students wanting better proficiency exam scores are transferring to Middlebury High School at a high rate, which will ultimately result in a lowering of the school's average score.

7. A study found that last year roughly 6,000 homeless people in the United States were admitted to hospitals because of malnutrition. In the same year, a little more than 10,000 nonhomeless people were admitted to hospitals for the same reason. These findings clearly show that the nonhomeless are more likely to suffer from malnutrition than are the homeless.

    The answer to which of the following questions would be most likely to point out the illogical nature of the conclusion drawn above?

    ○ What is the relative level of severity of the malnutrition suffered by each group cited in the study?

    ○ To what extent, on average, are the nonhomeless better off financially than the homeless?

    ○ To what extent are the causes of malnutrition in the nonhomeless related to ignorance of proper dietary habits?

    ○ What percentage of each group cited in the study suffered from malnutrition last year?

    ○ What effect would a large increase in the number of homeless shelters have on the incidence of malnutrition among the homeless?

8. History has shown that severe and sudden political instability strikes the Republic of Balanda roughly once every 50 years. The most recent example was the attempt on the president's life in 1992. The reaction of average investors in Balanda to crisis situations in the country cannot be predicted in advance. The government's fiscal affairs department has introduced an electronic protection mechanism into the market in the hopes of avoiding a prolonged large-scale selloff. The mechanism is triggered in specific instances based on estimations of how average investors will react to changes in corporate data and economic indicators.

    If the statements above are true, which of the following conclusions can be drawn regarding the electronic protection mechanism?

    ◯ Sometime within the next 50 years severe and sudden political instability in Balanda will trigger the protection mechanism.

    ◯ Whether the protection mechanism will function appropriately in response to a sudden political event depends on whether the event is seen by investors as positive or negative.

    ◯ It is unclear how well the protection mechanism would work in the event of a sudden political coup if such an event were partially or wholly unrelated to changes in corporate data and economic indicators.

    ◯ There would be no way for the protection mechanism to differentiate between market fluctuations resulting from economic factors and those that are caused by political instability.

    ◯ The protection mechanism would be purposely destroyed by political insurgents if they were able to infiltrate the government's fiscal affairs department.

9. Country X complains that Country Y's high tariffs on imported goods have artificially inflated the price of cars imported from Country X into Country Y, and that this is the reason that few of Country X's cars are sold in Country Y. On the other hand, Country X's very low tariffs allow Country Y to sell many cars there at relatively low prices. Country X says that if Country Y would lower its tariffs, then Country X's cars would be able to compete in Country Y and an equitable balance of trade would be achieved.

    Which of the following, if true, would most undermine the validity of Country X's explanation for the poor sales of its cars in Country Y?

    ◯ In places where the tariffs on goods from both countries are equal, Country Y's cars far outsell cars from Country X.

    ◯ Cars imported from Country Z sell poorly in Country Y.

    ◯ In countries where tariffs on imported goods are higher than in Country Y, Country X sells more cars than does Country Y.

    ◯ Other goods from Country X sell poorly in Country Y.

    ◯ Sales of Country Y's cars are high even in countries that have higher tariffs on imported goods than does Country X.

10. Many adults, no matter what their age, respond to adversity by seeking advice only from their parents. Consciously or not, they regress to a psychological state of childhood dependence in which the parent is seen as the only source of wisdom and comfort. Adults who do not regress to this childhood mode turn for advice in adversity only to other loved ones—a spouse or a best friend—whom they perceive and relate to as peers.

    If all of the above statements are true, which of the following must also be true?

    ○ One's parents offer more wisdom in adversity than those whom one perceives as peers.
    ○ Adults who do not suffer adversity look only to their parents for advice.
    ○ No adults seek advice in adversity from total strangers.
    ○ Adults who seek advice in adversity from their parents do not expect to receive wisdom and comfort.
    ○ Adults who regress to a state of childhood dependence lose touch with their peers.

11. Recent experiments in the Southern Ocean offer the promise of controlling the threat of global warming by creating organic "sponges" for carbon dioxide, which is widely considered the main culprit for rising global temperatures. Scientists were able to grow a lush strip of phytoplankton 150 kilometers long by fertilizing a patch of the ocean with hundreds of kilograms of an iron compound. Phytoplankton presently accounts for over half of the photosynthesis on Earth, the process by which carbon dioxide is absorbed and converted into oxygen. A major limiting factor in the production of phytoplankton is lack of iron, but by fertilizing oceans with iron compounds scientists hope to be able to reduce carbon dioxide levels and reverse the greenhouse effect.

    Which of the following, if true, casts the most serious doubt upon the advisability of using the fertilization method described above to control carbon dioxide levels?

    ○ In some oceans, the growth of phytoplankton is also limited by how much nitrogen, phosphorus, and silicon are available.
    ○ The cost of fertilizing the oceans with sufficient quantities of iron to reverse the greenhouse effect is likely to be very high.
    ○ Iron naturally reaches the seas in the form of wind-blown mineral dust, which becomes more or less abundant as conditions on land change.
    ○ Fertilization efforts will do nothing to curb the production of more carbon dioxide emissions.
    ○ The oceans are a complex system, and the long-term consequences of ocean fertilization may be the opposite of what is predicted.

12. University systems that use graduation rates to determine which campuses are allotted additional funds are acting counter to their stated goals. The universities say they are trying to raise academic standards, yet they are actually encouraging campuses to graduate students regardless of achievement.

    Which of the following statements, if true, would help to validate the approach taken by the university systems mentioned above?

    ○ Graduation rates for university systems with this policy are among the highest in the nation, but the graduates from these systems score poorly on tests of basic skills.

    ○ The campuses that need the additional funds the most are the ones that have the lowest graduation rates.

    ○ The new funds will be allotted for facility upgrades, not new faculty positions or staff pay increases.

    ○ Graduation examinations currently exist that require every graduate at each university to demonstrate a minimum level of achievement.

    ○ An opposing plan focuses on providing extra funding based not on graduation rates, but on the percent of students that pass basic skills tests.

ANSWERS AND EXPLANATIONS

1. C	5. E	9. A
2. C	6. A	10. C
3. B	7. D	11. E
4. E	8. C	12. D

1.

We're asked to find an assumption. The argument involves a question of cause and effect. Since enrollment in graduate and professional programs tends to be high when the economy is strong and low when it is weak, the reason must be, according to the author, a matter of people's perceptions of job availability. Sounds reasonable, but do all the terms match up with those in this conclusion? We know from the question stem that they do not. What's missing? Well, the evidence pertains to the state of the economy. But the conclusion strays into the area of psychology—people's perceptions. Are these the same things? The author treats them as such by arguing from evidence regarding the state of the economy to a conclusion based on people's *perceptions* of the economy. The author takes the relationship between these for granted, but technically, in order for the argument to work, this must be established. (C) reveals this basic assumption.

2.

Questions such as this one, which ask about the functions played by the bolded sentences in an argument, have become increasingly popular on the GMAT—so there's a good chance you'll see one on test day. Once again, your primary task is to break down the argument and identify its parts. Here the conclusion is in fact the first sentence of the passage; the rest of the passage goes on to explain why the university's decision is misguided. The first sentence, when it is phrased as an assertion, as here, is often the conclusion of the passage. So why is the university's decision misguided? (1) Students lacking a certain grounding cannot be considered fully educated. (2) The classics are the primary vehicle for instilling such knowledge. So the final sentence (second statement) provides evidence for the conclusion drawn in the first sentence (first statement), which is exactly what (C) says. You can also use the process of elimination. (A) is out because the second statement offers no *conflicting* evidence. (B) is out because the second statement does not describe a *phenomenon* and the first statement suggests no *alternative* explanation. (D) is out because the second statement does not have to be true in order for the first statement to be true, nor is the second statement an inference, or logically drawn conclusion, of the first statement, as (E) states.

3.

This question is a little unusual in that the conclusion—more of the band's shows will be canceled—appears in the actual question. You already know the argument's conclusion, so read the passage carefully and follow the flow of the evidence presented. Dismal performances led to a drop in ticket sales for future concerts, which in turn led concert promoters to cancel concerts, putting additional pressure on the band to make up the lost money from fewer shows. We're looking for the choice that leads to more canceled shows, and it's not easy to predict the answer here. But you can test each choice to see where it fits into this chain of events, if at all. Canceled concerts must now lead to a result that will trigger additional canceled concerts. What do you already know leads to canceled concerts? Dismal performances and lower ticket sales. Keep this in mind while testing out the choices. (B) works by turning the chain of events into a vicious cycle. If (B) were true, we would expect the events to follow the same course, culminating in the cancellation of more shows. Of the wrong choices, (A) indicates that some of the shows that have already been canceled might be rescheduled. Optimally, the band would get to perform the original number of shows, and at worst, the band will perform the current reduced number of concerts. But there is nothing here to indicate that even more shows will be canceled. (C) begins with the canceled concerts but then jumps beyond the scope of the argument to the issue of "profit." The impossibility of earning a profit under the current circumstances is an effect of the canceled shows—but it does nothing to suggest that more shows will be canceled. (D) discusses the long-term prospects for the band, but nothing here suggests that more shows on the current tour will be canceled. The effect that this tour ultimately has on the band's next album does not directly influence what happens now. (E) goes beyond the scope of the evidence. The accuracy of the management's predictions is not at issue.

4.

This is a Weaken "EXCEPT" question, so you're looking for the one choice that would *not* weaken the conclusion. This is a classic causal argument. The author concludes that the Water Park's admissions price cut is responsible for the increase in attendance over the same period last year. Of course, to weaken a causal argument, one needs only to point out another plausible explanation for the increase in attendance. (A), which notes an increase in park attendance nationally, (B), which notes the closing of a competitor, (C), which notes favorable publicity in a popular movie for the park, and (D), which notes an increase in the size and affluence of the local population, all offer other plausible reasons for the increase in attendance. Only (E), which notes that most people are aware of admission prices, would strengthen, rather than weaken, the conclusion, since public awareness of the price cut would be necessary for the price cut to have a positive effect on attendance.

5.

The argument here is a simple one: since students at the Willard Detention Center make their own decisions about free time, they should also make their own decisions about elective courses. The argument assumes that, for these students, decisions about what to do with free time are similar to decisions about what electives to take in school. Since we're looking for a premise to complete the argument, look for a choice that provides evidence that these things are similar. (E) provides the evidence we need. If it is true that elective courses are more akin to free time than to required activities, then the conclusion that students should be able to choose their own electives is more reasonable. You could have eliminated as follows: (A) is outside the scope of the argument; it's not the *importance* of the decision that's at issue here, it's who should have the power to make the decision. (B) is irrelevant; students' relative willingness to take the different types of courses doesn't matter. The argument concerns only who should make the decisions regarding activities. (C) may explain why staff members oversee decisions about required activities, but it tells us nothing about why students should be allowed to choose their own elective courses. In fact, it doesn't refer to elective courses at all. (D) follows the same general pattern of the other wrong choices, focusing on an irrelevant issue (in this case, the relative benefits of electives versus free-time activities), rather than the issue at hand: who should make the decisions.

6.

As you read the stem, you should have tried to identify the evidence and conclusion, and think about the possibility that an assumption glues the two together. An answer choice that validates that assumption will strengthen the author's argument. The author argues that since Middlebury High School students tend to get better math scores on the test, Ellingsford High School students who want better math scores should transfer to Middlebury the summer before they take the test. Think about the time frame employed here. The author assumes that former Ellingsford High School students will learn what they need to improve their math scores almost immediately after transferring to Middlebury. The correct answer will most likely offer a plausible reason why this might be the case. (A) provides a plausible reason to expect that students who transfer to Middlebury during the summer can significantly benefit before taking the test in September by taking advantage of the unique, week-long course offered just before test day. If (A) is true, then a major stumbling block to the potential efficacy of the proposal is removed, and the argument would be strengthened.

As to the wrong choices: (B) tells us nothing. The average score of only part of a group cannot be fairly compared to the average score of an entire group. A third of the students who remained at Ellingsford High School may also have scored at least 20 points higher than their school's average. (C) weakens the argument's conclusion. If Middlebury students who transfer to Ellingsford during the summer before they take the test still get higher math scores, then the notion that transferring the summer before is a cure-all seems less plausible. (D) presents an irrelevant comparison. The scores at Ellingsford High School may be rising faster than those at Middlebury High School, but the average score at Middlebury is still 20 points higher than the average score at Ellingsford. (E) goes beyond the scope of the argument because the argument does not concern itself with what will happen *ultimately*. The main issue is whether Ellingsford students can raise their scores by transferring. Even if (E) is true, and many students transfer and Middlebury's test score average drops, it's impossible for us to tell whether the transferees' scores are higher or lower than they would have been had they remained at Ellingsford.

7.

The question stem reveals that the argument in the stimulus is fatally flawed. As you read the passage, identify the evidence and conclusion, and watch for a questionable assumption or some other flaw along the way. The argument is based on numbers: Since only 6,000 homeless people suffering from malnutrition were admitted to U.S. hospitals last year, compared to 10,000 nonhomeless people, the nonhomeless must be more likely to suffer from malnutrition. But *total numbers* mean *nothing*. We cannot figure the odds of suffering from malnutrition solely from the number of malnourished people in each group. We need to know the *percentage* of homeless people suffering from malnutrition versus the *percentage* of nonhomeless people suffering from malnutrition. Clearly there are far more nonhomeless people than homeless people in the United States, so the argument contains a ludicrous assumption: that the two groups are comparably sized. The correct answer to the question will somehow point this out. (D) provides the question whose answer would provide the information we need to correctly understand the odds. It allows us to see how the raw numbers cited do not support the author's counterintuitive conclusion that the nonhomeless are more susceptible to malnutrition than are the homeless. As to the wrong answers, (A) goes beyond the scope of the argument. The argument involves the likelihood of suffering from malnutrition, not the relative levels of severity. (B) also introduces a new issue—finances. No matter how much people with homes are better off financially than the homeless, the fact remains that more nonhomeless were hospitalized for malnutrition than homeless. (C) introduces another new issue. The argument draws no conclusion about the causes of malnutrition within these groups, only about the likelihood of malnutrition. (E) is irrelevant to the argument as presented. The future possibility of remedying homelessness to some degree does not impact upon these numbers and this particular conclusion drawn from them.

8.

You must draw an inference in this question—so you are looking for a softly worded answer that must be true given the statements in the argument. It's difficult to predict the correct answer here, so your best bet is to test the choices rigorously, looking for the one that absolutely *must be true*. (C) draws a reasonable conclusion based on the evidence. If political instability involves changes in corporate data and economic indicators, then the mechanism should work the way it is designed to work. But if the incident does not involve those elements, then how the mechanism will work becomes unclear, because the behavior of investors will be unpredictable. Of the wrong answers, (A) goes too far when it infers that a severe and sudden political instability will occur within 50 years. The 1992 attempt was only an example of the political instability that occurs roughly every 50 years, and the 50-year period was an average, not an absolute limit. Furthermore, even if there is political instability, it is unclear how investors will react because their behavior in such situations cannot be predicted in advance. (B) goes beyond the scope of the argument. Whether investors perceive sudden political events positively or negatively isn't mentioned in the stimulus, so we can't infer that that perception makes any difference to the accuracy of the mechanism. (D) takes its inference too far. The mechanism might be able to differentiate between various types of market fluctuations, even though it might not be able to trigger appropriate responses to some of them. And (E) takes the argument far beyond its original scope. Nothing in the stimulus leads to a prediction of what might happen to the protection mechanism in the event of political instability.

9.

Find the author's conclusion and evidence, and the assumption linking them. Weaken the argument by invalidating that assumption. The argument develops from evidence that Y's high tariffs make X's cars relatively expensive, but X's low tariffs make Y's cars relatively cheap. The argument concludes that if Y lowers its tariffs, then real competition and an equitable balance of trade would result. Country X assumes that Y sells more cars in X than X sells in Y because of the price difference created by the different tariffs. This suggests a classic case of ignored alternatives. Look for a choice that suggests that there might be an alternative explanation besides the difference in tariffs that could explain the weakness of X's car sales relative to Y's. (A) weakens country X's argument by illustrating that the effect (more Y cars sold than X cars) is possible without the supposed cause (a tariff imbalance favoring Y). This implies that something other than tariffs—the reason offered by X for its poor performance in the car market—could very well explain the difference in sales (maybe X's car's are no good).

10.

The question stem sends us searching for a valid inference that can be drawn from the statements in the passage. You're looking for a conclusion *that must be true* based upon the statements in this argument. Reading the passage, you learn that adults can be divided into two groups: adults who seek advice in adversity only from their parents, and the remainder, who seek that advice only from other loved ones. There is not much room here for argument. All adults fall into one or the other of these categories, but not both. If these statements are true, then adults must turn either to parents or to other loved ones in times of adversity, and to no one else. (C) is a valid inference, given the evidence above. Adults seek advice from parents or other loved ones—not from strangers. Of the wrong answers, (A) introduces a concept foreign to the evidence. The passage tells us nothing about the relative wisdom of parents and peers. (For all we know, everyone gives terrible advice.) (B) introduces another concept foreign to the evidence. The passage tells us nothing about what people do for advice when they are not in adversity. (D) goes beyond the scope of the evidence. Expectations are not discussed in the passage. The issue here is where people in trouble go for advice—not what they expect to find. And (E) goes too far. Adults who regress will seek advice from parents if they face adverse circumstances and wish to get advice. This doesn't mean they will necessarily lose touch with peers.

11.

We're looking for the answer that does the best job at weakening the argument. This is a causal argument, which concludes that a plan to fertilize the oceans with iron compounds will be able to reverse the greenhouse effect. The chain of reasoning goes like this: by fertilizing the oceans to iron compounds, phytoplankton will grow, creating organic "sponges" to soak up carbon dioxide, widely believed to be responsible for global warming. We're looking for an answer that weakens this chain of causality. (E), which notes oceans are a complex system, and consequences of fertilization could be the *opposite* of what's predicted, does a good job of this. What if the plan ends up exacerbating the greenhouse effect? That would certainly cast doubt upon the advisability of the plan.

Of the wrong answers, (A), which discusses *some* oceans, is too weak to affect the argument. There's nothing in the argument to suggest that *all* the oceans need to be fertilized. (B), which mentions the high cost of the plan, is beyond the scope of the argument. The argument does not suggest the cost is a factor; after all, we're discussing a plan to save the planet! (C) is completely irrelevant to the issue at hand. Who cares about how iron naturally reaches the sea? And finally, (D) does nothing to invalidate the plan. Sure, emission-reduction plans may also be in order, but that doesn't mean we shouldn't try to reduce present carbon dioxide levels.

12.

The trickiest part of this question is understanding whose position we're trying to validate and whose we're trying to attack (it gets confusing when the argument involves opposing positions, as here). Here we're trying to validate the approach taken by the university systems, which the author argues is flawed; so, in other words, we're trying to weaken the author's critique. So what is the approach taken by the university systems? And what is the author's critique? The systems use graduation rates to determine which universities are awarded extra funds. This, the author argues, encourages campuses to graduate everyone, *regardless of achievement*. (D), which notes that exams exist that require every graduate to prove a minimum level of achievement, attacks the author's contention that the approach will lead to people graduating regardless of achievement.

Of the wrong answers, (A) strengthens the author's argument, as it agrees with his contention that achievement standards are being disregarded. (B) argues against the university systems' approach, although not for the same reasons as the author. (C) makes a completely irrelevant point. What's at issue is not how the money is *spent* by schools, but how it is *allotted* to them. And (E) doesn't validate the approach taken by the university systems, but in fact hints that there may be a fairer approach out there.

PART THREE

Practice Sets

SENTENCE CORRECTION PRACTICE SET ONE

Time: 25 Minutes/22 Questions

Directions: The following questions present a sentence, part or all of which is underlined. Below each sentence you will find five ways to phrase the underlined portion. Choice (A) repeats the original version, while the other four choices are different. If the original seems best, choose choice (A). If not, choose one of the revisions.

This question tests correctness and effectiveness of expression. Choose an answer that follows the norms of standard written English: grammar, word choice, and sentence construction.

Choose the answer that produces the most effective sentence, aiming to eliminate awkwardness, ambiguity, redundancy, and grammatical error.

1. To be a leading producer in the computer industry, a company must be international, achieve a turnover that makes efficient large-scale production possible, <u>and secure information about technical advances.</u>

    ⬭ and secure information about technical advances

    ⬭ and securing information about technical advances

    ⬭ while secure information about technical advances

    ⬭ and secure information of how to technically advance

    ⬭ and secure information in regards to technical advances

2. Of the people who brought about the Reformation, the religious revolution that grew out of objections to the doctrines of the medieval church, <u>Martin Luther is the best known of them.</u>

    ⬭ Martin Luther is the best known of them

    ⬭ the best known is Martin Luther

    ⬭ the better known of them was Martin Luther

    ⬭ Martin Luther is better known

    ⬭ the best known one was Martin Luther

3. Declining enrollments are forcing smaller private colleges to choose <u>between raising tuition and reduction of the staff.</u>

    ⬭ between raising tuition and reduction of the staff

    ⬭ among raising tuition and reducing staff

    ⬭ between raising tuition or reducing staff

    ⬭ between raising tuition and reducing staff

    ⬭ between the rise of tuition and the reduction of the staff

4. The bylaws of a corporation specify how the directors of the corporation are to be elected, whether the existing stockholders will have first right to buy any new stock issued by the firm, <u>as well as duties of management committees.</u>

    ⬭ as well as duties of management committees

    ⬭ as well as the duties that the management committees have

    ⬭ and that the management committees have duties

    ⬭ and the management committees have duties too

    ⬭ and what the duties of management committees will be

5. Although it is conceivable that certain electronic devices implanted in the brain may someday correct blindness caused by nerve damage, there is now no clear evidence <u>of their ability to do it</u>.

   ○ of their ability to do it

   ○ of their doing that

   ○ that they can do so

   ○ that they might one day be able to do it

   ○ to do so

6. Setting up a corporation requires more paperwork and legal provision <u>than to establish either a proprietorship or a partnership</u>.

   ○ than to establish either a proprietorship or a partnership

   ○ than what it requires to establish either a proprietorship or a partnership

   ○ than to either establish a proprietorship or a partnership

   ○ than establishing either a proprietorship or a partnership

   ○ than establishing proprietorships and partnerships

7. The Minnesota Multiphasic Personality Inventory, a test developed in the 1930s to assess character, attitudes, and behavior, <u>is finally being revised, after many attacks recently as dated and culturally biased</u>.

   ○ is finally being revised, after many attacks recently as dated and culturally biased

   ○ has recently been attacked as dated and culturally biased and is finally being revised

   ○ is finally under revision for receiving much recent attack as dated and culturally biased

   ○ was finally revised recently because it is being attacked as dated and culturally biased

   ○ is finally to be revised after recent attacks as dated and culturally biased

8. In the Champagne region of France, <u>wine growers still harvest grapes as they have done</u> for centuries, by carefully handpicking their crop and storing their precious fruit in specially aged casks.

   ○ wine growers still harvest grapes as they have done

   ○ the wine grower still harvests grapes as he has

   ○ wine growers still harvest grapes as was done

   ○ wine growers still harvest grapes as has been done

   ○ wine growers still harvest grapes as they did

9. A new generation of <u>sophisticated copy machines, capable of unprecedented detail and accuracy, are</u> prompting the development of more complex currency designs to prevent counterfeiting.

   ○ sophisticated copy machines, capable of unprecedented detail and accuracy, are

   ○ sophisticated copy machines, capable for unprecedented detail and accuracy, is

   ○ sophisticated copy machines, capable of unprecedented detail and accuracy, is

   ○ sophisticated copy machines, capable for unprecedented detail and accuracy, are

   ○ sophisticated copy machines that are capable of unprecedented detail and accuracy are

10. In an unusual move for a Republican, <u>the president's directive established price controls</u>.

   ○ the president's directive established price controls

   ○ the president's directive was to establish price controls

   ○ the president was successful in the establishment of controls on prices

   ○ the president had instituted controls on prices

   ○ the president established price controls

11. The United Automobile Workers returned to the A.F.L.-C.I.O. because <u>of the wish of both groups to strengthen labor's role not only in politics but also industry.</u>

    ◯ of the wish of both groups to strengthen labor's role not only in politics but also industry

    ◯ both groups wished to strengthen labor's role in politics as well as in industry

    ◯ the strengthening of labor's role in politics as well as industry was wished for by both groups

    ◯ it was wished by both groups to strengthen labor's role in politics and industry as well

    ◯ both groups wished to strengthen labor's role in both of the two areas of politics and industry

12. Of all the countries contiguous to China, <u>the Soviet Union's borders were most strongly defended.</u>

    ◯ the Soviet Union's borders were most strongly defended

    ◯ the borders of the Soviet Union were defended more strongly than any of the others

    ◯ the Soviet Union's borders stood out for the strength of their defensive capability

    ◯ the Soviet Union had the most strongly defended borders

    ◯ the Soviet Union's were the most strongly defended borders

13. Unlike <u>the people whom settled the Western states after the passage of the Homestead Act of 1862, the hope of the prospectors and adventurers who came to California during the gold rush was</u> to get rich quickly.

    ◯ the people whom settled the Western states after the passage of the Homestead Act of 1862, the hope of the prospectors and adventurers who came to California during the gold rush was

    ◯ the people who settled the Western states after the passage of the Homestead Act of 1862, the hope of the prospectors and adventurers who came to California during the gold rush was

    ◯ that of the people who settled the Western states after the passage of the Homestead Act of 1862, the prospectors and adventurers who came to California during the gold rush hoped

    ◯ that of the people whom settled the Western states after the passage of the Homestead Act of 1862, the hope of the prospectors and adventurers who came to California during the gold rush was

    ◯ the people who settled the Western states after the passage of the Homestead Act of 1862, the prospectors and adventurers who came to California during the gold rush hoped

14. <u>Before George Eliot became the popular and respected novelist known as George Eliot, she was</u> an anonymous translator and essayist of formidably far-ranging scholarship.

    ◯ Before George Eliot became the popular and respected novelist known as George Eliot, she was

    ◯ Before she had been the popular and respected novelist, George Eliot, she was

    ◯ George Eliot has been the popular and respected novelist, George Eliot, after such time as she was

    ◯ Before George Eliot became the popular and respected novelist, George Eliot, she was

    ◯ George Eliot, before she was the popular and respected novelist, George Eliot, had been

15. <u>Just like Congress is the legislative branch of the federal government of the United States, so</u> Parliament is the legislative body of the United Kingdom of Great Britain and Northern Ireland.

   ◯ Just like Congress is the legislative branch of the federal government of the United States, so

   ◯ As Congress is the legislative branch of the federal government of the United States,

   ◯ As Congress is the legislative branch of the federal government of the United States, in the same way

   ◯ Just as Congress is the legislative branch of the federal government of the United States, so

   ◯ Just as the federal government of the United States' legislative branch is Congress,

16. <u>The reason Frances Willard founded the Women's Christian Temperance Union was because she believed that national prohibition of alcohol will empty the poorhouses, jails, and asylums of the United States.</u>

   ◯ The reason Frances Willard founded the Women's Christian Temperance Union was because she believed that national prohibition of alcohol will empty the poorhouses, jails, and asylums of the United States

   ◯ Frances Willard founded the Women's Christian Temperance Union, the reason being that she believed that national prohibition of alcohol will empty the poorhouses, jails, and asylums of the United States

   ◯ The reason Frances Willard founded the Women's Christian Temperance Union was she believed that national prohibition of alcohol will empty the poorhouses, jails, and asylums of the United States

   ◯ Because she believed that national prohibition of alcohol would empty the poorhouses, jails, and asylums of the United States, so Frances Willard founded the Women's Christian Temperance Union

   ◯ Frances Willard founded the Women's Christian Temperance Union because she believed that national prohibition of alcohol would empty the poorhouses, jails, and asylums of the United States

17. The combination of technical expertise, commercial enterprise, and <u>that the government backs them judiciously should ensure Italian firms continuing</u> to innovate and gain competitively in world markets.

   ◯ that the government backs them judiciously should ensure Italian firms continuing

   ◯ the government backing them judiciously should ensure Italian firms of being about to continue

   ◯ judicious government backing should ensure that Italian firms will continue

   ◯ the government's judicious backing should ensure Italian firms that they will continue

   ◯ the government to back them judiciously should ensure Italian firms of continuing

18. The sloth, <u>which is a South American mammal related to armadillos and anteaters, live in tropical forests where they travel</u> through the trees upside down.

   ◯ which is a South American mammal related to armadillos and anteaters, live in tropical forests where they travel

   ◯ a South American mammal related to armadillos and anteaters, live in tropical forests where they travel

   ◯ a South American mammal related to the armadillo and the anteater, lives in tropical forests where it travels

   ◯ a South American mammal related to the armadillo and the anteater, lives in tropical forests where they travel

   ◯ a South American mammal in relation to the armadillo and the anteater, lives in tropical forests where it travels

19. Early derisive reactions from art critics and established painters <u>did not discourage the Primitivist painter Henri Rousseau to exhibit repeatedly, despite him completely lacking formal training and starting late</u> as a professional artist.

   ○ did not discourage the Primitivist painter Henri Rousseau to exhibit repeatedly, despite him completely lacking formal training and starting late

   ○ did not discourage the Primitivist painter Henri Rousseau exhibiting repeatedly, completely lacking formal training though he was, and starting late

   ○ did not discourage the Primitivist painter Henri Rousseau to exhibit repeatedly, despite their complete lack of formal training and late start

   ○ did not discourage the Primitivist painter Henri Rousseau in exhibiting repeatedly, despite his complete lack of formal training and late start

   ○ did not discourage the Primitivist painter Henri Rousseau from exhibiting repeatedly, despite his complete lack of formal training and late start

20. The poll taxes enacted in the Southern states between 1889 <u>and 1910 disenfranchised many citizens, since</u> payment of the tax was a prerequisite for voting.

   ○ and 1910 disenfranchised many citizens, since
   ○ to 1910 disenfranchised many citizens, since
   ○ and 1910 have disenfranchised many citizens since
   ○ to 1910 has been disenfranchising many citizens because
   ○ and 1910 had the effect of disenfranchising many citizens, inasmuch as

21. <u>With a population equal to Kansas in an area one three-hundredth its size, Singapore is the most densely populated nation in the world, averaging</u> almost ten thousand people per square mile.

   ○ With a population equal to Kansas in an area one three-hundredth its size, Singapore is the most densely populated nation in the world, averaging

   ○ With a population equal to that of Kansas in an area one three-hundredth its size, Singapore is the most densely populated nation in the world, averaging

   ○ With Kansas's population in one three-hundredth of its area, the densest population in the world is that of Singapore, with an average of

   ○ Singapore has the same population as Kansas but only one three-hundredth of its area, and makes it the most densely populated nation in the world, averaging

   ○ Singapore is the most densely populated nation in the world, with Kansas's population in one three-hundredth of its area, or an average of

22. Many medical schools offer courses in the ethics of treating terminal patients, partly to alert students about the legal implications involved in such treatment, <u>but primarily to prepare students, through discussion and forethought, to make responsible decisions that respect terminal patients' dignity.</u>

   ○ but primarily to prepare students, through discussion and forethought, to make responsible decisions that respect terminal patients' dignity

   ○ but primarily so as to prepare students, by discussing and by thinking ahead, for responsible decision making that respects terminal patients' dignity

   ○ but primarily for the purpose of preparing them, with discussion and forethought, to make responsible decisions that respect terminal patients' dignity

   ○ but primarily for preparing them, through discussion and forethought, for deciding responsibly so that they respect terminal patients' dignity

   ○ but primarily to prepare them, by discussing and thinking ahead, to responsibly decide so as to respect the dignity of terminal patients

KAPLAN)

ANSWERS AND EXPLANATIONS

1. A
2. B
3. D
4. E
5. C
6. D
7. B
8. A
9. C
10. E
11. B
12. D
13. E
14. A
15. D
16. E
17. C
18. C
19. E
20. A
21. B
22. A

1. A

All items in a list must be in parallel form. The word "secure" is used in its secondary meaning of "to make safe." "Secure" is in the same form as "be" and "achieve," so (A) is fine as is. (D) and (E) also use the correct form of "secure," but they contain unidiomatic phrases.

2. B

After you read the sentence, always scan the choices quickly to spot differences. Two choices, (C) and (D), here use "better," three use "best." "Better" is used when you compare two people or things. "Best" is used when you compare one person or thing to a whole group. Since you're comparing Martin Luther to *ALL* the people who brought about the Reformation, you have to use "best." "Them" and "one" in (A) and (E) are ambiguous and unnecessary.

3. D

Words linked by "and" must be in similar grammatical form. (A) is wrong because "and" links "raising" and "reduction." We're discussing two things, so we need "between," not "among" in (B). (C) uses "or" when it should use "and." (You choose between X and Y, not X or Y.) In (E), colleges aren't choosing "the rise."

4. E

Elements in a list must be parallel in form. In (A), there's a list of three things specified in the corporation's bylaws: "how . . . ," "whether . . . ," and "as well as . . . ." "As well as" doesn't fit, does it? "What," in (E), is in the same form as "how" and "whether."

5. C

On a question as short as this, you don't have to worry as much about scanning for differences. Just read quickly through the answer choices and you should be able to "hear" which one's best. In (C), "do so" is an academic-sounding but correct usage that can pop up on the GMAT. Watch out for it and other bookish-sounding phrases typical of GMAT style. If you can't use your ear for correct English, use logic and process of elimination. (E) is short. That might be a reason to prefer it. But if you plug in (E), you see it makes the sentence say that "evidence" is doing something. In (A), (B), and (D), "it" and "that" are ambiguous. That is, they don't clearly refer to one and only one noun.

6. D

"Than" must compare grammatically similar terms: for instance, *cooking chickens* is different from *cooking eggs*, not *cooking chickens* is different from *eggs*. Since "setting" is not underlined, you'll have to make the underlined portion agree with it. So let's look for an "-ing" form. That narrows it down to (D) and (E). "Corporation" is singular, so we have to compare it to singular nouns: "a proprietorship or a partnership," in (D).

7. B

Listen for things that sound funny in the original sentence, and find the choice that's most precise. In (A), "attacks recently" is illogical and awkward-sounding. The test isn't under revision "for being attackted," in (C). It's under revision *after* being attacked. In (D), it seems as though the attack happens before and after the revision. In (E), it's not clear that it's the test that's being attacked. (B) makes the sequence of events clear: The test has recently been attacked and is finally being revised.

8. A

If you can't spot an error in the original, scan the choices and look for reasons to cross some out. Then guess from the rest. (B) uses the singular "wine grower," but you need the plural to go with "their crop" and "their fruit" in the nonunderlined part of the sentence. (C) and (D) make the sentence switch from active ("harvest") to passive ("as was done," "as has been done") for no good reason. Avoid the passive if possible. In (E), "did" implies that the wine growers have stopped harvesting. Growers still harvest, so you need "have done" in (A) to indicate continuing action.

9. C

Like many GMAT sentences, this one is complex, but contains a predictable, relatively simple error. If you familiarize yourself with commonly tested errors and learn how to correct them, sentence corrections can be a breeze. As soon as you see a subject ("a generation") followed by a long phrase ("of sophisticated copy machines capable of unprecedented detail and accuracy") beware! GMAT sentence corrections often contain subjects and verbs that are separated. The verb "are" here is separated from the subject "generation," but they still need to agree. *Generation* is singular, so it should be "a new generation is prompting." This makes (A), (D), and (E) incorrect. In (B), it's unidiomatic to say "capable for." You need to say "capable of" detail.

10. E

What should an introductory phrase followed by a comma prompt you to do? Check to see if the phrase correctly modifies what follows it. You can't say that a directive is making "an unusual move for a Republican." No, it's a person, the president, that's making the move. This makes (A) incorrect. (C) is in the passive voice, and (D) is in the wrong tense. (E) says what the author of the sentence wants to say, clearly and simply. That's preferable on the GMAT.

11. B

Connectors like "as well as" or "not only . . . but also" must link like terms. So if you say "in politics," you have to say "in industry." Choices (A), (C), (D), and (E) do not use "in industry," so they are incorrect. Also, (E) is unnecessarily wordy.

12. D

This question contains the same type of recognizable error as number 9 does. "Of all the countries contiguous to China" can't modify "the Soviet Union's borders," (A); "the Soviet Union's," (E); or "the borders of the Soviet Union," (B) and (C). It has to modify "the Soviet Union."

13. E

"Like" or "unlike" signal comparisons, one of the test makers' favorite places to introduce errors. So when you see a sentence like this, which hits you with "unlike" first thing, make sure that the sentence compares similar things, things that can be logically compared and things that are in the same grammatical form. Here, "the people whom settled the Western states . . ." and "the hope of the prospectors . . ." are both nouns, but they can't be logically compared. You can't compare people to "hope," a feeling. You have to compare people to people, and that's what choice (E) does. In (E), "the people who settled the Western states" are compared to "the prospectors and adventurers." Also note that you need "who" instead of "whom." For more on this distinction, see the Grammar Reference Guide in the appendix.

14. A

Don't hypercorrect. About one-fifth of sentence corrections will be correct as is. Many of these sound like something you'd never say or write unless you were writing a term paper. George Eliot didn't become George Eliot, as (B), (C),

(D), and (E) have it. She became known as George Eliot. The word "before" determines the sequence of events in the sentence. Hence, "Before George Eliot became . . . *she was . . . .*"

15. D

Be on the lookout for connectors like "as," "just as," and "like." Here you have to decide which one to use. In everyday speech, this distinction isn't so important, but on the GMAT it is. If you're a native speaker of English, you should be able to use your sense of correct English to tell that "just as . . . so," (D), is correct. Otherwise, jot down this and other commonly used GMAT idioms as you come across them, and learn them.

16. E

Sentences like this one can be intimidating, but they don't have to be if you can spot the error quickly. Phrases like "the reason . . . was because," (A), are too wordy to be correct on the GMAT. Practice so you can quickly recognize and reject them. (D) would be okay if "so" were eliminated. As it is, stick with the most economical and logical phrase: "Willard founded the . . . Union because . . . ."

17. C

When you see a list or series, ask yourself, "Are all the listed items similar grammatically and logically?" The phrase that matches "technical expertise" and "commercial enterprise" is "judicious government backing," in (C). (D) is close but it's not as compact, and GMAT often rewards compact language. Also, (D)'s "ensure Italian firms that they will" is unclear.

18. C

Every pronoun must CLEARLY and LOGICALLY refer to ONE specific noun, and agree with that noun. You're talking about the sloth here. That's singular. To be correct, you have to compare the sloth to the armadillo and the anteater. That knocks out (A) and (B). (D) uses "they." "They" can't stand for "sloth." It can stand for only the plural noun "forests," which makes no sense. If you were working quickly, you might think it's okay to substitute "they" for "the sloth." But GMAT English is picky. If the noun "sloth" is singular, its pronoun must be singular too. (E) is wrong because the phrase "in relation to" is unidiomatic. You say "X is related to Y," not "X is in relation to Y."

19. E

The correct idiom is "discourage from exhibiting." Also, you can't say "despite him completely lacking," as in the original. You have to say "despite his complete lack of."

20. A

Here's another connector you should know: Between . . . and (as in "Between me and you . . ."). When you scan the choices, quickly narrow down the possibilities by picking out incorrect idioms like "between . . . to." In (C), you could use "have" only if you were talking about continuing action. You say "the recent poll taxes have disenfranchised many citizens," but if you're talking about action that started and finished in the past, you simply say "the taxes disenfranchised many citizens." In (E), "had the effect of" and "inasmuch as" are wordy and therefore wrong.

21. B

Be sensitive to the small variations in answer choices. They allow you to zero in on subtle errors like the one in this sentence. When you got to the answer choices here, you may have noticed that each one plays with the wording of "population equal to Kansas." You can compare only like terms. You can't say "a population equal to Kansas," because you can compare a population only to another population; you can't compare a population to a state. In (B), "that of" should have sounded really good to you; "that" stands for "population." "With a population equal to that of Kansas" is just a shorter and more elegant way of saying "With a population equal to the population of Kansas." In (C), the population isn't "with an average" of ten thousand people per square mile. (E) introduces a comma splice—a new error—and is thus another wrong answer.

22. A

In (A), "but" connects two similar phrases: "To alert . . . " and "to prepare." Answers (B), "so as to prepare," (C), "for the purpose of preparing," and (D), "for preparing," break this parallel construction. (E) has "to prepare," but the pronoun "them" is ambiguous, and "so as to" is too wordy.

SENTENCE CORRECTION PRACTICE SET TWO

Time: 25 Minutes/22 Questions

Directions: The following questions present a sentence, part or all of which is underlined. Below each sentence you will find five ways to phrase the underlined portion. Choice (A) repeats the original version, while the other four choices are different. If the original seems best, choose choice (A). If not, choose one of the revisions.

This question tests correctness and effectiveness of expression. Choose an answer that follows the norms of standard written English: grammar, word choice, and sentence construction.

Choose the answer that produces the most effective sentence, aiming to eliminate awkwardness, ambiguity, redundancy, and grammatical error.

1. The chairman of the board of directors <u>have decided that this year's profits will be used</u> for research and development, rather than for a shareholder dividend.

   ○ have decided that this year's profits will be used

   ○ has decided that this year's profits will be used

   ○ have decided on using this year's profits

   ○ has decided on using this year's profits

   ○ decided this year's profits will have been used

2. <u>Like most religions, the teachings of Sikhism are codified in</u> a book.

   ○ Like most religions, the teachings of Sikhism are codified in

   ○ Like most other religions, the teachings of Sikhism are codified in

   ○ Sikhism's teachings, like those of most other religions, are codified in

   ○ For their codification, like the teachings of most religions, Sikhism has

   ○ Like those of most religions, Sikhism has codified its teachings in

3. <u>Not only do deep-sea divers risk nitrogen narcosis, often called "raptures of the deep," if they descend below 200 feet, but</u> they also fall prey to decompression sickness, commonly known as "the bends," if they ascend too quickly.

   ○ Not only do deep-sea divers risk nitrogen narcosis, often called "raptures of the deep," if they descend below 200 feet, but

   ○ Deep-sea divers risk nitrogen narcosis, often called "raptures of the deep," if they descend below 200 feet, but

   ○ Nitrogen narcosis, often called "raptures of the deep," is risked by deep-sea divers if they descend below 200 feet, in addition

   ○ The descending of deep-sea divers to below 200 feet causes them risking nitrogen narcosis, often called "raptures of the deep," and

   ○ Not only does a deep-sea diver risk nitrogen narcosis, often called "raptures of the deep," if they descend below 200 feet, but

KAPLAN

4. <u>A 32 percent wage hike, working four days a week, and above all a higher standard of factory safety is a demand</u> that management must meet if it wishes to avoid a crippling strike.

    ◯ A 32 percent wage hike, working four days a week, and above all a higher standard of factory safety is a demand

    ◯ A 32 percent wage hike, a four-day work-week, and above all a higher standard of factory safety is a demand

    ◯ A 32 percent wage hike, a four-day work-week, and above all a higher standard of safety in the factory are demands

    ◯ A 32 percent wage hike, working four days a week, and above all a higher standard of factory safety are demands

    ◯ Hiking wages 32 percent, working four days a week, and above all heighten the standard of factory safety are demands

5. Although new farm subsidy legislation is presently being considered in the House of Representatives, <u>significant revision is to be expected if it is to be passed</u>.

    ◯ significant revision is to be expected if it is to be passed

    ◯ they do not expect it passing without significant revision

    ◯ they do not expect it passing without it being significantly revised

    ◯ it is not expected to pass without it being significantly revised

    ◯ it is not expected to pass without significant revision

6. At a recent conference, the Transit Authority <u>has stated that the provisions in the Clean Air Act fail</u> to promote mass transit as an alternative to private transportation.

    ◯ has stated that the provisions in the Clean Air Act fail

    ◯ stated that the provisions of the Clean Air Act fail

    ◯ has stated that the provisions of the Clean Air Act will fail

    ◯ stated that the provisions in the Clean Air Act are a failure

    ◯ has stated the provisions in the Clean Air Act failed

7. A revolution has taken place in medical science as a result of <u>the introduction of new methods of surgically implanting artificial and human organs</u>.

    ◯ the introduction of new methods of surgically implanting artificial and human organs

    ◯ the introduction of new surgical implantation methods of human and artificial organs

    ◯ the surgical introduction of new artificial and human organ implantation methods

    ◯ the introduction of implantation methods of new artificial and human organs

    ◯ the introduction of methods of surgically implanting new artificial and human organs

8. <u>Added to worries about budget cuts and cost of living increases</u>, the administrators of public healthcare facilities must contend with the possibility of a strike by employees.

    ◯ Added to worries about budget cuts and cost of living increases

    ◯ Added to budget cuts and increases in the cost of living

    ◯ In addition to worry about cuts in the budget and as the cost of living increases

    ◯ Added to their worrying about budget cuts and cost of living increases

    ◯ In addition to worrying about budget cuts and increases in the cost of living

9. Renaissance scientist Copernicus found that his rejection of the Ptolemaic system placed him at odds <u>not only with the Church and the scientific community of his day, but also with ship captains, who navigated according to a geocentric universe.</u>

    ◯ not only with the Church and the scientific community of his day, but also with ship captains, who navigated according to a geocentric universe

    ◯ opposing the Church and the scientific community of his day, and also the ship captains, who navigated according to a geocentric universe

    ◯ not only in opposition to the Church and the scientific community of his day, but with ship captains, who navigated according to a geocentric universe

    ◯ not only with the Church and the scientific community of his day, but with ship captains, who calculated their navigations on a geocentric basis

    ◯ opposing not only churchmen and scientists, but the ship captains, who navigated according to a geocentric universe

10. Despite <u>them attempting to do it</u>, doctors have not yet found a cure for the common cold.

    ◯ them attempting to do it

    ◯ their attempts to do so

    ◯ them attempting to do so

    ◯ the fact that they have attempted to do it

    ◯ their attempts to do it

11. Unlike the Pulitzer, which is given for a specific work, <u>an author receives the Nobel Prize for a lifetime's achievement in literature.</u>

    ◯ an author receives the Nobel Prize for a lifetime's achievement in literature

    ◯ an author's lifetime achievement in literature receives the Nobel Prize

    ◯ the Nobel Prize is awarded to an author's lifetime's achievement in literature

    ◯ the Nobel Prize is awarded for a lifetime of achievement in literature

    ◯ the Nobel Prize is awarded for a lifetime of achievement in literature by an author

12. Medical researchers, who have identified a genetic abnormality in parents of children with Down syndrome, <u>which they believe, instead of the age of the mother, may be</u> the cause of this congenital birth defect.

    ◯ which they believe, instead of the age of the mother, may be

    ◯ which, they believe, may be more important than the age of the mother as

    ◯ believe this abnormality and not the age of the mother as being

    ◯ believe that this abnormality, other than how old the mother is, may be

    ◯ believe that this abnormality, rather than the age of the mother, may be

13. Unable to walk without assistance, <u>radio provided Franklin Roosevelt with a medium for conveying</u> a message of vigor and confidence that would have been belied by the visual image presented on television.

    ◯ radio provided Franklin Roosevelt with a medium for conveying

    ◯ Franklin Roosevelt conveyed in radio

    ◯ Franklin Roosevelt used radio to convey

    ◯ radio allowed Franklin Roosevelt to convey

    ◯ through radio it was possible

KAPLAN)

14. Modern inventions such as the pneumatic drill
may seem to have improved the work conditions
of manual laborers, but in fact, <u>have increased
the incidence of health hazards such as silicosis
because it has aggravated the dust hazard</u> involved
in excavation and demolition.

  ○ have increased the incidence of health
  hazards such as silicosis because it has aggravated the dust hazard

  ○ has increased the incidence of health hazards
  such as silicosis because it has aggravated the
  dust hazard

  ○ have increased the incidence of health
  hazards such as silicosis because they have
  aggravated the dust hazard

  ○ increased the incidence of health hazards
  such as silicosis because they aggravated the
  dust hazard

  ○ increased the incidence of health hazards
  such as silicosis because of aggravating the
  dust hazard

15. The Federal Reserve <u>Board assumes primary
responsibility of the regulation for</u> this nation's
commercial banks and savings institutions.

  ○ Board assumes primary responsibility of the
  regulation for

  ○ Board's assumption of primary responsibility
  for the regulation of

  ○ Board's assuming primary responsibility to
  regulate

  ○ Board assumes primary responsibility for the
  regulation of

  ○ Board regulates primary responsibility for

16. The groundswell of public opinion made <u>it
inevitable that the Senate would approve</u> the
president's energy proposals.

  ○ it inevitable that the Senate would approve

  ○ it inevitable that the Senate had approved

  ○ it inevitable of the Senate to approve

  ○ inevitable the approval of the Senate of

  ○ the approval of the Senate inevitable of

17. Though caterpillars transform large amounts of
plant matter into animal tissue and wastes, and
therefore hold an important place in the food chain,
<u>they are so voracious that they have become an
economic</u> threat to farmers whose crops they eat.

  ○ they are so voracious that they have become
  an economic

  ○ they are of such voracity, they have become
  an economical

  ○ so voracious are they as to become an
  economical

  ○ such is their voracity, they become an
  economic

  ○ there is so much voracity that it has become
  an economical

18. The nations with nuclear capabilities have
restrained the proliferation of nuclear weapons less
by reaching military understandings than <u>by the
refusal to sell</u> associated technologies.

  ○ by the refusal to sell

  ○ not selling

  ○ the refusal to sell

  ○ refusing to sell

  ○ by refusing to sell

19. During and immediately after the California gold
rush, the way for a merchant to generate the most
profit was to move a limited amount of scarce
goods to San Francisco as quickly as possible,
rather than <u>to carry larger loads more slowly,
determining</u> the design of the clipper ship.

  ○ to carry larger loads more slowly, determining

  ○ to carry larger loads more slowly, a situation
  that determined

  ○ carry larger loads more slowly, which determined

  ○ slowly carry larger loads which determined

  ○ carrying larger loads more slowly, and this
  was a situation in determining

20. <u>Compared with the time period of John Steinbeck's *The Grapes of Wrath*</u>, the poor of today would be considered wealthy.

    ○ Compared with the time period of John Steinbeck's *The Grapes of Wrath*

    ○ Compared with the time period during which John Steinbeck's *The Grapes of Wrath* took place

    ○ Compared with the characters in John Steinbeck's *The Grapes of Wrath*

    ○ In comparison to the time of John Steinbeck's *The Grapes of Wrath*

    ○ In comparison to John Steinbeck's *The Grapes of Wrath*

21. According to the teachings of the Buddhist and Hindu religions, <u>attaining nirvana is to enter</u> a state of supreme liberation, leaving behind the desires that perpetuate the cycle of death and rebirth.

    ○ attaining nirvana is to enter

    ○ to attain nirvana is entering

    ○ to attain nirvana is

    ○ to attain nirvana is to enter

    ○ attaining nirvana is to be entering

22. Uninformed about students' experience in urban classrooms, critics often condemn schools' performance as gauged by <u>an index, such as standardized test scores, that are called objective and can be quantified and overlook less measurable progress, such as that</u> in higher-level reasoning.

    ○ an index, such as standardized test scores, that are called objective and can be quantified and overlook less measurable progress, such as that

    ○ an index, such as standardized test scores, that are called objective and can be quantified and overlook less measurable progress, such as what is made

    ○ an index, such as standardized test scores, that is called objective and can be quantified and overlook less measurable progress, such as what is made

    ○ a so-called objective index, such as standardized test scores, that can be quantified and overlook less measurable progress, such as what is made

    ○ a so-called objective index, such as standardized test scores, that can be quantified and overlook less measurable progress, such as that

KAPLAN

ANSWERS AND EXPLANATIONS

1. B
2. C
3. A
4. C
5. E
6. B
7. A
8. E
9. A
10. B
11. D
12. E
13. C
14. C
15. D
16. A
17. A
18. E
19. B
20. C
21. D
22. D

1. B

GMAT likes to introduce errors by separating the subject and verb. Practice with Sentence Corrections, so you anticipate and ignore distracting phrases like "of the board of directors." The verb has to agree with the singular subject "chairman," rather than with the plural "directors." Only (B) and (D) use "has." (B) is correct because the idiom is "decided that," not "decided on."

2. C

When you see "like" or "unlike," watch out for faulty comparisons. You can't compare "most religions" to the "teachings of Sikhism." You have to find the choice that compares teachings to teachings or religions to religions. (C) uses "those" to stand for "teachings." But in (E), it's not clear what "those" stands for. A pronoun like "those" must refer to an already expressed noun, so "those" must follow "teachings." (D) also has an unclear pronoun, "their."

3. A

"Not only . . . but also" must connect similar terms. "Deep-sea divers not only risk" and "but also fall prey" are correctly paralleled in (A). (B) would work if "and" was substituted for "but." There are two problems with (C): "nitrogen narcosis . . . is risked" and the fact that (C) is actually two complete sentences incorrectly linked with a comma. You'd need a period after "feet," and a capital "i" in "in." In (E), "they" doesn't refer clearly and unambiguously to one specific plural noun. In (A), "they" can mean only "divers." In (D), the beginning is a bit wordy, and "causes them risking . . ." sounds awkward. The infinitive "to risk" is needed in place of "risking."

4. C

Whenever you see a list on the GMAT, check that the items in it are in grammatically similar form. If you quickly scan the choices, you see that only (B) and (C) put the three listed items in similar form: *wage hike, workweek,* and *standard.* The subject is plural. That is, the three things listed in the sentence *are* demands the management must meet. So, (B) can't work.

5. E

On GMAT Sentence Correction, the wrong choices often contain unnecessary words. That's why, if you're clueless, you should favor the shorter choices. Correct choice (E) is one of the shortest. So is (B), but in (B), "they do not expect it passing" is unidiomatic. You'd have to say "they do not expect it *to* pass."

6. B

When you scan the choices, notice you have to choose between three that begin with "has stated" and two that begin with "stated." Many GMAT Sentence Corrections exhibit this "3-2 split" answer choice pattern. Use this to your advantage. Begin by deciding which of the two forms, "has stated" or "stated," is correct. This is strategic: You deal with one small problem at a time, and narrow down your choices. The Transit Authority made its statement and it was over. The action didn't continue. So you should say "the Transit Authority *stated*." (B), "the provisions fail to promote mass transit," is more concise and more ideomatic than (D), "the provisions are a failure to promote mass transit."

7. A

The original is long-winded and probably not the best sentence you've ever read. GMAT sentences don't have to be beautiful; they just have to be correct (about one-fifth of the Sentence Corrections in each set *will be* correct as written in the stem). The wrong choices here are nonsensical. In (B), what's "methods of . . . organs"? There's no such thing. In (C), what's "surgical introduction of . . . methods"? (D) and (E) say that the artificial and human organs are new. But it's *the methods* that are new.

8. E

An intro phrase set off by a comma is your signal to watch out for modification errors. Simply put, that means you should make sure the sentence is logical. Here, you have a "3-2" pattern in the answer choices, so you can use this to quickly narrow down the possibilities. It's not *the administrators* that are added to worries, budget cuts, or worrying, so (A), (B), and (D) are out. (C) may seem to make sense, but look at it closely: "Worry" is wrong, and administrators are worrying "about cuts in the budget *and* as the cost of living increases." "And" must link similar terms, but it doesn't in (C).

9. A

The correct phrase is "at odds with," not "at odds . . . opposing," in (B) and (E), or "at odds . . . in opposition," in (C). It's better to say "navigated according to a geocentric universe" than "calculated their navigations on a geocentric basis," in (D).

10. B

Here you have another "3-2 split," this time between "to do it" and "to do so," in the answer choice endings. "It" is an ambiguous pronoun. You might assume "it" stands for "cure," but if you substitute "cure" for "it" in the sentence, you get the unidiomatic "despite them attempting to do a cure." This rules out (A), (D), and (E). If you're not familiar with idiomatic expressions like "to do so," learn to recognize them. As you practice Sentence Correction, write down any usages that are correct but unfamiliar to you. "Doctors" is the subject. You use the pronoun "their," not "them," (C), to stand for "doctors." For more discussion of pronouns, see the Grammar Reference Guide in appendix 1.

11. D

Like number 8, this question contains an intro phrase set off by a comma. This time you've got to rearrange the rest of the sentence to fit the intro. So what can correctly follow "Unlike the Pulitzer"? You can compare only similar things; the Pulitzer Prize must be compared to some other prize. Hence (A) and (B) are incorrect. In (C), the prize isn't awarded to an author's achievement, it's awarded to an author. In (E), "author" incorrectly follows "literature" ("literature by an author"), making it unclear who exactly is doing the achieving. (D) makes it clear whose achievement is being awarded.

12. E

To finish the Sentence Correction section on time, you have to cut through the wordiness of these questions. You can often do this by temporarily ignoring parts of the sentence that are set off by commas. Here, that's "who have identified . . . with Down syndrome" and "instead of the age of the mother." The rest of the sentence should make sense and be complete without these. But in the original you get "Medical researchers . . . which they believe . . . may be the cause of this congenital birth defect." In (C), (D), and (E), the subject "medical researchers" has a verb, "believe." In (C), "believe . . . as being" is unidiomatic. ("Being" is wordy and often appears in wrong choices.) In (D), you need "rather" instead of "other," and "how old the mother is" isn't parallel to "abnormality."

13. C

In (A), (D), and (E), you are saying that radio was unable to walk without assistance. You want to say that Franklin Roosevelt was. So the noun "Franklin Roosevelt" must follow the intro phrase, as it does in (B) and (C). In (B), it's wrong and awkward to say that Roosevelt "conveyed in radio a message." (C) puts it best: Roosevelt "*used* radio to convey a message."

14. C

(A) has to be wrong, because "it" illogically refers to "silicosis." Actually, "modern inventions," plural, have "aggravated the dust hazard." So you need "they" to follow "because," as in (C) and (D). There's no reason to use the past, in (D) and (E), because the hazard is still happening.

15. D

You say "assumes responsibility for." You don't take responsibility *of* (A) or *to* (C) completing your work, you take responsibility *for* completing it. If you plug in (B), you get an incomplete sentence. You need a noun, "Board," and a verb, "assumes." In (E), the Board isn't regulating responsibility.

16. A

You can say, "It was inevitable that I would miss my bus." But you can't say, "It was inevitable of me to miss my bus." You need "that." (B) says that it's "inevitable" that the Senate had approved the proposals, past tense. But something that's already happened can't be said to be inevitable. In (C) and (E), the idiom is not "inevitable of." In choice (D), the word "it" has been removed for no reason.

17. A

The wrong choices use illogical and unidiomatic phrases. In (B), caterpillars can't be "of such voracity." In (C), you can't say something is so voracious *as* to become a threat to farmers. Choice (D) is not a clear or idiomatic way of conveying the meaning of the sentence. In (E), there is no way to tell that the caterpillars are the ones being voracious.

18. E

The phrase "less by . . . than by" is another connector that must link similar terms. What follows the first "by"? "Reaching." So what must follow the second "by"? "Refusing." Only (B) and (D) do this. (D) won't work. It takes out the second "by," which you need to complete the comparison.

19. B

In this long sentence, the connector "rather than" should jump out at you right away. In the phrase "to move . . . rather than to carry," "to move" and "to carry" need to be kept in parallel form. That narrows the possibilities to (A) or (B). Think about what the sentence is saying. In (A), the way for a merchant to generate profit isn't determining the design of the clipper ship. The way for a merchant to generate profit is a *situation* determining the design of the clipper ship. (E) is too wordy.

20. C

Notice that the very first word you read is *compared*. Right away you should start hunting for comparison errors as you read. In standard English, only similar things can be compared. So "the poor" can be compared only with other people, including fictional characters, (C). People cannot be compared with a "time period," as in (A) and (B); or with a "time," as in (D); or with a book, as in (E). Only (C) presents a valid comparison.

Also note the 3-2 split between "compared with" and "in comparison to." The GMAT prefers shorter constructions whenever possible; if you can say the same thing with two words instead of three, choose the two-word version. (D) and (E) could be eliminated for this reason as well.

21. D

"Attaining" and "to enter" must be parallel. (D) gives this to you, with "to attain" and "to enter." The other choices are not parallel.

22. E

The beginning of the underlined part should be "an index… that is called objective," not "an index … that are called objective." If you catch an obvious error like this, quickly scan the other choices for versions that repeat it. That knocks out (B). (Remember you don't need to reread (A); it's the same as the original, and we already know that's wrong.) Now we are left with (C), (D), and (E). The crucial difference here is between the wordy phrase "progress, such as what is made"—in (C) and (D)—and (E)'s "progress such as that." (E)'s wording is preferable.

Also note the 3-2 split between "that are/is called objective" and "so-called objective." This is an important GMAT style point—as long as the meaning is unchanged, the phrase with fewer words is preferable. (This is true for essays as well, by the way!)

SENTENCE CORRECTION PRACTICE SET THREE

Time: 25 Minutes/22 Questions

Directions: The following questions present a sentence, part or all of which is underlined. Below each sentence you will find five ways to phrase the underlined portion. Choice (A) repeats the original version, while the other four choices are different. If the original seems best, choose choice (A). If not, choose one of the revisions.

This question tests correctness and effectiveness of expression. Choose an answer that follows the norms of standard written English: grammar, word choice, and sentence construction.

Choose the answer that produces the most effective sentence, aiming to eliminate awkwardness, ambiguity, redundancy, and grammatical error.

1. One student at the school was not yet fifteen, yet he was already a <u>master in both chess and in bridge.</u>

   ○ master in both chess and in bridge
   ○ master of both chess and in bridge
   ○ master of both chess and of bridge
   ○ master both chess and bridge
   ○ master of both chess and bridge

2. It has been demonstrated that individuals who participated in competitive sports <u>when they are in college tend towards remaining</u> physically active in their later years.

   ○ when they are in college tend towards remaining
   ○ when they were in college are likely to be
   ○ when they were in college were apt to be
   ○ when they are in college are apt to be
   ○ when they were in college were liable to be

3. <u>Unlike the Puritan ethic, extolling hard work as the supreme virtue, many modern psychologists focus on the goals of inner peace and self-discovery.</u>

   ○ Unlike the Puritan ethic, extolling hard work as the supreme virtue, many modern psychologists focus on the goals of inner peace and self-discovery
   ○ Unlike believers in the Puritan ethic, which extols as the supreme virtue hard work, the goals of inner peace and self-discovery are focused on by many modern psychologists
   ○ Unlike the Puritan ethic, which extols hard work as the supreme virtue, the focus of the doctrines of many modern psychologists are the goals of inner peace and self-discovery
   ○ Unlike the Puritan ethic, which extols hard work as the supreme virtue, the doctrines of many modern psychologists focus on the goals of inner peace and self-discovery
   ○ Unlike those of the Puritans, who extol hard work as the supreme virtue, many modern psychologists focus on the goals of inner peace and self-discovery

KAPLAN

4. <u>The customer will not be responsible for transactions made with lost or stolen credit cards after issuing replacement cards.</u>

   ⬭ The customer will not be responsible for transactions made with lost or stolen credit cards after issuing replacement cards

   ⬭ No customer will be responsible for transactions made with lost or stolen credit cards after they are issued replacement cards

   ⬭ The customer will not be responsible for transactions made with lost or stolen credit cards after replacement cards have been issued

   ⬭ Responsibility for transactions made with lost or stolen credit cards will not be the customer's after he is issued replacement cards

   ⬭ The customer will not be responsible for transactions made with lost or stolen credit cards after such time as they will have been issued replacement cards

5. <u>Despite that they were able to calculate faster than ever before possible</u>, the earliest computers, built with tubes instead of transistors, were too bulky, expensive, and unreliable to be useful to businesses.

   ⬭ Despite that they were able to calculate faster than ever before possible

   ⬭ Even though it could calculate faster than previously possible

   ⬭ Although faster in its calculating than ever before possible

   ⬭ Despite their calculations being faster than ever before possible

   ⬭ Despite their unprecedented speed of calculation

6. As genetics researchers achieve greater success in their attempt to map the exact locations and functions of human genes, the <u>close connection between genes and birth defects has become</u> increasingly clear.

   ⬭ close connection between genes and birth defects has become

   ⬭ closeness of the connection between genes and birth defects has become

   ⬭ close connection genes have with birth defects has been becoming

   ⬭ close connection between genes and birth defects has been becoming

   ⬭ close connection between genes and birth defects becomes

7. At Agincourt, Charles D'Albret's battle plan was thwarted <u>as a direct result of the irrepressible desire the French nobility had to</u> charge headlong into any enemy offering a challenge.

   ⬭ as a direct result of the irrepressible desire the French nobility had to

   ⬭ because the French nobility had an irrepressible desire to

   ⬭ insofar as the French nobility desired to

   ⬭ because the French nobility would have an irrepressible desire to

   ⬭ by the French nobility's desire to irrepressibly

8. At their birthday party, the twins were eager to begin opening their presents, but <u>finishing was hard for them.</u>

   ⬭ finishing was hard for them

   ⬭ reluctant to finish

   ⬭ finishing them reluctant

   ⬭ were reluctant after finishing

   ⬭ their finishing reluctant

9. <u>That young girls score as well if not better than young boys on standardized tests disprove</u> one prevalent male-supremacy myth.

   ○ That young girls score as well if not better than young boys on standardized tests disprove

   ○ That young girls score as well if not better than young boys on standardized tests disproves

   ○ That young girls score as well as if not better than young boys on standardized tests disproves

   ○ That young girls score so well as if not better than young boys on standardized tests disprove

   ○ The fact of young girls' scoring as well if not better than young boys on standardized tests disprove

10. A common social problem in the workplace occurs <u>when workers accept supervisory positions, and it causes them to lose</u> the trust of their former coworkers.

    ○ when workers accept supervisory positions, and it causes them to lose

    ○ by a worker accepting supervisory positions, which causes him to lose

    ○ when workers accept supervisory positions and so lose

    ○ when a worker who accepts a supervisory position, thereby losing

    ○ if a worker accepts a supervisory position, he would lose

11. To restore fishing grounds damaged by pollution, marine engineers can create an artificial reef by towing old barges to an offshore location <u>and sinking</u> to the sandy bottom.

    ○ and sinking

    ○ and sinking them

    ○ and sinking it

    ○ where it sinks

    ○ having sunk them

12. Popular child psychologists have advocated that parents discipline male children <u>similarly to the fashion in which they discipline</u> daughters.

    ○ similarly to the fashion in which they discipline

    ○ in the same manner that they would use with

    ○ like they would handle

    ○ as they discipline

    ○ as they would

13. In the Middle Ages, philosophers <u>were so devoted to Aristotle that they neglected</u> the evidence of their own senses and accepted whatever he wrote.

    ○ were so devoted to Aristotle that they neglected

    ○ were so devoted to Aristotle as to neglect

    ○ were devoted to Aristotle to such a degree that they were to neglect

    ○ were so devoted to Aristotle that they had to neglect

    ○ were as devoted to Aristotle as to neglect

14. <u>To rely on anecdotal evidence of social phenomena is ignoring</u> decades of increasing sophistication in the use of statistics in sociology.

    ○ To rely on anecdotal evidence of social phenomena is ignoring

    ○ To rely on anecdotal evidence of social phenomena is to ignore

    ○ To rely on anecdotes for demonstration of social phenomena is ignoring

    ○ Relying on anecdotal evidence of social phenomena is to ignore

    ○ Relying on anecdotal evidence of social phenomena amounts to the ignoring of

KAPLAN

15. The team streamed into the locker room, donned their uniforms, <u>and, before commencing its first practice, they joined in a brief strategy session.</u>

    ○ and, before commencing its first practice, they joined in a brief strategy session

    ○ and its first practice was preceded by a brief strategy session

    ○ and a brief strategy session preceded its first practice

    ○ and, before commencing their first practice, they joined in a brief strategy session

    ○ and, before commencing their first practice, joined in a brief strategy session

16. Records of the first 736 British convicts deported to Australia reveal <u>convictions for crimes against property in all cases and they ranged</u> from highway robbery to forgery.

    ○ convictions for crimes against property in all cases and they ranged

    ○ convictions in all cases were for crimes against property and ranging

    ○ the ranging of convictions for crimes against property in all cases

    ○ that all were convicted of crimes against property ranging

    ○ that all of them had convictions for crimes that were against property; the range was

17. A turning point in U.S. labor history was reached when most of the nation's air traffic controllers supported their union's strike and ignored President Reagan's demand <u>that they go back to work</u>.

    ○ that they go back to work

    ○ that these people go back to work

    ○ for them to go back to work

    ○ that they would go back to work

    ○ they should go back to work

18. One of the informants eventually professed <u>ignorant of the crime, having</u> fear that his testimony would lead to reprisals against him by his former confederates.

    ○ ignorant of the crime, having

    ○ ignorantly to the crime, with

    ○ ignorance of the crime, since

    ○ ignorance of the crime, for

    ○ to have ignorance of the crime, since

19. The nineteenth-century Russian composers known as "The Five" <u>were united by their holding</u> an ideal of a national music based on folk melodies and themes.

    ○ were united by their holding

    ○ had as their uniting ideal

    ○ united each other with

    ○ united based on

    ○ were united with

20. The symphonies of Mahler are characterized by <u>a much freer use of dissonance than Haydn.</u>

    ○ a much freer use of dissonance than Haydn

    ○ a much freer usage than Haydn of dissonance

    ○ a much freer use of dissonance than are those of Haydn

    ○ a usage much freer than the dissonance of Haydn

    ○ a use of dissonance that is much freer than Haydn

21. King James I of England tried unsuccessfully to merge the legislature of Scotland—his original kingdom—<u>with England</u>.

    ◯ with England

    ◯ and England

    ◯ with that of England

    ◯ and England's

    ◯ and England's legislature

22. In a convincing test of Newtonian physics, <u>it was anomalies in the orbit of Uranus that</u> led astronomers to predict the discovery of Neptune.

    ◯ it was anomalies in the orbit of Uranus that

    ◯ it was the orbit of Uranus showing anomalies that

    ◯ the orbit of Uranus showing anomalies was what

    ◯ the orbit of Uranus being anomalous was what

    ◯ anomalies in the orbit of Uranus

KAPLAN

ANSWERS AND EXPLANATIONS

1.   E
2.   B
3.   D
4.   C
5.   E
6.   E
7.   B
8.   B
9.   C
10. C
11. B
12. E
13. A
14. B
15. E
16. D
17. A
18. D
19. D
20. C
21. C
22. E

1.   E

When you use the "both . . . and" formula, the things being linked have to be grammatically parallel. If you say "*both* of chess," you have to follow it with "*and* of bridge." If you say "of *both* chess," you have to follow it with "*and* bridge." And idiomatically, one speaks of a master *of* chess or bridge, not a master *in* chess or bridge. So (E) is the best answer.

2.   B

The main differences in the answer choices have to do with verb tense. Notice that "participated," which is not underlined, is in the simple past tense. Since the people in question participated in sports while in college, we need the past tense "were," not the present tense "are," which eliminates (A) and (D). The next question is whether the next verb should be past or present: were or are? Well, the sentence seems to be describing a general truth, rather than merely facts about specific individuals in the past, and general truths are usually expressed in the present tense.

3.   D

This sentence makes a comparison, so we have to make sure it's logical. You can't compare "the Puritan ethic" with "many modern psychologists" as in (A), nor with "the focus of the doctrines of many modern psychologists," as in (C). You can't compare "believers in the Puritan ethic" with "the goals of inner peace and self-discovery" in (B). You can't compare "those of the Puritans" (those what?) with "many modern psychologists," in (E). Only (D) makes a logical comparison, between "the Puritan ethic" and "the doctrines of many modern psychologists."

4.   C

The problem here has to do with modification. Who or what will issue replacement cards? Not the customer, certainly, but that's what (A) seems to be saying. Choices (B) and (E) have a pronoun reference problem: The plural "they" refers to the singular "customer." "Responsibility . . . will not be the customer's" in (D) is more awkward than "the customer will not be responsible."

5.   E

This question presents problems of idiom. "Despite that" in (A) is unidiomatic, and "than ever before possible" in (A), (C), and (D) is awkward. Choice (B) has a clear pronoun reference problem: The singular "it" is used to refer to the plural "computers."

6. E

Logically, both things must be going on in the present. The genetics researchers are achieving success and the connection between genes and birth defects is becoming clear. So there's no need to switch to the past "has become" or "has been becoming" as (A), (B), (C), and (D) do.

7. B

This question presents problems of style. There is no reason to say "as a direct result of" when "by" or "because" will do, so (A) is out. "Insofar" in (C) does not make the logical connection between the parts of the sentence clear enough. There is no reason to use "would have" in (D). Finally, "irrepressibly charge," in (E), makes less sense than "irrepressible desire," in (B).

8. B

Here, we want an answer that's grammatically parallel to "were eager to begin."

9. C

This question tests your knowledge of a common idiom. The correct expression is "as well as . . . if not better than." Choices (A), (B), and (E) lack the "as." Choice (D) turns "as well as" into "so well as."

10. C

Perhaps you noticed the poor usage of the pronoun *it* in the sentence as written. It is meant to refer to "workers accept[ing] supervisory positions." But that's an action, not a thing. Therefore "it" is incorrect. Eliminate (A). All of the other answers focus instead on the cause-and-effect dynamic. Among them, (B) is wordiest and could be eliminated on those grounds.

Scanning the beginning of the choices, we see a 3-1-1 split among *when, by,* and *if.* Your ear probably recognizes "a problem occurs when" or "a problem occurs if " as correct usage and "a problem occurs by" as awkward. Eliminate (B). There's another split between "workers" and "a worker." The end of the sentence says "their," so clearly we need the plural. Eliminate (B)—if you hadn't done so already—as well as (D) and (E).

By this point, you've eliminated everything but (C), so you know that (C) is correct. On test day, you'd select it and move on. Just two more things for you to focus on for your prep. First, read (D) closely. Notice that it sounds okay on its

own, but by including the word *who,* the answer choice put the verb *accepts* into a subordinate clause. As a result, the sentence has no main verb. This is a sneaky trick the GMAT will use from time to time. Secondly, most people don't say things like "and so lose" in everyday speech. Sometimes the GMAT uses construction that is correct according to the rules of standard English but sounds a little "stuffy" for common usage. Don't eliminate an answer just because you think, "I would never say it that way."

11. B

A good place to start is with pronoun reference. First, let's be clear that you do need some pronoun in the answer to serve as the object of "sinking"; (A) seems to say that it is the engineers who sink to the bottom. The pronoun must refer to barges, which is plural; we need "them," not "it," so (C) and (D) can be eliminated. "Having sunk," in (E), illogically suggests that the engineers sunk the barges before towing them into position. The correct answer is (B).

12. E

Here, the main things to look for are clarity and brevity. The shortest choice, (E), is best: None of the other, longer, choices are any clearer. In (A), "discipline male children" is parallel to "discipline female children," but the word "discipline" need not be repeated. Choices (A) and (B) use other, wordier, grammatical constructions. Choice (C) uses "like" instead of "as." You use "like" when there's no verb, implied or stated, in the second half of the comparison. You say "He acts *like* me," but "He is *as* tall *as* I (am)." (D) changes the sentence's meaning, suggesting that parents discipline sons and daughters simultaneously.

13. A

What's needed here is the "so . . . that" construction. Choice (A) provides that. "So . . . as to" in (B) and "as . . . as to" in (E) are unidiomatic. "To such a degree that they were to neglect" in (C) and "they had to neglect" in (D) introduce unnecessary verbiage.

14. B

The rule that's being tested here is the one that says that things joined by "is" have to be parallel. You can join an infinitive (to rely) with an infinitive (to ignore), or a participle (relying) with a participle (ignoring), but not a participle with an infinitive or an infinitive with a participle. Hence, choice (B) is correct.

15. E

The question tests parallelism: The three things that the team did have to be expressed in the same form. To match "streamed" and "donned," you need "joined." This eliminates (B) and (C). You just say "the team streamed, donned, and joined . . . ." There's no need to say "and they joined," in (A) and (D). This leaves (E) as the correct answer. Notice, by the way, that the team, though technically singular, is construed as plural in the part of the sentence that's not underlined; it must be construed in the same way throughout the sentence, and this is another reason why (A), (B), and (C) are wrong.

16. D

If you have the option, it's usually more concise to put a modifying idea in a phrase instead of in a clause. Here you really don't need the clause "and they ranged." You should strongly suspect that there will be a more efficient choice than this. A scan of the tail ends shows that only (D) works. In (B), "and ranging" is needlessly wordy, made worse by the fact that (B) also uses "in all cases" where (D) has the more concise "all." In (E), "the range was" is too verbose, and its wordiness is compounded by the use of "that were against property" where "against property" would do just fine. (C) uses the awkward, wordy phrase "the ranging of convictions." After eliminating everything else, select (D).

17. A

This question tests your knowledge of the subjunctive of requirement, used after a word like "demand," and employing the word "that," a subject, and the infinitive form of a verb without the "to." The choice that uses this form correctly is (A). Actually, (B) uses it correctly too, but "they" is much more concise than "these people."

18. D

Here we have another question of idiom. You profess "ignorance," not ignorant or ignorantly; this eliminates (A) and (B). "To have ignorance," in (E), is unnecessarily wordy. Finally, before a noun like "fear," we need a preposition like "for," not a conjunction like "since."

19. D

You don't say people were "united by their holding," so (A) is wrong. (B) unnecessarily repeats "ideal." In (C), what does it mean to say the composers "united each other"?

This makes no sense. In (E), the composers didn't unite *with* the ideal. (D) is the only choice that makes sense. On GMAT Sentence Correction, favor concise answer choices.

20. C

Finding the most effective expression is not as simple as just going for the shortest choice. You must distinguish between necessary and unnecessary omissions, and you must be careful not to eliminate *necessary* words. In this sentence, the word "than" indicates a comparison, so make sure that like things are being compared. Here Mahler's symphonies are compared to "Haydn." That's no good. Eliminate (A).

(E) repeats the mistake of (A). (B) and (D) contain the unGMAT-like "usage" where "use" would do just fine. (D) actually is neither parallel nor logical, since "usage" is said to be "freer" than the "dissonance of Haydn." (B) contains the misplaced modifier "of dissonance," which should come after "usage." After the eliminations, only (C) is left standing.

21. C

Here's another example of how you have to distinguish between necessary and unnecessary omissions. You need to compare legislature to legislature. So don't go for the shortest choice. You need "that of" to complete the comparison. Eliminate (A).

Also, the correct idiom is "merge . . . with." You don't merge one thing and another—you merge one thing *with* another. Select (C). If you knew only one of the two things tested here, you could still have eliminated two or three choices. The need to compare likes eliminates (A) and (B), while the need to use proper idiom eliminates (B), (D), and (E).

22. E

"It was anomalies" should jump out at you as bad style for the GMAT. Look for more concise versions in the choices. There are only three ways to begin this clause, so if you don't like the original "it was anomalies," see whether "the orbit," in (C) and (D), or "anomalies," in (E), works out any better. "The orbit" didn't lead to the discovery (the anomalies did), so (C) and (D) can't be right. The answer has to be (E), because it is much more concise than (A).

READING COMPREHENSION PRACTICE SET ONE

Time: 25 Minutes/18 Questions

Directions: The questions in this group are based on the content of a passage. After reading the passage, choose the best answer to each question. Base your answers only according to what is stated or implied in the text.

Questions 1-4 refer to the following passage.

Line   The relevance of formal economic models to real-world policy has been a topic of some dispute. The economists R. D. Norton and S. Y. Rhee achieved some success in
(5) applying such a model retrospectively to the Korean economy over a fourteen-year period; the model's figures for output, prices, and other variables closely matched real statistics. The model's value in policy terms, however,
(10) proved less clear-cut. Norton and Rhee performed simulations in which, keeping long-term factors constant, they tried to pinpoint the effect of short-term policy changes. Their model indicated that rising prices for imported
(15) oil would increase inflation; reducing exports by five percent would lower Gross Domestic Product and increase inflation; and slowing the growth of the money supply would result in slightly higher inflation.

(20)   These findings are somewhat startling. Many economists have argued that reducing exports will lessen, not increase, inflation.

And while most view escalating oil costs as inflationary, few would think the same of
(25) slower monetary growth. The Norton-Rhee model can perhaps be viewed as indicating the pitfalls of a formalist approach that stresses statistical "goodness of fit" at the expense of genuine policy relevance.

1. The author is primarily concerned with

   ◯ proposing a new type of economic analysis

   ◯ criticizing an overly formal economic model

   ◯ advocating the use of statistical models in determining economic policy

   ◯ suggesting an explanation for Korean inflation

   ◯ determining the accuracy of Norton and Rhee's analysis

2. The author mentions "a fourteen-year period" (line 6) in order to

   ◯ indicate how far into the future Norton and Rhee's model can make accurate predictions

   ◯ acknowledge the accuracy of Norton and Rhee's model in accounting for past events

   ◯ explain the effect of reducing exports on inflation

   ◯ demonstrate the startling nature of Norton and Rhee's findings

   ◯ expose the flaws in Norton and Rhee's model

3. The most significant criticism leveled against Norton and Rhee's model is that it

   ◯ excludes key statistical variables

   ◯ is too abstract to be useful in policy making

   ◯ fails to adjust for Korea's high rate of inflation

   ◯ underestimates the importance of economic growth

   ◯ fails to consider the effect of short-term variations in the economy

KAPLAN

4. It can be inferred that the most surprising finding of the Norton-Rhee study is that

   ○ reducing exports would reduce inflation

   ○ high oil prices worsen inflation

   ○ an increase in exports can slow the rate of growth

   ○ slower monetary expansion would worsen inflation

   ○ long-term factors do not affect economic growth

Questions 5-11 refer to the following passage.

Line   A basic principle of ecology is that population size is partly a reflection of available food resources. Recent experiments suggest that the relationship is more complex than for-
(5) merly thought. Specifically, the browsing of certain rodents appears to trigger chemical reactions in food plants that, in turn, affect the size of the rodent populations. Two examples of such regulation have been reported.

(10)   Berger has demonstrated the power of a naturally occurring chemical called 6-MBOA to stimulate reproductive behavior in the mountain vole, a small mouselike rodent. 6-MBOA forms in young grass in response to browsing
(15) by voles. Berger experimented by feeding oats coated with 6-MBOA to nonbreeding winter populations of voles. After three weeks, she found a high incidence of pregnancy among females. Since the timing of reproduction is
(20) crucial to the short-lived vole in an environment in which the onset of vegetative growth may be considerably delayed, the phytochemical triggering of reproductive behavior represents a significant biological adaptation.

(25)   In an example reported by Bryant, plants appear to have developed a phytochemical defense against the depredations of snowshoe hares in Canada. Every ten years, for reasons that are unclear, the hare population swells.
(30) The result is overbrowsing of certain deciduous trees and shrubs. Bryant found that trees favored by the hare produce young shoots high in terpene and phenolic resins, which discourage hare browsing. After treating non-
(35) resinous willow twigs with resinous extracts and placing treated and untreated samples at hare feeding stations, Bryant found that samples containing at least half of the resin concentration of natural twigs were untouched.
(40) The avoidance of resinous shoots, he concludes, may play a role in the decline of the hare population to normal levels.

   Both of these reports suggest areas for further research. For example, data should be
(45) reviewed to determine if periodic population explosions among lemmings (another small rodent living in a northern environment) occur during years in which there is an early onset of vegetative growth; if so, a triggering
(50) mechanism similar to that prompted by the vole may be involved.

5. The author provides specific information to answer which of the following questions?

   ○ What factors other than food supply affect the population size of rodents?

   ○ Why is the timing of the voles' reproductive effort important?

   ○ Are phytochemical reactions found only in northern environments?

   ○ How does 6-MBOA trigger reproductive activity in the mountain vole?

   ○ What are the causes of the periodic increase in the snowshoe hare population?

6. The passage describes the effect of 6-MBOA on voles as a "significant biological adaptation" (line 24) because it

   ○ limits reproductive behavior in times of food scarcity

   ○ prompts the vole population to seek new food sources

   ○ supports species survival during periods of fluctuating food supply

   ○ maximizes the number of offspring in individual litters

   ○ minimizes territorial competition

7. Which of the following statements can be inferred about plant shoots containing large amounts of terpene and phenolic resins?

   I. They serve as a form of natural defense.

   II. Their growth is stimulated by increases in the hare population.

   III. They are unappetizing to hares.

   ○ I only

   ○ II only

   ○ III only

   ○ I and III only

   ○ I, II, and III

8. It can be inferred that the study of lemmings proposed by the author would probably

   ○ strengthen the conclusions of Bryant

   ○ cast doubt on the conclusions of Bryant

   ○ support the specific findings of Berger

   ○ provide evidence as to whether Berger's conclusions can be generalized

   ○ disprove common beliefs about the relationship between population size and food supply

9. The author of the passage is primarily concerned with

   ○ reviewing findings about phytochemical regulation of rodent populations

   ○ outlining the role of 6-MBOA in regulating population size

   ○ summarizing knowledge on population size of rodents

   ○ explaining why earlier studies of population size were wrong

   ○ describing mechanisms used by plants to protect themselves

10. Bryant's interpretation of the results of his experiment (lines 37–39) depends on which of the following assumptions?

    ○ The response of hares to resinous substances may be different in nature than under experimental conditions.

    ○ The periodic rise in the hare population is triggered by an unknown phytochemical response.

    ○ Many hares will starve to death rather than eat resinous shoots.

    ○ Hares alter their breeding behavior in response to the declining availability of food.

    ○ Significant numbers of hares die from ingesting the resins in shoots.

11. The experiments described in the passage did each of the following EXCEPT

    ○ measure changes in the behavior of test animals

    ○ measure changes in the populations of experimental animals

    ○ simulate a hypothesized phytochemical effect in nature

    ○ measure the consumption of foods by test animals

    ○ analyze the effects of food on breeding behavior

Questions 12-18 refer to the following passage.

Line   There is an intriguing note to the current
call upon civil rights law to help remedy the
undervaluation of women's work. Until fairly
recently, government was not expected to
(5) solve workers' economic grievances, however
valid they might be. Many assumed that the
responsibility lay with workers themselves.
Collective bargaining was the preferred instru-
ment for pursuing pay equity for women.
(10) Rather than call upon the law to regulate the
market from the outside, one could try to
reshape or otherwise influence the market so
that women themselves would be better able
to address the problem. This could be done
(15) by raising absolute wage levels in low-paying,
predominantly female industries (such as
retail clothing) or by changing the pay relationship between largely female and largely
male occupations within a single industry,
(20) such as auto manufacturing. Through union
representation, employees in traditionally
female jobs in an industry could identify the
actual degree of underpayment of their work
and then, as a group, pressure their employer
(25) to remedy it. In addition, this process would
encourage those affected—men and women
alike—to be sensitive to the limits of available
resources, to be pragmatic about the pace at
which the wage structure could be revised.

(30)   I do not mean to suggest that collective
bargaining is a foolproof means for closing
the gender gap in wages. To the extent that the
problem involves the undervaluation of non-
union female occupations in an otherwise
(35) unionized industry, political hurdles will discourage unionized employees from supporting revisions in the wage structure. And to the
extent that the problem is the concentration
of women in low-paying industries—textiles,
(40) for example—the product market imposes

serious economic constraints on a substantial
closing of the wage gap.

Despite the imperfections of tools like collective bargaining for redressing wage dispari-
(45) ties between men and women, a reliance on
law or government is favorable for neither
individual firms nor our economy as a whole.
Nonetheless, although opponents of mandatory public remedies may correctly fear
(50) those remedies as being a cure worse than the
disease, they are wrong when they imply that
the current system of wage determination by
business management is perfectly healthy.

12. In line 14, "This" most likely refers to

   ◯ increasing the wages of women and men in a
       single industry

   ◯ bringing about changes in market conditions

   ◯ changing the dynamic of collective bargaining

   ◯ relying on civil rights law to remedy
       economic grievances

   ◯ applying group pressure on an employer

13. According to the author, the process of
     unionization and collective bargaining could do all
     of the following EXCEPT

   ◯ overcome market pressures that keep wages
       in some industries lower than in others

   ◯ encourage worker flexibility in adjusting a
       new pay scale to economic conditions

   ◯ help workers to apply group pressure on
       employers

   ◯ aid in determining the degree to which
       women are being underpaid

   ◯ sensitize workers to the limits of their indus-
       try's ability to institute change

14. Which of the following best summarizes the author's main point?

    ◯ Pay inequity for women exists because of the lack of unionization in traditionally female occupations.

    ◯ Government regulation of industry to achieve pay equity for women is unnecessary because management has the power to effectively determine wages.

    ◯ Unionization would solve all industry problems relating to the valuation of women's work.

    ◯ Government regulation of women's wages is necessary only in those industries where collective bargaining is ineffective.

    ◯ Collective bargaining is preferable to government actions in redressing the under-valuation of women's work.

15. The author mentions textiles (line 39) in order to

    ◯ demonstrate the potential harm of govern-ment regulation of industry

    ◯ outline a strategy for achieving pay equity for women

    ◯ indicate how quickly employees can reason-ably expect to achieve pay equity

    ◯ give an example of a situation in which collective bargaining may be ineffective

    ◯ show why civil rights laws are the most important tool for increasing women's wages

16. It can be inferred that the author's attitude towards opponents of government regulation of wage determination mentioned in the last paragraph is characterized by which of the following?

    I.   Distrust of their motives
    II. Sympathy with some of their concerns
    III. Disagreement with some of their assumptions
    IV. Opposition to their political principles

    ◯ I only
    ◯ III only
    ◯ I and II only
    ◯ II and III only
    ◯ I, II, and IV

17. In the final paragraph, the author addresses "opponents of mandatory public remedies" (lines 48–49) by

    ◯ arguing that those remedies would benefit the economy

    ◯ implying that alternative methods of correcting wage disparities would be worse

    ◯ asserting that the present approach to setting wages is flawed

    ◯ defending civil rights legislation as a solution to social problems

    ◯ insisting that those remedies are a viable means of correcting wage disparities

18. The passage refers to which of the following as reasons for preferring collective bargaining to legislation as a method of ending the undervaluation of women's work?

    I.   The greater responsiveness of collective bargaining to existing conditions that affect wage levels

    II. The general desirability of using private rather than public remedies

    III. The potential of collective bargaining for achieving a uniform national solution to the problem of gender wage disparities

    ◯ I only
    ◯ III only
    ◯ I and II only
    ◯ II and III only
    ◯ I, II, and III

ANSWERS AND EXPLANATIONS

1. B
2. B
3. B
4. D
5. B
6. C
7. D
8. D
9. A
10. C
11. E
12. B
13. A
14. E
15. D
16. D
17. C
18. C

PASSAGE 1—THE NORTON AND RHEE MODEL

Topic and Scope: A discussion of the relevance of formal economic models to real-world policy. The author uses the model applied to Korea by Norton and Rhee to show shortcomings of such models.

Purpose and Main Idea: Author wants to reveal the shortcomings of formal economic models.

Paragraph Structure: Paragraph 1 describes the Norton and Rhee model. Paragraph 2 shows how the results of the application contradict the general trends of real-world economic policy.

1.   B

The passage begins by posing the question of how useful formal models are, and concludes by calling Norton and Rhee's model an example of the "pitfalls" of formalism. (B) captures this critical approach, though it misses the broader implications hinted at in the opening sentence. There's nothing that indicates that Norton and Rhee's method of analysis was "new," (A), nor is the author "proposing" it; on the other hand, she doesn't propose any *other* approach. (C) is what the author is very skeptical about; certainly she doesn't "advocate" using such models. (D) is a mess. Norton and Rhee were not trying to explain Korean inflation as a whole, but to see how various economic factors would affect inflation; and the author is not even trying to do that, but to discuss Norton and Rhee's work. (E) is incidental to the broader purpose of criticizing "formalism."

2.   B

The passage says that Norton and Rhee "achieved some success in applying such a model retrospectively to the Korean economy over a fourteen-year period." In other words, the model is fairly effective in analyzing past events, as (B) suggests.

Since the "fourteen-year period" refers to the past, not the future, (A) is clearly wrong; in fact, one of the main points of the passage is that Norton and Rhee's model is not particularly useful for predicting the future. Choices (C), (D), and (E) refer to matters discussed later in the passage.

3. B

The whole passage is critical of Norton and Rhee, but the last sentence offers the only explicit criticism: Their approach is "formalist" (or abstract) and lacks "policy relevance." (B) paraphrases this criticism. The only economic factors specifically excluded from the model, (A), are the long-term factors mentioned in the middle of paragraph 1; there is no suggestion that Norton and Rhee should be criticized for this procedure. (C) is something that the model does do, since it is aimed at finding the effect of various factors on inflation. The "importance" of economic growth, (D), is not discussed at all and certainly not underestimated. (E) is contradicted by paragraph 1: These are exactly the factors Norton and Rhee *did* consider.

4. D

The last paragraph calls Norton and Rhee's findings "startling," and then cites other economists' views on three points discussed in the preceding paragraph. The most surprising finding is the one "few" economists would agree with; the *least* surprising is the one "most" economists would agree with; and the one that "many" economists dispute lies somewhere in between. The finding "few" economists would agree with, that slower monetary growth is inflationary, is summarized in correct choice (D). (B) refers to the least controversial point, that rising oil costs are inflationary (Norton and Rhee share the orthodox view on this question). Choices (A) and (C) refer to the "in between" finding, on the effects of reduced exports, and are wrong for this reason. In addition, they distort the finding. Norton and Rhee contended that reduced exports would *increase* inflation (the choice paraphrases the "orthodox" view). And they argued that lower (not higher) exports would lower GDP, (C)—no finding about higher exports is implied. Lastly, keeping the long-term factors constant, (E), does not mean that they don't affect growth, simply that Norton and Rhee were not examining their effects on growth.

PASSAGE 2—ECOLOGY

Topic and Scope: A basic scientific principle: "Population size is partly a reflection of available food resources." Specifically, author uses two experiments (one by Berger, one by Bryant) to illustrate how changes in food supply can dramatically affect the size of rodent populations.

Purpose and Main Idea: Author wants to demonstrate that the relationship between population and food supply "is more complex than formerly thought."

Paragraph Structure: In paragraph 1, the second sentence is key: "Recent experiments suggest that the relationship is more complex than formerly thought." *You can guess from these words that the passage will go on to discuss these experiments.* The next sentence identifies the nature of the complexity—rodent browsing affects plant chemicals, which in turn affect the rodents. Paragraph 2 details Berger's experiment, which studied how plant chemicals *trigger reproductive activity among voles.* Paragraph 3 details Bryant's experiment, which studied the effect of plant chemicals on *declining populations of snowshoe hares.* Paragraph 4 discusses possible future research involving lemmings, another rodent with fluctuating populations.

5. B

With a question like this, you need to check each choice against the passage. A faster way to eliminate choices is to remember that the right answer often fits with the main idea, here the food-population relationship. Thus, (A) is wrong because it ventures away from this. (B) looks excellent, because the author devotes several lines at the end of paragraph 2 to explaining the importance of timing for vole reproduction. (C) is simply never covered. (D) is wrong because the author discusses the significance of 6-MBOA, but not its biologic mechanism. With (E), why the hares overpopulate is dismissed in the third paragraph with the words "for reasons that are unclear." The answer is (B).

6. C

This question asks about a detail from paragraph 2. The cited sentence says that timing is crucial because voles are short-lived and the timing of plant growth is unpredictable. You can infer that the plant-rodent relationship increases the vole population at times when food is more plentiful. The best restatement of this inference is (C). (A) goes the wrong way; 6-MBOA triggers breeding—it doesn't discourage it. (B), (D), and (E) are never mentioned anywhere.

7. D

The resinous shoots are discussed in the third paragraph. There, we are told that these shoots function as part of "a phytochemical defense against the depredations of snowshoe hares in Canada." This means that statement I is correct. We are also told the resins in these shoots "discourage hare browsing," and that hares avoid shoots artificially treated with these resins. This means that statement III must also appear in the correct answer. But the passage does not say that increases in the hare population cause plants to produce more resinous shoots, so statement II is not supported by the passage. Therefore, the answer is (D).

8. D

The lemmings are mentioned in the last paragraph, which speculates that lemmings might, like voles, be affected by a plant trigger for breeding behavior. Some answer choices mention Berger and some mention Bryant. The lemmings are likened to voles, so Berger is the pertinent researcher here. This eliminates (A) and (B). (E) conflicts with the main idea. The author wants to prove something, not disprove it.

That leaves (C), supporting Berger's specific findings, and (D), indicating whether Berger's findings can be generalized. The paragraph doesn't talk about proving Berger's specific results with the voles; those are accepted as given. It does say that the lemmings, like voles, may be affected by a plant trigger. This implies (D), that Berger's findings may be applicable to other animals.

9. A

The answer to this global question has to focus on something about the complex relationship between food and population size, including the rodent examples; it should also encompass the entire passage. Thus, the best answer is (A). (B) is a detail appearing only in the second paragraph, while (E) appears only in paragraph 3. (C) is too general, and (D) mentions a topic the author never covers.

10. C

When you read about the hares, notice that Bryant's conclusion is pure speculation. He sees that the hares don't eat resinous shoots, and concludes that this "may play a role" in population decline. The assumption is that there's a connection between not eating the plants and a population reduction. Choice (C) corresponds: the avoidance of plants would lead to starvation, and population decline.

(A), if true, would *weaken*, not strengthen, Bryant's conclusion. (B) is irrelevant—the cause of the rise is unknown and doesn't concern Bryant; it's the decline that interests him. (D) mixes up the hares with the voles and

their breeding behavior. The hare experiment has nothing to do with breeding and reproduction. Finally, (E) is never suggested. Bryant concluded that the population decline was caused by *avoiding* the shoots, not by *eating* them.

11. E

Because the question stem refers to both experiments, you need to find the statement that describes only one of the experiments. Choice (A) was part of both: Berger measured how voles changed breeding behavior and Bryant measured how hares changed eating behavior. (B) also appears in both: Berger measured the rise and fall of vole populations, while Bryant measured hare populations. (C) and (D) apply to both experiments, since both scientists fed the animals chemically treated foods and noted consumption. (E) is correct: Only Berger's experiment dealt with the effect of food on breeding behavior. Bryant's hare experiment dealt with the effect of food on *eating* behavior.

PASSAGE 3—CIVIL RIGHTS LAW

Topic and Scope: Unfair differences between women's and men's wages; specifically, how to remedy such pay inequities.

Purpose and Main Idea: The author argues that collective bargaining is a more desirable way of solving wage disparities than are government-sponsored remedies such as civil rights laws.

Paragraph Structure: Paragraph 1 cites the use of civil rights law for remedying women's pay inequities, but immediately jumps to the topic of collective bargaining, asserting that it's a better alternative. A number of reasons are then given. Paragraph 2 acknowledges that collective bargaining is not foolproof and explains why. Paragraph 3 confirms the author's preference for collective bargaining. Note the conclusion: While the author agrees with opponents of "public remedies," he also issues a warning: That "the current system of wage determination" is far from "perfectly healthy."

12. B

Since "This" is the first word in the sentence, you have to check the previous sentence to determine its meaning. The previous sentence says that instead of invoking civil rights law, one could try to influence the market so that women could address their own problems. The correct answer will paraphrase "influence the market," (B).

(A) and (E) appear after "This," and thus cannot be what the pronoun refers to. (C) mentions collective bargaining, but "changing its dynamic" is never discussed. (D) goes against the main idea, by favoring use of civil rights law over collective bargaining.

13. A

Figuring out where in the passage to look for an answer is vital! For something that collective bargaining *can't* do, you look at paragraph 2, which lists the shortcomings. There the author states that "the product market imposes serious economic constraints on a substantial closing of the wage gap," which makes (A) correct. Choices (B), (C), (D), and (E) are identified in paragraph 1 as things that collective bargaining *can* accomplish.

14. E

The bold and efficient approach here is to restate the main idea in your own words and then look for an equivalent. Here, (E) is close to the idea we came up with earlier: collective bargaining isn't perfect, but it's preferable to civil rights law for addressing women's labor issues. (E) "jumps out."

As for the wrong answers, (A) offers a detail. (B) distorts the passage—the author believes that government regulation is bad, but not that management should have unlimited power to set wages. (C) is a sweeping generalization—a negative sign in itself. Correct choices seldom use absolute words such as "all," "never," "always," and "every." And the passage explicitly states that unionization doesn't solve all problems. (D) runs counter to the author's attitude: the author never endorses any type of government remedy.

15. D

The textile industry is mentioned in the course of the author's admission that collective bargaining is not "foolproof." The passage says that "the concentration of women in low-paying industries" raises problems that are not easily resolved by collective bargaining. Thus, (D) is the best answer.

Choice (A) is wrong, because the second paragraph is not where the author makes a case against government

regulation. Choices (B) and (C) refer to matters discussed earlier in the passage. And (E) contradicts the author's argument.

16. D

The answer to this question is in the last paragraph, where the author refers to the "opponents" of government regulation. The author says that they aren't right about everything, although they are right about the evils of government intervention. This confirms options II and III—the author is sympathetic, but disagrees with part of their argument. Since only (D) includes both II and III, it must be the correct answer.

Statements I and IV suggest that the author's hostile to the opponents. The author generally agrees with them! The author takes issue with one point only.

17. C

Questions are sometimes consistent with each other! You examined the last paragraph in the previous question and found that the author agrees with the conclusion that public remedies are bad, but sharply questions the assumption that the present system is fine just the way it is. (C) restates this latter point. The four wrong choices run counter to the author's argument—at no point does the author endorse any form of government regulation or civil rights law.

18. C

As always, knowing where to look is crucial. The answer to this question will appear in the first paragraph, which lists all the reasons collective bargaining is good. Option I is implied at the end of the paragraph with "sensitive to the limits." Option II occurs at the beginning of the paragraph, which endorses self-help over civil rights law. Option III, however, is not found here. In fact, option III appears in the discussion of the weaknesses of collective bargaining in paragraph 2.

KAPLAN

READING COMPREHENSION PRACTICE SET TWO

Time: 25 Minutes/18 Questions

Directions: The questions in this group are based on the content of a passage. After reading the passage, choose the best answer to each question. Base your answers only according to what is stated or implied in the text.

Questions 8-13 are based on the following passage.

Line   In many underdeveloped countries, the state plays an important and increasingly varied role in economic development today. There are four general arguments, all of them related,
(5) for state participation in economic development. First, the entrance requirements in terms of financial capital and capital equipment are very large in certain industries, and the size of these obstacles will serve as
(10) barriers to entry on the part of private investors. One can imagine that these obstacles are imposing in industries such as steel production, automobiles, electronics, and parts of the textile industry. In addition, there
(15) are what Myint calls "technical indivisibilities in social overhead capital." Public utilities, transport, and communications facilities must be in place before industrial development can occur, and they do not lend themselves to
(20) small-scale improvements.

    A related argument centers on the demand side of the economy. This economy is seen as fragmented, disconnected, and incapable of using inputs from other parts of the economy.
(25) Consequently, economic activity in one part of the economy does not generate the dynamism in other sectors that is expected in more cohesive economies. Industrialization necessarily involves many different sectors;

(30) economic enterprises will thrive best in an environment in which they draw on inputs from related economic sectors and, in turn, release their own goods for industrial utilization within their own economies.

(35)   A third argument concerns the low-level equilibrium trap in which less developed countries find themselves. At subsistence levels, societies consume exactly what they produce. There is no remaining surplus for
(40) reinvestment. As per capita income rises, however, the additional income will not be used for savings and investment. Instead, it will have the effect of increasing the population, which will eat up the surplus and
(45) force the society to its former subsistence position. Fortunately, after a certain point, the rate of population growth will decrease; economic growth will intersect with and eventually outstrip population growth. The
(50) private sector, however, will not be able to provide the one-shot large dose of capital to push economic growth beyond those levels where population increases eat up the incremental advances.

(55)   The final argument concerns the relationship between delayed development and the state. Countries wishing to industrialize today have more competitors, and these competitors occupy a more
(60) differentiated industrial terrain than previously. This means that the available niches in the international system are more limited. For today's industrializers, therefore, the process of industrialization cannot be a
(65) haphazard affair, nor can the pace, content, and direction be left solely to market forces. Part of the reason for a strong state presence, then, relates specifically to the competitive international environment in which modern
(70) countries and firms must operate.

KAPLAN

1. According to the passage, all of the following are arguments for state economic intervention EXCEPT:

    ○ The start-up costs of initial investments are beyond the capacities of many private investors.

    ○ The state must mediate relations between the demand and supply sides of the economy

    ○ The pace and processes of industrialization are too important to be left solely to market trends.

    ○ The livelihoods and security of workers should not be subject to the variability of industrial trends.

    ○ Public amenities are required to facilitate a favorable business environment.

2. Which of the following best states the central point of the passage?

    ○ Without state intervention, many less developed countries will not be able to carry out the interrelated tasks necessary to achieve industrialization.

    ○ Underdeveloped countries face a crisis of overpopulation and a lack of effective demand that cannot be overcome without outside assistance.

    ○ State participation plays a secondary role as compared to private capital investment in the industrialization of underdeveloped countries.

    ○ Less developed countries are trapped in an inescapable cycle of low production and demand.

    ○ State economic planning can ensure the rapid development of nonindustrialized countries' natural resources.

3. The author suggests all of the following as appropriate roles for the state in economic development EXCEPT

    ○ safeguarding against the domination of local markets by a single source of capital

    ○ financing industries with large capital requirements

    ○ helping to coordinate demand among different economic sectors

    ○ providing capital inputs sufficient for growth to surpass increases in per capita consumption

    ○ developing communication and transportation facilities to service industry

4. The author suggests which of the following about the "technical indivisibilities in social overhead capital" (lines 15–16) and the "low-level equilibrium trap" (lines 35–36)?

    ○ The first leads to rapid technological progress; the second creates demand for technologically sophisticated products.

    ○ Both enhance the developmental effects of private sector investment.

    ○ Neither is relevant to formulating a strategy for economic growth.

    ○ The first is a barrier to private investment; the second can attract it.

    ○ The first can prevent development from occurring; the second can negate its effects.

5. Which of the following, if true, would cast doubt on the author's argument that state participation is important in launching large-scale industries?

   I. Coordination of demand among different economic sectors requires a state planning agency.

   II. Associations of private sector investors can raise large amounts of capital by pooling their resources.

   III. Transportation and communications facilities can be built up through a series of small-scale improvements.

   ○ I only

   ○ II only

   ○ I and II only

   ○ II and III only

   ○ I, II, and III

6. According to the passage, the "low-level equilibrium trap" in underdeveloped countries results from

   ○ the tendency for societies to produce more than they can use

   ○ intervention of the state in economic development

   ○ the inability of market forces to overcome the effects of population growth

   ○ the fragmented and disconnected nature of the demand side of the economy

   ○ one-shot, large doses of capital intended to spur economic growth

Questions 7-12 refer to the following passage.

Line   Desert plant populations have evolved sophisticated physiological behavioral traits that aid survival in arid conditions. Some send out long, unusually deep taproots; others
(5)   utilize shallow but widespread roots, which allow them to absorb large, intermittent flows of water. Certain plants protect their access to water. The creosote bush produces a potent root toxin which inhibits the growth of com-
(10)   peting root systems. Daytime closure of stomata exemplifies a further genetic adaptation; guard cells work to minimize daytime water loss, later allowing the stomata to open when conditions are more favorable to gas exchange
(15)   with the environment.

       Certain adaptations reflect the principle that a large surface area facilitates water and gas exchange. Most plants have small leaves, modified leaves (spines), or no leaves at all.
(20)   The main food-producing organ is not the leaf but the stem, which is often green and non-woody. Thick, waxy stems and cuticles, seen in succulents such as cacti and agaves, also help conserve water. Spines and thorns
(25)   (modified branches) protect against predators and also minimize water loss.

7. The passage refers to the spines and thorns of desert plants as

   I. genetically evolved structural adaptations that protect against predation

   II. genetic modifications that aid in the reduction of water loss

   III. structures that do not participate directly in food production

   ○ I only

   ○ III only

   ○ I and II only

   ○ II and III only

   ○ I, II, and III

KAPLAN

8. The author suggests that the guard cells of desert plants act to do which of the following?

    I.   Facilitate gas and water exchange between the plants and their surroundings
    II. Cause the stomata of desert plants to remain closed during daytime hours
    III. Respond to sudden, heavy rainfalls by forcing the plants' stomata to open

    ○ I only
    ○ II only
    ○ III only
    ○ I and II only
    ○ I, II, and III

9. The passage suggests that which of the following weather-related conditions would most benefit plants with shallow root systems?

    ○ An unusually prolonged drought
    ○ A windstorm
    ○ A flash flood
    ○ A light spring rain
    ○ A winter snowfall

10. The adaptations of desert plants to their environment would tend to support the statement that

    ○ the rate of genetic evolution is greater in the desert than in more temperate surroundings
    ○ structures in a plant that usually perform one function may, under certain conditions, perform different functions
    ○ while the amount of leaf surface area is critical for a desert plant, it is much less so for plants in most other environments
    ○ desert plants do not have many physiological and behavioral traits in common with other plants
    ○ desert plants could probably adapt to life in a variety of harsh ecosystems

11. All of the following are mentioned as examples of adaptation by desert plants EXCEPT

    ○ deep roots
    ○ shallow roots
    ○ poisonous roots
    ○ food-producing leaves
    ○ spines and thorns

12. The passage suggests that the adaptations of desert plants function to do all of the following EXCEPT

    ○ protect the plants' access to water
    ○ prevent the loss of water during the day
    ○ maximize the water and gas exchange
    ○ shield the plants from daytime heat
    ○ guard against predators

Questions 13–18 refer to the following passage.

Line   The great migration of European intel-
        lectuals to the United States in the second
        quarter of the twentieth century prompted a
        transformation in the character of Western
(5)   social thought. The influx of Continental
        thinkers fleeing fascist regimes had a great
        impact on American academic circles, leading
        to new developments in such diverse fields as
        linguistics and theology. But the greatest
(10)   impact was on the emigrés themselves. This
        "migration experience" led expatriates to
        reexamine the supposedly self-evident
        premises inherited from the Continental
        intellectual tradition. The result, according to
(15)   H. Stuart Hughes in *The Sea-Change*, was an
        increased sophistication and deprovinciliza-
        tion in social theory.

        One problem facing newly arrived emigrés
        in the U.S. was the spirit of anti-intellectual-
(20)   ism in much of the country. The empirical

orientation of American academic circles, moreover, led to the conscious tempering by many European thinkers of their own tendencies towards speculative idealism. In addition, (25) reports of oppression in Europe shook many Old World intellectuals from a stance of moral isolation. Many great European social theorists had regarded their work as separate from all moral considerations. The migration (30) experience proved to many intellectuals of the following generations that such notions of moral seclusion were unrealistic, even irresponsible.

This transformation of social thought is (35) perhaps best exemplified in the career of the German theologian Paul Tillich. Migration confronted Tillich with an ideological as well as a cultural dichotomy. Hughes points out that Tillich's thought was "suspended (40) between philosophy and theology, Marxism and political conformity, theism and disbelief." Comparable to the fusion by other expatriate intellectuals of their own idealist traditions with the Anglo-American empiricist tradition (45) was Tillich's synthesis of German Romantic religiosity with the existentialism born of the twentieth-century war experience. Tillich's basic goal, according to Hughes, was to move secular individuals by making religious sym- (50) bols more accessible to them. Forced to make his ethical orientation explicit in the context of American attitudes, Tillich avoided the esoteric academic posture of many Old World scholars, and was able to find a wide (55) and sympathetic audience for his sometimes difficult theology. In this way, his experience in America, in his own words, "deprovincialized" his thought.

13. The author's main concern in the passage is to

○ characterize the effects of migration on U.S. history

○ show how Paul Tillich's career was representative of the migration experience

○ discuss the effects of the great migration on modern social thought

○ reveal the increased sophistication of post-migration thought

○ contrast European social thought with that of the United States

14. The author probably mentions H. Stuart Hughes (line 15) in order to

○ give an example of a European intellectual who migrated to America

○ cite an important source of information about the migration experience

○ demonstrate how one American academic was influenced by European scholars

○ pay tribute to Americans who provided European thinkers with a refuge from fascism

○ name a leading disciple of Paul Tillich

15. Which of the following statements describe Tillich's achievement?

I. He elucidated religious symbols in a secular context without sacrificing their impact.

II. He shunned the esotericism of much theological scholarship.

III. He adapted a traditional religiosity to the temper of the modern world.

○ I only

○ II only

○ I and II only

○ II and III only

○ I, II, and III

16. According to the passage, "reports of oppression in Europe" (line 25) affected social thinkers by forcing them to

    ○ rethink their moral responsibilities

    ○ reexamine the morality of European leaders

    ○ analyze the effects of migration on morality

    ○ reconsider their antisocial behavior

    ○ justify the moral value of social thought

17. It can be inferred that postmigration social thought is distinguished from premigration thought by its

    ○ less secular nature

    ○ greater social consciousness

    ○ more difficult theology

    ○ diminished accessibility

    ○ more theoretical nature

18. The passage suggests that the migration experience

    ○ had little major effect on American academic circles

    ○ led to the abandonment of the idealist philosophical tradition

    ○ made American intellectuals sensitive to oppression in Europe

    ○ caused emigré social thinkers to question certain of their beliefs

    ○ negated Tillich's influence on modern social thought

ANSWERS AND EXPLANATIONS

1. D
2. A
3. A
4. E
5. D
6. C
7. E
8. D
9. C
10. B
11. D
12. D
13. C
14. B
15. E
16. A
17. B
18. D

PASSAGE 1—STATE ROLE IN DEVELOPMENT

Topic and Scope: The underdeveloped countries' economies; specifically, the four arguments for state participation in economic development.

Purpose and Main Idea: The author's purpose is to argue for state participation in economic development in underdeveloped countries.

Paragraph Structure: The first paragraph introduces the Topic and mentions the first argument: size of obstacles. The second paragraph mentions the next argument: many sectors of industrialization. The third paragraph addresses the third argument: the low-level equilibrium trap and population. The fourth paragraph mentions the final argument: the relationship between delayed development and the state.

1. D

Here's a good example of why it's helpful to be done with the passage quickly. Some of the answers to this Detail question are pretty tricky. We're looking for a reason *not* given in the passage, which means that the four wrong answers are in there somewhere. *Start-up costs of initial investments* from (A) fits with *entrance requirements in terms of financial capital* in lines 6–7. (B) is trickier. *Demand* is pretty clearly mentioned at the top of Paragraph 2, but what about *supply*? Following are lots of details that might plausibly have something to do with supply. Best to strike (B) out for now, coming back to it if all the others get eliminated as well. (C) mirrors the author's explicit opinion in lines 64–66. Spotting those Emphasis keywords would make for quick elimination of this answer choice. (D) talks about *livelihoods and security of workers*, two subjects mentioned nowhere in the passage. Could public *amenities* in (E) mean *public utilities, transport, and communications facilities* from lines 16–17? It's certainly plausible. So (E) should be eliminated as well. Only (D), the correct answer, remains.

2. A

The passage as a whole presents reasons state intervention is necessary for the industrialization of many less developed countries. (B) focuses only on Paragraph 2 and Paragraph 3. It also introduces the new idea of outside assistance (*state presence* doesn't mean *foreign presence*). (D) also draws only on those two paragraphs and confuses them to boot. (C) is the opposite of the author's main point, and (E) overstates the case with the extreme words *rapid* and *ensure*.

3. A

You need what's *not* in the passage. (B) and (E) are mentioned in Paragraph 1, (C) in Paragraph 2, and (D) in Paragraph 3. "Safeguarding against the domination of local markets by a single source of capital" is not mentioned.

4. E

Context is critical for any question that references a specific part of the passage, and Inference questions are no exception. Notice that the sentence talking about "technical indivisibilities in social overhead capital" (whatever that means) begins with a nice clear keyword—*in addition*. Whatever this difficult jargon means, it's another example of whatever was discussed in the previous sentence. That sentence lists imposing obstacles. So "technical blah blah blah" must be another obstacle. That eliminates everything but (D) and (E).

Now on to "low-level equilibrium trap." The context here isn't as clear, but at this point our job is simpler—we only need to figure out which of the two remaining answers is supported by the passage. There is no language in Paragraph 3 that fits with attracting investment. But lines 41–46 say "additional income . . . [will] force society back to its former subsistence position." That fits (E) nicely.

5. D

Every now and again you'll see a Weaken question in Reading Comprehension. Don't panic, as you can deal with it just as you would in a Critical Reasoning question. The author makes four arguments here, and it wouldn't be efficient to try to analyze them all and create four different predictions. It'll be best, as it often is in Roman numeral questions, to go statement by statement.

Statement I fits with the author's main point, so it's hardly reasonable to think that it would weaken any of his arguments. We can eliminate (A), (C), and (E). Note that we now know for sure that Statement II is part of the correct answer. No need to waste your time with it! Statement III directly contradicts the end of Paragraph 1, thus knocking out part of the author's evidence. That would certainly

weaken his argument, so (D) is the correct answer. (If you're curious, Statement II contradicts both Paragraph 1 and Paragraph 3.)

6. C

This question is technically a Detail question, but even so it tests your big-picture knowledge of the passage, as will many seemingly detail-oriented questions. We know from our Passage Map that we need to look in Paragraph 3 for the answer. Perhaps you read for context only the first two sentences of that paragraph. Even so, you could have eliminated (A), which is the exact opposite of the second sentence. It's not likely that state intervention is the problem, as we know from the author's Purpose that he's arguing in favor of such intervention. (B), then, should be eliminated. (D) also is out on big-picture grounds, as it is drawn from the wrong paragraph. (E) seems to be in the paragraph, but read the whole sentence—the author doesn't mention "one-shot, large doses of capital" as a cause of the trap. Rather, it's the private sector's inability to provide those doses that's the culprit. (C), then, is correct.

PASSAGE 2—DESERT PLANTS

Topic and Scope: Desert plant adaptations and how they aid in these plants' survival.

Purpose and Main Idea: The author is trying to describe the physiological traits that desert plants have adapted in order to survive in arid conditions.

Paragraph Structure: The first paragraph describes some general adaptations. The second paragraph discusses adaptations based on the principle that a large surface area facilitates water and gas exchange.

7. E

The whole passage focuses on structural and behavioral adaptations that desert plants have made in order to survive. While the word "genetic" is used only once (in the last sentence of paragraph 1), it's clear that many of these modifications are genetic. Spines and thorns, which are identified in the second paragraph as modified leaves and branches, are inferably among these genetic adaptations. In the last sentence, it's further stated that they protect against predation (I) and also that they help minimize water loss (II). Option III is confirmed in the third sentence of the second paragraph; most of a desert plant's food is produced in its stem, not in its leaves, so it's pretty clear that spines and thorns (again, modified leaves and branches) have little or nothing to do with food production.

8. D

Like question 7, this is another detail question, this time focusing on the functioning of guard cells, mentioned in the sentence that concludes paragraph 1. This sentence discusses two closely related plant features: the stomata and the guard cells. You read first that daytime closing of the stomata is an adaptation that helps to minimize daytime water loss. The second half of the sentence clearly implies that it's the guard cells that control this opening and closing of the stomata. So, the guard cells force the stomata to close during the day, to minimize water loss, and then they later cause the stomata to open, when conditions for gas exchange between the plant and its environment are more favorable. The first two options are thus clearly suggested. The third option, however, is an unjustified inference. Nothing at all is stated to link the functioning of guard cells to sudden downpours.

9. D

The stem is looking for the weather-related condition that would especially benefit plants with shallow root systems. Shallow root systems are mentioned up in the second sentence, and the point is that these specially adapted roots allow desert plants to take advantage of heavy, irregular flows of water. One example would be a very heavy, torrential downpour. The only choice that comes close to this is a flash flood. Flash floods result from unexpected, torrential rainfall. (A) and (B) are impossible; neither drought nor windstorms provide water. (D) won't work because a light rain doesn't fit with the idea of a large, sudden quantity of water. (E), finally, is also unsuitable. First, this choice doesn't suggest a *heavy*, intermittent snowfall, and second, nothing is said in the passage to suggest snow would be of special benefit to shallow rooted plants.

10. B

The second paragraph contains several examples of structures that in desert plants perform different functions than those they normally perform in plants in other environments. Spines and thorns in desert plants are modified leaves and branches, to reduce water loss. And,

as a result of their lack of normal leaves, most desert plants produce their food in their green, fleshy stems. As for the wrong choices, three of them—(A), (D), and (E)—simply can't be answered. There's no information to support any of these statements. Finally, in choice (C), while the passage does indicate that a small leaf surface area is a critical factor for desert plants, nothing suggests that leaf surface area isn't critical for plants in most other environments. Since the general principle is that a large surface area facilitates gas and water exchange, one can infer that the larger leaf surface area of other plants helps in this process.

11. D

We are told in the second paragraph that most desert plants produce food in their stems, not their leaves. Therefore, (D) is the correct answer: it names something that's not mentioned in the passage. Choices (A), (B), and (C) are mentioned in the first paragraph, and (E) is mentioned in the second paragraph.

12. D

The passage mentions several different adaptations and the purpose of each. The creosote bush produces a toxin that prohibits competing root systems from intruding on its space, therefore protecting its access to water. Guard cells function to "minimize daytime water loss." The second paragraph starts by talking about adaptations that facilitate gas and water exchange. Spines and thorns are adaptations that protect against predators. There is no mention of any adaptation shielding plants from the heat, so (D) must be the answer.

PASSAGE 3—MIGRATION

Topic and Scope: The great migration; specifically, how the migration experience transformed the social thought of European intellectuals who came to America, especially Tillich.

Purpose and Main Idea: The author's purpose is to describe the changes in the social thought of European intellectuals who immigrated to America, using Tillich as an example. The main idea is simply that, as a consequence of the migration experience, European thinkers in America transformed their ideas to have more relevance to "real world" issues.

Paragraph Structure: The first paragraph introduces the topic and scope of the passage. The second paragraph describes in general terms how the social thought of European intellectuals was transformed. And the third paragraph provides a specific example of this transformation by describing the case of Tillich.

13. C

To answer this question, it's important to realize that the author's purpose is to discuss the transformation of social thought that resulted from the great migration. Tillich is merely an example of how this transformation manifested itself among European emigrés; he is not the primary focus of the passage. Therefore, (B), which places emphasis on Tillich, is out. (A) fails to mention "social thought." (D) mentions only "thought," not "social thought." Finally, (E) gets in the idea of social thought but leaves out the migration experience. (C), which includes the important elements of the author's purpose—the effects of the great migration on social thought—is correct.

14. B

Hughes is mentioned in the first paragraph as the author of a book that says something about European expatriates in the United States. He's also cited in the third paragraph in the course of analysis of Tillich's thought. In other words, Hughes is cited as a source of information, as (B) suggests.

Choices (A), (C), and (D) can't be right, because the passage doesn't tell us whether Hughes was a European or an American, or whether he had any direct contact with the emigrés. Choice (E) is a bit more tempting, since the author cites Hughes's interpretation of Tillich's ideas. But that doesn't mean that Hughes is a disciple—a follower—of Tillich. Choice (B) is the only answer that's really supported by the passage.

15. E

Before you check the options, review the information about Tillich in the last paragraph. He combined religiosity with existentialism and made religious symbols more meaningful to people. These achievements are echoed in options I and III. None of the choices includes just I and III, so you know the correct answer must be (E), which includes all three options. To confirm option II, again look back at the passage,

which does say that Tillich "avoided the esoteric academic posture of many Old World scholars." Option II makes more or less the same point, so it's indeed part of the correct answer.

16. A

This is a detail question, so the correct answer is there in the text—in this case, in the second paragraph, which says that oppression forced social thinkers to reject moral isolation. (A) gets at this notion. (B) brings in "leaders," but they aren't mentioned in the passage. (C) substitutes "morality" for "moral isolation." They are not the same, and the morality of the emigrés was never in question. (D) is entirely wrong; the passage doesn't accuse the emigrés of "antisocial behavior." The most tempting wrong choice is (E). However, "rethink" in (A) is much more characteristic of the thrust of the passage than the word "justify" in (E). Don't answer detail questions on a hunch. Go back to the text and find the answer.

17. B

The passage uses the word "deprovincialization" twice to characterize the transformation of social thought. Among the choices, the closest paraphrase is (B), greater social consciousness. Notice that two choices, (A) and (C), allude to Tillich, but the question asks about social thought in general, not about him. Besides, these choices distort Tillich's approach. (D) and (E) are *au contraire* choices.

18. D

This question doesn't zero in on a particular piece of the text, so just read through the choices and look for one that "jumps out" as consistent with the purpose of the passage. (D) is consistent with what the author's trying to accomplish. "Prephrasing" his purpose would have made it easy to pick this choice.

Looking at the other choices, (A) is contradicted in the first paragraph. Also, it deals with a minor point that the author doesn't pursue in the remainder of the text. The word "abandonment" makes (B) too broad a choice. Be suspicious of choices that make sweeping generalizations. (C) focuses on American rather than European thinkers. Finally, (E) is an *au contraire* choice. If anything, the migration experience enhanced Tillich's influence.

READING COMPREHENSION PRACTICE SET THREE

Time: 25 Minutes/18 Questions

Directions: The questions in this group are based on the content of a passage. After reading the passage, choose the best answer to each question. Base your answers only according to what is stated or implied in the text.

Questions 1-7 refer to the following passage.

Line   Although it is well documented that women face difficulties in reaching senior positions in business, studies indicate that business proprietorship offers one way for-
(5) ward. Stanworth and Curran suggest that members of ethnic and religious minorities have often started their own businesses as a means of advancement. One advantage of ownership is the absence of "organizational
(10) selectors"—proprietors need not meet employment criteria based on age, gender, or experience. Recent data confirm that women perceive self-employment as a means for overcoming subordination. In 1985, 4 percent
(15) of employed women in Britain were self-employed; more recent estimates are put at 6 percent. Between 1977 and 1980, the number of woman-owned enterprises in the U.S. increased by 33 percent.

(20)   Goffee and Scase classify self-employed women into four types by considering commitments to both entrepreneurial and conventional female values. Innovative entrepreneurs question conventional assumptions about
(25) the social position of women. Innovators seek business ownership because of their inability to fulfill ambitions within more common career structures. Work is a cen-

tral interest and is much more important
(30) than conventional female roles. In a related category are radicals—proprietors who are active in collective political and economic ventures which promote female issues. Unlike innovators, their businesses are not oriented
(35) mainly to profit making; rather, accumulated assets are used to further the long-term interests of women. Goffee and Scase designate a number of women as conventionals. Committed to entrepreneurship, they also
(40) remain attached to conventional female roles. Unlike many innovators, resentment about limited career prospects is rarely a motive for business start-up. Conventionals "are less likely to have been previously employed in
(45) large-scale organizations. Before starting their businesses, most were 'secondary' workers who moved in and out of the labor market depending upon employment prospects and according to domestic commitments." Goffee
(50) and Scase suggest that entrepreneurs in a fourth category, domestics, have a limited commitment to entrepreneurial ideals and are strongly attached to a traditional female role. These women "regard their business as
(55) secondary to their roles as mothers and wives. Proprietorship offers opportunities for self-fulfillment and autonomy within parameters delineated by their other obligations."

KAPLAN)

1. Which of the following correctly describes one of the four types of female entrepreneurs discussed in the passage?

    ○ A conventional has a strong attachment to conventional gender roles and a weak attachment to entrepreneurial ideals.

    ○ An innovator has a limited attachment to both conventional gender roles and entrepreneurial ideals.

    ○ A radical has a limited attachment to conventional gender roles and a strong attachment to entrepreneurial ideals.

    ○ An innovator has a strong attachment to both conventional gender roles and entrepreneurial ideals.

    ○ A domestic has a limited attachment to entrepreneurial ideals and a strong attachment to conventional gender roles.

2. Which of the following summarizes a main idea of the passage?

    ○ There are few fundamental distinctions among female entrepreneurs.

    ○ Women entrepreneurs, in their motives and objectives, do not differ significantly from their male counterparts.

    ○ Entrepreneurship is increasingly seen by women as providing access to formerly unavailable economic opportunities.

    ○ The development of a single set of policy guidelines designed to facilitate female entrepreneurship is desirable.

    ○ Numbers of female entrepreneurs continue to grow despite opposition within the predominantly male business world.

3. Which of the following addresses a distinction made in the passage between innovators and radicals?

    ○ Innovators attempt to revise current definitions of women's social roles; radicals do not.

    ○ Innovators are committed to organizing cooperative business ventures; radicals are not.

    ○ Innovators view work primarily as a means of securing personal and financial success; radicals do not.

    ○ Radicals are motivated by antagonism towards previous employers; innovators are not.

    ○ Radicals direct themselves mainly towards profit-making goals; innovators do not.

4. According to the passage, which of the following is true of conventionals?

    ○ A commitment to entrepreneurship affects their attachment to a traditional female role.

    ○ Their entrepreneurial values are shaped by past job-related experiences.

    ○ Their political values are similar to those of domestics.

    ○ Their previous participation in the labor market was often irregular.

    ○ An attachment to a conventional female role inhibits their business activities.

5. It can be inferred from the passage that the author believes that the work of Goffee and Scase offers

    ○ a compelling though narrow view of self-employed women

    ○ a well-intended but unfinished analysis of female entrepreneurial behavior

    ○ an effective assault on the system men have used to circumscribe women's careers

    ○ a necessary alternative to the views of Stanworth and Curran

    ○ a meaningful contribution to current studies of female entrepreneurship

6. The information given in the passage about the work of Goffee and Scase supports each of the following generalizations about female proprietorship EXCEPT that it

   ○ fosters links among minority groups

   ○ offers opportunities for nonmonetary rewards

   ○ provides a means for political advances

   ○ allows access to previously unattainable economic goals

   ○ curtails the importance of the conventional female role

7. Goffee and Scase's distinction between innovators and radicals would be most weakened if it were shown that relatively few women

   ○ become self-employed because of anger towards former employers

   ○ use business profits to combat male dominance in society

   ○ start a business in order to avoid organizational selectors

   ○ are able to enter and leave the labor force at will

   ○ feel that sex discrimination plays a major role in their lives

Questions 8-12 refer to the following passage.

Line   In 1943, Baade obtained photographs of stars in the galaxy Andromeda. Using these photographs, Baade divided stars into two groups. The brightest members of Population I
(5) were hot, blue stars with surface temperatures up to 30,000 kelvins. The brightest Population II stars (called "red giants") were large, cool, and red, and fainter than Population I stars. Later observations showed that most
(10) Population I stars occur in the arms of spiral galaxies, while Population II stars are most common between the arms and in the centers of spiral galaxies, and in elliptical galaxies.

According to Baade, the two populations
(15) compose distinct stellar age groups. Since the rate at which stars consume their fuel is directly proportional to their brightness, and brightness increases with mass, large, bright stars burn their fuel more quickly than dim-
(20) mer stars. Baade concluded that the brightest Population I stars were probably less than one million years old while Population II stars were older.

Baade found support for his views in the
(25) distribution of red giants. It is believed that most of a star's hydrogen fuel is gradually converted to helium. When the helium core comprises about one tenth of a star's mass, the star expands and its surface cools. This
(30) phase lasts until the red giant consumes all of its fuel and disintegrates in either a single explosion or a series of outbursts. Most red giants occur in Population II.

The composition of red giants supports
(35) Baade's conception. It is thought that all elements evolved from hydrogen as a result of nuclear reactions in stars. When a star explodes, it throws out heavy elements. Thus, the dust and gas from which new stars are
(40) produced gradually become richer in heavier elements. Studies of red giants in both populations reveal that heavier elements are more abundant in Population I giants. Thus, Population II stars evolved from material
(45) poor in heavier elements and are older.

While Baade's basic insights have been sustained, analyses of stars in our galaxy have shown variations in concentrations of heavy elements, indicating that the stars must be of
(50) assorted ages. As a consequence, stars are now classified into five distinct populations.

8. The primary purpose of this passage is to

   ◯ explain how to determine the age of a star

   ◯ describe a system of star classification and some of the evidence supporting it

   ◯ discuss Population II stars

   ◯ compare and evaluate competing theories of stellar evolution

   ◯ examine the importance of Baade's contributions to astronomy

9. According to the passage, Baade considered all of the following to be characteristics of Population I stars EXCEPT:

   ◯ They are relatively young stars.

   ◯ The brightest members are hot, blue stars.

   ◯ They are found mainly between the arms of spiral galaxies.

   ◯ They are brighter than Population II stars.

   ◯ They have surface temperatures of up to 30,000 kelvins.

10. According to the passage, when the core in which hydrogen has been totally consumed amounts to approximately one-tenth of a star's mass, then

    ◯ the star will expand and its outer layer will cool

    ◯ its life as a normal star will end

    ◯ the star may disintegrate in a single explosion

    ◯ the star will throw out the heavy elements it has produced

    ◯ its classification will change from Population I to Population II

11. Which of the following statements can be inferred from the passage as characteristic of red giants?

    I.   They are all Population II stars.

    II. Each red giant is cooler than it once was.

    III. They all have a low percentage of heavy elements.

    ◯ I only

    ◯ II only

    ◯ I and II only

    ◯ I and III only

    ◯ I, II, and III

12. The passage provides support for all of the following statements EXCEPT:

    ◯ The death of a star involves either one major or several minor explosions.

    ◯ The chemical compositions of red giants support the classification of stars into different age groups.

    ◯ Population II stars are older than Population I stars.

    ◯ Elliptical galaxies have existed for a longer period of time than spiral galaxies.

    ◯ The chemical composition of a star is indicative of its age.

Questions 13–18 refer to the following passage.

Line   Many aspects of coral reefs remain puz-
         zling to scientists. One mystery concerns the
         relationship between Scleractinia, the coral
         type whose colonization produces reefs, and
    (5) their symbiotic partners, a unicellular algae
         present in the coral's endodermic tissues. It is
         known that both organisms play an integral
         part in the formation of a reef's foundation
         by together secreting and depositing calcium
   (10) carbonate, which reacts with sea salt to form
         a hard limestone underlayer. Scientists also
         know that, because of algal photosynthesis,
         the reef environment is oxygen-rich, while
         similarly high amounts of carbon dioxide are

(15) removed rapidly. All of this accounts for the amazing renewability of coral reefs despite the erosion caused by waves. The precise manner in which one symbiotic organism stimulates the secretion of calcium carbonate
(20) by the other, however, remains unclear.

In addition to the above unanswered question, scientists have proposed various theories to explain the transformation of "fringing reefs" (those connected above sea level to land
(25) masses) into "barrier reefs" (those separated from shorelines by lagoons) and finally into island atolls. Although Darwin's view of the transformation is considered partially correct, some scientists feel that the creation of reef
(30) formations has more to do with the rise in sea level that occurred at the end of the last Ice Age than with a gradual submergence of the volcanic islands to which fringing reefs were originally attached. However, recent drillings at
(35) one atoll have revealed a substantial underlayer of volcanic rock, which suggests that Darwin's explanation may be largely correct.

The term "coral reef" is something of a misnomer. The *Scleractinia* themselves gener-
(40) ally comprise only 10 percent of the total mass of life forms of an average reef community: Algae, along with foraminifera, annelid worms, and assorted molluscs, can account for up to 90 percent of the reef mass.
(45) Moreover, the conditions under which reef growth occurs are determined by the needs of the algae, not those of the coral. Reefs flourish only in shallow, highly saline waters above 70° F, because the algae require such an environ-
(50) ment. Non-reef-building coral, meanwhile, occur worldwide.

13. The author cites which of the following as characteristic of coral reefs?

I.   The coexistence of a multitude of organisms
II. Widely varying environmental conditions
III. A tough limestone underlayer

- ○ II only
- ○ III only
- ○ I and II only
- ○ I and III only
- ○ I, II, and III

14. The author suggests that coral reefs are able to survive the process of erosion

- ○ primarily through the activities of algae
- ○ despite the high oxygen content of the reef environment
- ○ as a result of the combined relations of coral and algae
- ○ only if they have an above-surface connection to the shoreline
- ○ because of the volcanic rock at their base

15. It can be inferred from the passage that Darwin

- ○ believed that reefs became atolls through the sinking of volcanic islands
- ○ should have expanded his studies of reefs to include those found at atolls
- ○ theorized that each reef formation was formed by an entirely different process
- ○ is less persuasive on the topic of reef formation in light of recent discoveries
- ○ was more interested in algae and coral than in other organisms living at reefs

16. The passage does NOT discuss the relationship between

   ○ algal photosynthesis and high oxygen content
   ○ Darwin's views and evidence supplied by recent research
   ○ volcanic rock and the life forms found at reefs
   ○ sea salt and calcium carbonate
   ○ wave action and the renewal of reefs

17. Which of the following questions is most completely answered by the passage?

   ○ What percentage of coral worldwide is of the reef-building type?
   ○ How do rises in sea level affect reef formation?
   ○ What are the requisite environmental conditions for coral reef formation?
   ○ How does coral stimulate the calceous secretions of symbiotic algae?
   ○ What is the principal reason for the transformation of fringing reefs into atolls?

18. It can be inferred that the author would agree with all of the following statements EXCEPT:

   ○ Coral cannot produce reefs without algae.
   ○ The water around a coral reef contains high levels of oxygen.
   ○ Darwin's theory about the causes of reef formation is at least partly accurate.
   ○ The term "coral reef" should be abandoned by scientists.
   ○ Coral are more resistant to cold temperatures than the algae that live in their tissues.

ANSWERS AND EXPLANATIONS

1. E
2. C
3. C
4. D
5. E
6. A
7. B
8. B
9. C
10. A
11. B
12. D
13. D
14. C
15. A
16. C
17. C
18. D

PASSAGE 1—SELF-EMPLOYED WOMEN

Topic and Scope: Different motives and values that motivate different women to start their own businesses.

Purpose and Main Idea: The author summarizes the four categories into which Goffee and Scase have divided female entrepreneurs.

Paragraph Structure: The first paragraph provides a general introduction to the topic. It says that a significant number of women have started their own businesses as a way of avoiding the discrimination to which they are often subject in male-owned businesses. The second paragraph sorts women who start their own businesses into four categories: *innovators*, who are motivated mainly by the desire for career success; *radicals*, whose motivation is primarily ideological; *conventionals*, who are committed both to their businesses and to traditional female roles; and *domestics*, for whom traditional female roles are the first priority.

1. E

This is a detail question, so the answer's in the text itself. In fact, all this question requires is that you check the choices against the definitions in the second paragraph. (A), (B), (C), and (D) are "half-right, half-wrong" choices. Each combines a correct piece of information with an incorrect piece. Only (E) gets the definition completely right.

2. C

"Prephrasing" the answer to this global question would have allowed you to move quickly and confidently through the answer choices. The first paragraph makes the point that comes up in (C).

(A) is an *au contraire* choice; the second paragraph reveals that there are many fundamental distinctions among female entrepreneurs. (B) is outside the scope of the passage, since the text never even mentions male entrepreneurs. (D) is wrong because the author describes "female entrepreneurship" without advocating any particular official actions to "facilitate" it. Finally, (E) distorts information in the first paragraph, which mentions that women have difficulty reaching senior positions in business. However, the author never claims that female entrepreneurship is opposed by the business world; certainly, this is not a main idea of the passage.

3.   C

Paying close attention to terms can sometimes make it easy to relocate details. According to the second paragraph, innovators are very committed to their work and start their own businesses to fulfill their ambitions—sentiments that often clash with conventional gender roles. Radicals, though they also reject traditional female roles, start businesses not for profit but primarily to advance general female interests. The choice that gets at this distinction is (C): innovators work primarily for personal and financial success but radicals do not. (A) and (B) ascribe the motives of radicals to innovators, while (D) and (E) do the precise opposite, attributing innovator qualities to radicals.

4.   D

This is yet another detail question, so, again, the answer is right there in the text. Conventionals, according to the passage, are committed to both entrepreneurship and traditional female roles. They are not motivated by resentment about limited careers, and tend to be people who have "moved in and out of the labor market." These facts contradict (A), (B), and (E), while political values (C) are never even mentioned. However, (D), irregular participation in the labor market, is a nice paraphrase of "in and out of the labor market."

5.   E

Since the author quotes Goffee and Scase at considerable length and without criticism, it may be assumed that she thinks that they have something significant to say about women in business. That makes (E) the correct answer. (A) and (B) can be eliminated because the author never presents the work of Goffee and Scase as "narrow" or "unfinished." The other two choices are inaccurate as well. (D) implies that Goffee and Scase oppose the views expressed in the first paragraph, whereas the author presents their ideas as a logical complement. Notice how (C), like wrong answers from previous questions, exaggerates the "male versus female" issue—an issue that never rated more than a brief mention in the passage.

6.   A

The correct answer to this "all/EXCEPT" question either will not be mentioned at all in the passage or will refer to something in the wrong part of the passage. This question concerns Goffee and Scase, who are featured in the second

paragraph. Since the only mention of minorities is in the first paragraph, (A) is correct: The work of Goffee and Scase pertains to women, not minorities. The remaining four choices are all supported by the research of Goffee and Scase: "non-monetary rewards," (B), for domestics; "political advances," (C), for radicals; "access . . . to goals," (D) for all; and "curtails the importance of the conventional female role," (E), for innovators.

7.   B

First look at the distinction at issue. You've already examined it in question 3, where it was noted that innovators want personal success while radicals want to further the interests of women in general. Thus, you're looking for an answer that denies this difference in motivation. You can eliminate (C), which plays on information in the first paragraph, and applies to many women in business. Choice (D) is also poor, because it applies to conventionals, not the two categories mentioned. (A) is mentioned in regard to innovators, but you can get rid of it because it does not address the difference between personal and political motivation. (B) and (E) address this distinction, but (B) is stronger because it directly states that few women are in business to advance a political agenda. This does deny the main difference between the two groups. (E) is fuzzier— even if most women don't feel discriminated against, they may still have distinctly different goals.

PASSAGE 2—BAADE

Topic and Scope: Baade's star observations; specifically, his system for classifying stars.

Purpose and Main Idea: The author's purpose is to describe Baade's star classification scheme and the evidence behind it. Since this is a descriptive passage, the author doesn't offer a specific main point of his own.

Paragraph Structure: The first paragraph introduces Baade's scheme by differentiating Population I and II stars. The second paragraph picks up on this contrast, distinguishing the two groups by age. The third and fourth paragraphs provide evidence in support of the notion that Population II stars are older: first, the more frequent occurrence of red giants in this population and, second, the composition of red giants themselves. The last paragraph indicates that, although Baade's basic insights are still considered valid, his two star categories have now been expanded to five.

8.   B

If you put the purpose of the passage into your own words, you should have come up with something like "describe Baade's star categories and show how evidence supports them." (B) contains these ideas, though in more general terms.

Remember that the correct response to a global question must cover everything in the passage. (A) ignores the first and last paragraphs, which are not concerned with star ages. (C) focuses only on Population II stars, while the passage clearly differentiates between Population I and II stars. No theories of stellar evolution are presented, so (D) is wrong. (E) might have been tempting because it focuses on Baade, but it does so without mentioning his star categories, which are the main focus of the passage; (E) would be appropriate for a more general and biographical passage than this one.

9.   C

"According to the passage" indicates a detail question, so the correct answer is to be found in the text itself. Population I stars are discussed in the first two paragraphs: They are bright (brighter than Population II stars), they are hot (up to 30,000 kelvins), the brightest among them are blue, they are young, and they occur *in* the arms of spiral galaxies. Since this is an "all/EXCEPT" question, the correct answer cannot be one of these facts. This eliminates (A), (B), (D), and (E). That leaves (C), which is indeed correct, because it is Population II stars that are found *between* the arms of spiral galaxies.

10.   A

This development is discussed in the third paragraph. "When the helium core comprises about one-tenth of a star's mass, the star expands and its surface cools." (A) paraphrases this development. Notice that (B), (C), and (D) come from either too far along in the third paragraph or from the fourth paragraph. Choice (E), logical as it may appear, is never mentioned at all.

11.   B

According to the passage, red giants occur primarily among Population II stars, and they are older, cooler, dimmer,

and redder than Population I stars. Their hydrogen has mostly changed to helium, and they are poorer in heavier elements than other stars. Option I is not a valid inference because of the word "all." The author says at the end of the third paragraph that "most," but not "all," red giants are in Population II. (B), therefore, must be the correct choice. Option II is supported by information in the third paragraph. Option III, on the other hand, is another absolute assertion that the passage doesn't support; the passage says that Population I red giants have "more abundant" heavy elements than Population II red giants. They are not all alike, nor do we know anything about a "low percentage."

12.   D

Remember to look for the choice that is *not* supported by information in the passage. (A) appears nearly verbatim at the end of the third paragraph. (B) and (E), which get at the same point, constitute the principal focus of the fourth paragraph. (C)'s point is made several times in the passage. (D), however, looks different immediately. Elliptical galaxies are mentioned only once—at the end of the first paragraph—where it's stated that older Population II stars are found in them. But these stars are found in spiral galaxies as well, so it can't be concluded that elliptical galaxies are older than spiral galaxies. (D), therefore, is correct.

PASSAGE 3—CORAL REEFS

Topic and Scope: Coral reefs; specifically, the renewability, transformation, and composition and environment of coral reefs.

Purpose and Main Idea: The author's purpose is to discuss several aspects of coral reefs. Since this is a descriptive passage rather than an argumentative passage, the author makes no specific point.

Paragraph Structure: The first paragraph talks about the renewability of coral reefs. The second paragraph discusses their transformation, summarizing two theories on this issue. And the third paragraph describes the composition of coral reefs and the environment in which they can exist.

13.   D

The third paragraph mentions that coral reefs are made up of many different creatures, so option I is part of the answer. Therefore, you can eliminate (A) and (B). Option II is contradicted by the same paragraph, which says that reefs can flourish only in a very specific environment because the algae have very specific needs. Thus, since option II isn't part of the answer, you can eliminate (C) and (E) as well. So (D), I and III only, must be correct. Checking option III just to be sure, it can be found in the first paragraph.

14. C

The answer to this question appears in the first paragraph. The paragraph's next-to-last sentence states that "All of this accounts for . . . renewability . . . despite . . . erosion." Thus, the answer must appear in the previous sentences. These sentences discuss the symbiotic relationship between coral and algae, so the correct answer is (C). (A) might have been tempting because the sentence before "All of this accounts . . . " refers to algae, but the focus of the first paragraph is on symbiosis, so the correct answer must include both coral and algae. (B) distorts the logic of the passage—oxygen contributes to renewability; "despite" is not appropriate here. (D) and (E) come from the wrong part of the passage—from later paragraphs that don't deal with the issue of erosion.

15. A

Darwin is discussed in the second paragraph of the passage. This paragraph mentions his theory of reef transformation: the theory of gradual submergence of volcanic islands. That makes (A) correct. (B), (C), and (D) are *au contraire* choices. (E) is outside the scope of the passage; the text does not address the question of what parts of the reef most interested Darwin.

16. C

The relationships in (D), (A), and (E) are discussed in the third, fourth, and fifth sentences of the first paragraph, respectively. (B) is mentioned in the second paragraph. (C), however, connects items that are not associated with each other in the passage. Volcanic rock is discussed in the second paragraph, while life at reefs is brought up in the third.

17. C

(A) is tricky because it tries to get you to look at the third paragraph and see "10 percent." This percentage, however, refers to a particular type of reef life form; no

percentage is given for reef-building coral worldwide. (B) appears promising since sea level and reefs appear in the second paragraph, but the mechanism by which sea level contributes to reef-building is never explained. (C), though, looks good; the second-to-last sentence provides considerable detail about where reefs can form. Checking the last two choices, (D) can be eliminated because the author specifies in the last sentence of the first paragraph that the answer to this question is unknown. Likewise, (E), the transformation of reefs, is never resolved. Two theories are presented and the author leans towards one of them, but never gives a definitive answer.

18. D

It might seem that the author would agree with statement (D), since the term "coral reef" is described in lines 38–39 as "something of a misnomer" (rather misleading, that is). But the fact a term is a misnomer doesn't necessarily mean that people need to stop using it. While the author calls the term a misnomer because of the large variety of life forms in a reef community, there is never any reason to believe the author wants to change it.

CRITICAL REASONING PRACTICE SET ONE

Time: 25 Minutes/16 Questions

Directions: Select the best of the answer choices given.

1. One problem with labor unions today is that their top staffs consist of college-trained lawyers, economists, and labor relations experts who cannot understand the concerns of real workers. One goal of union reform movements should be to build staffs out of workers who have come up from the ranks of the industry involved.

   The argument above depends primarily on which of the following assumptions?

   ○ Higher education lessens people's identification with their class background.

   ○ Union staffs should include more people with firsthand industrial supervisory experience.

   ○ People who have worked in a given industry can understand the concerns of workers in that industry.

   ○ Most labor unions today do not fairly represent workers' interests.

   ○ A goal of union reform movements should be to make unions more democratic.

2. Opening a plant in war-torn Country X is not inadvisable, despite what critics of the plan may say. Ten years ago we opened our plant in Country Y in the middle of a revolution; that plant has been generating substantial profits ever since.

   Which of the following is the author of the argument above most reasonably intending the reader to conclude?

   ○ Wars are profitable for the author's particular business.

   ○ Country X is a more politically stable nation than is Country Y.

   ○ Critics of the proposed plant in Country X are likely to be biased.

   ○ The proposed plant in Country X will generate profits in spite of its present war.

   ○ The proposed plant in Country X will be more successful than the plant in Country Y.

3. The local high school students have been clamoring for the freedom to design their own curricula. Allowing this would be as disastrous as allowing three-year-olds to choose their own diets. These students have neither the maturity nor the experience to equal that of the professional educators now doing the job.

   Which of the following statements, if true, would most strengthen the above argument?

   ○ High school students have less formal education than those who currently design the curricula.

   ○ Three-year-olds do not, if left to their own devices, choose healthful diets.

   ○ The local high school students are less intelligent than the average teenager.

   ○ Individualized curricula are more beneficial to high school students than are the standard curricula, which are rigid and unresponsive to their particular strengths and weaknesses.

   ○ The ability to design good curricula develops only after years of familiarity with educational life.

KAPLAN)

4. One Zydol capsule contains twice the pain reliever found in regular aspirin. A consumer will have to take two aspirin in order to get the relief provided by one Zydol. And since a bottle of Zydol costs the same as a bottle of regular aspirin, consumers can be expected to switch to Zydol.

   Which of the following, if true, would most weaken the argument that consumers will be discontinuing the use of regular aspirin and switching to Zydol?

   ◯ A regular bottle of aspirin contains more than twice as many capsules as does a bottle of Zydol.

   ◯ The pain reliever in Zydol is essentially the same pain reliever found in regular aspirin.

   ◯ Some headache sufferers experience a brief period of dizziness shortly after taking Zydol but not after taking regular aspirin.

   ◯ Neither regular aspirin nor Zydol is as effective in the relief of serious pain as are drugs available only by prescription.

   ◯ A Zydol capsule is twice as large as the average aspirin.

5. At a certain college, graduate teaching assistants conduct discussion sections but have no input into grading. It has been suggested that graduate assistants be given some grading responsibility, but many undergraduates oppose that proposal. They argue that if grades are assigned by graduate assistants, regular full-time faculty will devote less time and attention to undergraduate work.

   The information in the passage above answers which one of the following questions?

   ◯ Are grades assigned by graduate teaching assistants inherently as fair as those given by regular faculty?

   ◯ Are some undergraduates in favor of maintaining the full-time faculty's interest in their schoolwork?

   ◯ May regular full-time faculty conduct discussion sections at the college?

   ◯ Does graduate student contact with undergraduates' work make the grades assigned by regular faculty less valid?

   ◯ Are regular faculty members in favor of giving graduate assistants some teaching responsibility?

6. Air travel is becoming increasingly dangerous. In the last year there have been seven major collisions resulting in over 700 deaths, more deaths than in any previous year.

   Which statement, if true, would most weaken the argument above?

   ◯ Since the volume of air traffic has been increasing all the time, an increase in the number of deaths due to collisions does not necessarily mean greater danger.

   ◯ The increase in collisions can be explained by statistical coincidence, hijackings, and unusual weather.

   ◯ Mortality per passenger mile is lower for air travel than for any kind of surface transportation.

   ◯ The increase in deaths due to collision in air travel has proceeded at a rate identical to that for deaths in all other major forms of transportation.

   ◯ Last year the average number of passengers per flown plane was significantly lower than that of previous years.

7. According to a recent study, attending a single-sex high school aids an adolescent's physical growth. Cited as evidence is the finding that during the first two years of high school, the average boy in an all-boys school grew five inches, and the average girl in an all-girls school grew four inches.

   The answer to which of the following questions is needed in order to evaluate the reasoning presented in the study?

   ◯ Why was it that the first two years of high school were chosen as the focus of the study?

   ◯ Did some of the boys in the study grow less than five inches while they were in high school?

   ◯ How much do the average male student and the average female student in a coeducational school grow during their first two years of high school?

   ◯ Did the girls in the study have as nutritious a diet as the boys during the time the study was being conducted?

   ◯ What was the average height of the boys and the average height of the girls upon entering high school?

8. Although most people know that exercise is good for the body, few realize the extent to which it is valuable to the mind. The blood circulates more rapidly after physical exertion, thus allowing all of the body's organs to operate more efficiently. This increased activity enables the brain to receive more oxygen, thereby creating a higher capacity for concentration.

   The main point in the argument above is that

   ○ the greater the amount of oxygen the brain receives, the better the brain functions

   ○ exercise is a mental, as well as physical, activity

   ○ exercise helps the brain more than it does the rest of the body

   ○ people can greatly improve their powers of concentration by exercising more often

   ○ exercise serves more than one purpose

9. The education offered by junior colleges just after World War II had a tremendous practical effect on family-run businesses throughout the country. After learning new methods of marketing, finance, and accounting, the sons and daughters of merchants returned home, often to increase significantly the size of the family's enterprise or to maximize profits in other ways.

   Which of the following statements is best supported by the information above?

   ○ The junior colleges principally emphasized methods of increasing the size of small businesses.

   ○ The business methods taught in the junior colleges were already widespread before World War II.

   ○ The business curricula at junior colleges did not include theoretical principles of management.

   ○ Without the influence of junior colleges, many family-run businesses would have been abandoned as unprofitable.

   ○ Business methods in many postwar family-run businesses changed significantly as a result of the junior colleges.

10. Archaeologists have discovered various paintings on the walls and ceiling of a Chinese cave whose entrance was blocked by a volcanic eruption in the 25th century B.C. and only recently cleared by an earthquake. Since the paintings depict warriors using Type C bronze weapons, these archaeologists have concluded that Type C bronze weapons were already widely used in this area by 2500 B.C., far earlier than was previously believed.

    Which of the following pieces of additional evidence would most seriously weaken the archaeologists' conclusion?

    ○ Another entrance to the cave remained clear until a second volcanic eruption 1,000 years after the first.

    ○ Archaeologists have evidence that Type C bronze weapons were in wide use in areas of present-day India as early as 2500 B.C.

    ○ Alternative methods of dating place the time of the volcanic eruption somewhat earlier, at around 3000 B.C.

    ○ Most experts believe that Type C bronze weapons were not in use anywhere in present-day China until 2000 B.C.

    ○ The paintings were very faded when the archaeologists found them, making identification of the depicted weapons difficult.

KAPLAN

11. Considering the current economy, the introduction of a new brand of cereal is unlikely to expand total sales of cereal, but rather will just cause some existing buyers of cereal to switch brands. So it makes no sense for the Coolidge Corporation to introduce another brand of cereal, since they will only hurt sales of the brands of cereal they already produce.

    Which of the following, if true, would most seriously weaken the argument above?

    ○ Total sales of cereal will increase as the total population increases.

    ○ Many new brands of cereal sell extremely well for the first year of their existence.

    ○ Coolidge Corporation currently produces fewer brands of cereal than its competitors do.

    ○ Some cereal buyers regularly switch from brand to brand, even when no new brands have been introduced.

    ○ Research indicates that the new brand will attract more buyers of competitors' cereals than buyers of other Coolidge brands.

12. A public health official reported that 60 percent of the children at summer school have never had the measles or chicken pox, and that of this 60 percent not one child has ever been observed to eat the cheese served in the school lunches. From this he concluded that children who abstain from cheese products protect themselves from most childhood disease.

    Each of the following, if true, would strengthen the official's argument EXCEPT:

    ○ Medically speaking, whatever serves to inhibit measles and chicken pox will generally inhibit the entire spectrum of childhood diseases.

    ○ The observations the official carried out were extremely accurate, and all those observed to abstain from cheese at school did, in fact, abstain.

    ○ The children's eating habits are the same at school as anywhere else, and those who abstain from cheese products at school do so in general.

    ○ Recent research has pointed to a deficiency in cheese products as one of the major causes of measles and chicken pox infections.

    ○ Most cheeses and cheese products harbor bacteria that are known to be causative agents for many childhood diseases, such as measles and chicken pox.

13. A confidential survey revealed that 75 percent of the employees of Company P are dissatisfied with their jobs. However, an investigation into working conditions at the company showed nothing uncommonly bad. Therefore, Company P's consulting firm concluded that the employees' dissatisfaction must result from an unusually high incidence of psychological problems on their part.

Each of the following, if true, casts doubt on the consulting firm's conclusion EXCEPT:

○ In the investigation of working conditions, no account was taken of the fact that for the past year many Company P employees worked on a joint venture with Company O, at Company O's facilities.

○ Workers in many companies are dissatisfied although there are no apparent problems with their working conditions.

○ The consulting firm's conception of what constitutes uncommonly bad working conditions is not identical to that of Company P's employees.

○ The reasons given by Company P's employees for their dissatisfaction varied greatly from employee to employee.

○ A battery of tests performed on Company P's employees one month ago revealed no significant psychological stresses or problems.

14. Director: Our engineers are considering two different sites—one on the Abaco River and one on the Bornos River—for a hydroelectric plant. Although we have the technical expertise to build roughly the same plant in either place, producing roughly the same amount of electricity per hour, building the plant on the Abaco site will cost over twice as much money. With our budget currently in deficit, we should build the dam at the Bornos site.

Which of the following, if true, best explains the difference in building costs for the two proposed dam sites?

○ Many farms along the lower Bornos River valley would benefit from the controlled flow of water a dam would make possible.

○ The Abaco site is in an inaccessible area, requiring the building of new roads and the importation of laborers.

○ The Bornos site is near a large city whose residents could use the resulting lake for inexpensive recreation.

○ The Abaco site is in an area that contains many endangered species that would be threatened by the new dam.

○ The Abaco River has a relatively low volume of flow, making it impossible to expand an Abaco plant to meet future electricity needs.

15. In 1998, 50 people with emotional disturbances underwent hypnosis to be cured of their mood swings. A follow-up survey in 2003 revealed that 5 had fairly stable emotional conditions at the time of the survey. These 5 subjects can therefore serve as models of the types of people for whom hypnosis is likely to be successful.

    Which of the following, if true, casts the most doubt on the suitability of those five subjects as models in the sense described?

    ◯ The five subjects have very different personalities and backgrounds.

    ◯ Since 1998, the five subjects have experienced dramatic mood swings interspersed with periods of relative stability.

    ◯ Those people who were still suffering from unstable emotional conditions at the time of the 2003 survey had shown no improvement since 1998.

    ◯ Many psychologists are less concerned about a patient's mood swings than about the patient's willingness to express his or her problems and fears.

    ◯ The emotional condition of most of the 45 subjects who were still unstable at the time of the 2003 survey had actually worsened since 1998.

16. The cause of the peculiar columnar growth pattern displayed by junipers growing near burning underground veins of lignite coal has never been convincingly explained. Until recently, the accepted theory posited that the abundance of carbon monoxide in the local atmosphere caused the columnar growth. However, a new theory holds that the cause is the persistent heat present near these underground fires that, while not intense enough to inflame the trees, can nonetheless change their normal growth pattern.

    The existence of which of the following would provide the strongest support for the new theory?

    ◯ A columnar juniper growing in an atmosphere of intense heat and an absence of carbon monoxide

    ◯ A normal juniper growing in an atmosphere of intense heat and an absence of carbon monoxide

    ◯ A columnar juniper growing in an atmosphere of normal heat and a high concentration of carbon monoxide

    ◯ A normal juniper growing in an atmosphere of intense heat and a high concentration of carbon monoxide

    ◯ A columnar juniper growing in an atmosphere of intense heat and a high concentration of carbon monoxide

ANSWERS AND EXPLANATIONS

1. C
2. D
3. E
4. A
5. B
6. A
7. C
8. E
9. E
10. A
11. E
12. D
13. D
14. B
15. B
16. A

1. C

The Conclusion: Union reform movements should build staffs out of workers who have come up the ranks.

The Evidence: Union movements are currently suffering from a problem: Their staffs consist of college-educated professional types who don't understand the concerns of the worker.

If the author believes that hiring up-from-the-ranks workers (an idea introduced in the conclusion) will cure that problem, he must be assuming that these former workers do understand workers' real concerns.

There's no need to assume that higher education lessens people's identification with their class background, (A), since the author hasn't said that the lawyers, economists, and experts who don't understand workers come from a working-class background. Supervisory experience, (B), isn't the same as coming up through the ranks. Labor unions having problems, which the author admits, isn't the same as (D), most of them unfairly representing workers' interests. That's an overstatement. "Democratic," (E), is a new term, and one the argument doesn't need.

2. D

The Conclusion: None is stated, but as the question stem alerts us, one is implied.

The Evidence: A plant opened in Country Y during a revolution ten years ago has always generated substantial profits.

The author draws an analogy between the two plants. Since the one in Country Y has made money, so too, she implies, will the one in Country X.

The author's point is that the plant can be successful despite the war, (A), not that the plant will be successful because of the war. The author presents the two countries as similar, so she's not arguing that (B), one is more stable than the other. The author is attacking her opponents' argument, but not (C), their motives. She makes no judgment, (E), as to which plant will be more successful. Remember, comparing and contrasting things that are considered equivalent in the stimulus is a common wrong answer type for inference questions.

3. E

The Conclusion: High school students should not design their own curricula.

The Evidence: The maturity and experience of professional educators is required.

First, we have to understand the argument. The author claims that high school students should not design their own curricula, because they don't have the maturity or experience of professional educators. What if experience and maturity weren't necessary for the design of good curricula? The author's argument would completely fall apart. So to strengthen it, we need the answer to explain why curriculum design requires both experience and maturity. (E) does exactly that and is the correct answer.

(A) just restates the last piece of evidence, and correct answers on the GMAT always deal with the assumption, not the evidence. (B) reinforces the author's rhetorical flourish about three-year-olds, but that is just window dressing, not the heart of the author's point; we didn't need to bring three-year-olds into our paraphrase at all. So (B) does not strengthen the main argument. The comparison made in (C) is irrelevant; teenagers who don't go to the local high school are outside the scope of the argument, which is about what one needs to design curricula. Besides, "intelligence" is not the same thing as "experience and maturity." (D) is also out of scope, as it discusses what kind of curriculum is best, not who designs it (and if anything, (D) weakens the argument, as it suggests that a change in curriculum design is needed).

4. A

The Conclusion: Consumers can be expected to switch to Zydol.

The Evidence: Although one has to take two aspirins to get the relief provided by one Zydol, nevertheless a bottle of Zydol costs the same as a bottle of aspirin.

The implication is that Zydol is more cost-effective than aspirin: You get a much better bargain with a bottle of Zydol. But if the aspirin bottle contains more than twice as many tablets as the Zydol bottle, then it's the aspirin bottle that gives you more pain reliever for your money.

The argument concerns which is the better bargain, not which is the better pain reliever. Thus, it doesn't matter (B) that the ingredient is the same. (C) points to some consumers who won't want Zydol. Perhaps, but one, these may be very few, and two, this doesn't attack the author's reasoning, which is based on cost. Pain sufferers who don't have a doctor's prescription are left with the same choice between Zydol and aspirin, so (D) doesn't weaken Zydol's

case against aspirin. The size of the capsules, (E), has no bearing on the author's argument.

5. B

The Undergraduates' Conclusion: If grades are assigned by graduate assistants, regular full-time faculty will devote less time to undergraduate work.

Their Evidence: There really isn't any; just the idea that giving grading responsibilities to graduate students will somehow move regular full-time faculty away from the undergraduates' work.

The only thing to do is go through the choices to see which question we can answer. Since the undergraduates are against the proposal, it's safe to conclude that they want the full-time faculty to stay interested in their work. We have no information about the fairness of graduate assistants' grades, (A). All we know about the discussion sections, (C), is that graduate assistants now hold them; we aren't told whether or not full-time faculty may hold them. (D) asks about the validity of the faculty's grades. We know that some people have proposed that graduate assistants be given some grading responsibility, but that doesn't imply (D), that they believe the faculty's grades have been made less valid by the graduate students' "contact" with undergraduates. And we're told absolutely nothing about (E), the faculty's opinion of the proposal.

6. A

The Conclusion: Air travel is becoming more dangerous.

The Evidence: In the last year, there have been seven collisions and over 700 deaths, the highest number of deaths ever.

We want something that suggests that the increase in fatalities doesn't prove an increase in danger. If more and more people are traveling by airplane, an increase in the number of deaths doesn't prove that air travel is becoming more dangerous. The question of how dangerous air travel is can't be answered unless we know the proportion, not the number, of passengers who get killed.

The author's contention isn't undermined by (B), the reasons for the lack of safety. Pointing out more dangerous methods of transportation, (C), doesn't deny that the danger of air travel is increasing. Likewise, the fact that other forms of transportation are also getting more dangerous, (D), doesn't dent the author's claim. Fewer passengers per plane, (E), means more collisions, but we already know how many collisions there were.

7. C

The Conclusion: Attending a single-sex high school promotes growth.

The Evidence: During the first two years, the average student in an all-boys school grew five inches and the average girl in an all-girls school grew four inches.

The question stem tells you that something has been left out of the argument. The conclusion compares single-sex schools to coed schools, but the evidence only cites data from single-sex schools. Until we know how much the average student grows in co-educational schools, we have no evidence that the growth in single-sex schools is greater.

Even if we knew the answer to (A), we'd still have no evidence from the coed schools. (B) is a rather silly question; we're dealing with average growth, so we'd expect some boys to grow more than the average and some less. The reasons for the growth difference between boys and girls, (D), isn't relevant to the growth differences between coed and single-sex schools. Since the study is only interested in how much students grow during the first two years of high school, it's irrelevant how tall they are to start with, (E).

8. E

The Conclusion: Exercise is good for the mind as well as for the body.

The Evidence: Exercise increases the speed at which blood circulates, allowing the brain to receive more oxygen and thus concentrate better.

The main point is the conclusion, that exercise is good for the mind as well as the body. More generally, exercise serves more than one purpose.

(A) goes out on a limb; the author's point is the beneficial effects of exercise, not the unlimited benefits of oxygen. While exercise aids mental activity, it's not (B), a mental activity as such. Whether exercise aids the brain more or less than the rest of the body, (C), isn't discussed. This is a classic wrong answer type: the choice that compares two items the stimulus treats equally. While the author argues that exercise is beneficial to the mind, "greatly improving" concentration, (D), is an overstatement.

9. E

Conclusion: Junior college education had a big impact on family-run businesses after World War II.

Evidence: New methods of accounting, marketing, and finance allowed business size to grow and profits to be maximized.

This question asks, "Which of the following is best supported by the information above?" In other words, what can be inferred from the stated material?

It's difficult to make a specific prediction on most Inference questions. It's often best to say, "The answer *must* be true based on the stimulus; it won't go beyond the Scope or read a detail in an extreme way."

In (A), the disqualifying word is *principally*. The information presented does not specify what the junior colleges emphasized. This choice reads too much into the fact that often family businesses increased in size because of the newly acquired knowledge. (B) is wrong because we really can't infer how popular or widespread these methods were before the war. For all we know, these could have been revolutionary techniques or well-kept secrets. In (C), we know junior colleges taught new methods of marketing and finance and stuff like that; we do not know how much management theory was or was not presented. This choice relies on data we aren't given—a sure sign of an incorrect or unwarranted inference. (D) takes the facts in the stimulus too far. We're told that profits increased thanks to the influence of junior colleges, so we could infer that family-run businesses would have been less profitable without them. But there's a world of difference between *less profitable* and *unprofitable*. (E) is certainly true. Business methods did change because of the education—the stimulus calls them "new methods," after all. It's a common mistake to throw out an answer because it seems somehow "too obvious." Some Inference answers are tough to prove right, yes . . . but many are very straightforward.

10. A

The Conclusion: People must already have been using Type C weapons in this area by 2500 B.C.

The Evidence: Depictions of the weapons exist on the walls of a cave that was sealed off in 2500 B.C.

We need to show that the paintings either don't depict weapons that were in use or that the paintings were made after 2500 B.C. The archaeologists are assuming that there was only one entrance to the cave. If there's another entrance to the cave that was only sealed much later, then people could have entered the cave and made the paintings long after the first entrance was sealed.

KAPLAN

If anything, the existence of the weapons in India, (B), might be considered to strengthen the argument, since it shows Type C weapons were in existence as early as 2500 B.C. Pushing the date of the eruption back, (C), also strengthens the argument by making it likely that the paintings were done even earlier than claimed. Without some evidence to back it up, the opinion of the experts, (D), isn't worth much. That identification was difficult, (E), is not the same as its being uncertain or controversial.

11. E

The Conclusion: Introducing a new cereal will only hurt the brands Coolidge already produces, so Coolidge shouldn't introduce another brand of cereal.

The Evidence: The introduction of a new brand of cereal doesn't increase the total number of cereal buyers, but only encourages those who already buy cereal to switch brands.

The assumption here is that the new brand will only attract those who currently buy other brands of Coolidge's cereal. If the new brand steals buyers from competitors' cereals, then it will help Coolidge by adding to its total sales.

Even if the population does increase and total cereal sales with it, (A), a new brand might still hurt the sales of Coolidge's established cereals. The new cereal may sell well, (B), but if that just means it's stealing lots of buyers from other Coolidge cereals, what good is it? The fact that Coolidge has only a few brands, (C), doesn't make it likely that a new cereal brand would steal buyers from competitors' brands rather than from other Coolidge brands. Neither does the fact that some brand switching is usual even when a new brand isn't introduced, (D).

12. D

The Conclusion: Not eating cheese protects children from childhood diseases.

The Evidence: All the children at summer school who have never had measles or chicken pox have also never eaten the cheese served in the school lunches.

The author deduces a causal relationship: not eating cheese leads to protection from childhood diseases. I hope you saw that this has numerous holes. Four of the choices help to fill those holes; the fifth does not. That fifth choice is (D). If research shows that abstaining from cheese products is a major cause of some childhood diseases, then the health official's claim that children can protect themselves from disease by not eating cheese is flat-out wrong.

It's important that the author be able (A) to connect measles and chicken pox (in the evidence) to other childhood diseases. Also necessary is that the observations be accurate, (B), and the students' behavior at home mirror their behavior at school (C). Each of those speaks to the legitimacy of the correlation. Most important, though, is that there really be a causal connection, (E), rather than just a correlation, between cheese eating and childhood illness.

13. D

The Consulting Firm's Conclusion: The employees' dissatisfaction is all in their heads.

Its Evidence: Of the employees, 75 percent are dissatisfied. An investigation showed no uncommonly bad working conditions.

We need the one choice that doesn't weaken the consulting firm's conclusion; that's a good tip that the conclusion isn't solidly based. The mere fact that the complaints vary doesn't hurt the firm's conclusion that the complaints are based on psychological problems. In fact, it might even strengthen the firm's argument: every employee has a different mental hang-up, so every employee comes up with a different irrational complaint.

If many employees had been working at a different company's facilities, (A), then it could be these facilities, not mental problems, that are responsible for the complaints. If the situation in Company P is fairly normal, (B), there's no need for the firm to hypothesize an unusual incidence of psychological problems among the workforce. If the firm's definition of uncommonly bad conditions differs from that of the workers, (C), then the firm may well have overlooked the real causes of employee dissatisfaction. And if a battery of tests, (E), showed no significant psychological problems, then the very cause cited by the firm is attacked.

14. B

The Director's Conclusion: We should build the dam at the Bornos site.

Her Evidence: Although the same plant can produce the same amount of electricity at either site, building at Abaco will cost twice as much money.

Looking at the question stem first here really helps you narrow your focus when reading the stimulus. The only thing you're interested in is why the Abaco site will cost more than twice as much as the Bornos site. The stimulus doesn't give you any hint as to how the sites are different, so you'll have to rely on the correct answer to provide a complete explanation by itself. If the Abaco site is in the middle of nowhere, and requires constructing new roads and importing laborers, then, of course, it's going to be more expensive to build there.

The benefits of the Bornos plant to farms, (A), don't explain its lower cost of construction. Neither do the benefits to nearby city residents, (C). Possible environmental damage caused by a plant built at Abaco, (D), is another reason for building at Bornos, but it's a different reason. The issue of expansion, (E), like the environment, might merit consideration, but it's not a factor in determining the cost of building.

15. B

The Conclusion: These five people can serve as models for the type of person who can be helped by hypnosis.

The Evidence: A study showed that these five previously disturbed hypnosis subjects had stable emotional conditions.

The survey only found that at the time of the study the five seemed to be doing okay. Remember, these people were originally suffering from mood swings; maybe the study just caught them on a good day. If that's the case—if since 1998 these people have been experiencing dramatic mood swings and occasional periods of health—then hypnosis hasn't really helped them and they're not good models.

The author presented the people as models of different types of people who can be helped, not as a single model of a single personality type, so they needn't be similar, (A). It doesn't matter that the other 45 people who underwent hypnosis didn't get better (C); the argument is based on and concerns only the 5 who were stable. (E) fails to weaken the argument for the same reason. The concern of many psychologists, (D), is well outside the scope. We need a statement that speaks about hypnosis and these 5 subjects.

16. A

The New Theory's Conclusion: Heat (from the burning coal) causes columnar growth in junipers near burning underground coal veins.

The New Theory's Evidence: None really, except the correlation of columnar growth with these areas with underground fires.

The Old Theory's Conclusion: The abundance of carbon monoxide causes columnar growth.

The Old Theory's Evidence: None really, except the correlation of columnar growth with these areas with high carbon monoxide.

When you scan the choices, you see that each presents a case of the cause with or without the effect or the effect with or without the cause. Since the two theories are in opposition, weakening the old theory is a way of strengthening the new one. Bearing in mind from the lesson the key issues in a causal argument, we recognize that a case of columnar growth where the cause claimed by the new theory (heat) is present, but the cause claimed by the old theory (carbon monoxide) is absent, strengthens the new theory at the expense of the old.

(B), where we get the new theory's alleged cause (intense heat), without the alleged effect (columnar junipers), is of no help at all. A columnar juniper in an atmosphere with high carbon monoxide but no extra heat, (C), strengthens the old theory. A case with both alleged causes without the expected effect, (D), weakens both theories. Likewise, columnar growth in the presence of both causes, (E), does nothing to promote one theory over the other.

CRITICAL REASONING PRACTICE SET TWO

Time: 25 Minutes/16 Questions

Directions: Select the best of the answer choices given.

1. Although air pollution was previously thought to exist almost exclusively in our nation's cities, the recent increase in the number of persons suffering from illnesses attributed to excessive air pollution leaves us no choice but to conclude that other, nonurban areas are now affected.

   Which of the following, if true, would most seriously weaken the conclusion of the argument above?

   ○ The nation's cities have seen a marked decrease in levels of air pollution.

   ○ The nation has experienced a sharp decrease in the number of people moving out of its cities.

   ○ Illnesses due to air pollution are among the least common causes of death to urban dwellers.

   ○ Many illnesses previously thought unrelated to air pollution are now considered to be caused by it.

   ○ As a result of the problems in urban areas, nonurban areas have passed strict pollution control measures.

2. Statistics show that although consumption of low-calorie, alternative sweeteners has gone up in each of the past five years, so has the percentage of the population that is obese. According to sugar manufacturers, this shows that the low-calorie, alternative sweeteners are not effective weight loss aids.

   Which of the following assertions, if true, would most weaken the sugar manufacturers' conclusion?

   ○ Many people who use low-calorie, alternative sweeteners eat some foods that are not low-calorie.

   ○ Some low-calorie, alternative sweeteners can increase the appetite, making a person eat more than he or she normally would.

   ○ Many people use low-calorie, alternative sweeteners to accompany a well-balanced, low-calorie diet.

   ○ Obesity has declined among people who have consistently used low-calorie, alternative sweeteners.

   ○ The rise in the consumption of low-calorie, alternative sweeteners is primarily due to an increase in the number of users rather than an increase in the amount each user consumes.

KAPLAN

3. It has long been commonplace in medical literature that the ingestion of drug L, in combination with the application of lotion M, causes the appearance of adverse reaction O. Recently, however, doubts have been cast on the role of lotion M in the appearance of adverse reaction O.

   Which one of the following research findings could most reasonably have created the doubts referred to above?

   ○ The appearance of adverse reaction O following the ingestion of drug L and the application of lotion M

   ○ The absence of adverse reaction O following the ingestion of drug L and the application of lotion M

   ○ The ingestion of drug L and the appearance of adverse reaction O in the absence of lotion M

   ○ The absence of adverse reaction O following the ingestion of drug L without the application of lotion M

   ○ The disappearance of adverse reaction O following the ingestion of drug L and the application of lotion M

4. The candy manufacturer's claim that employee "theft" costs the company thousands of dollars a year in potential sales is greatly overstated. Most of the candy eaten on the job and not paid for is eaten one piece at a time, by workers who would not be willing to buy an entire box of it anyway.

   Which of the following, if true, most weakens the argument above?

   ○ The workers eat only defective candies that could not be sold.

   ○ Candy eaten by employees represents lost potential sales to nonemployees.

   ○ A few workers account for most of the candy that is eaten but not paid for.

   ○ Most of the candies eaten by employees are consumed during the holiday season, when production outputs are at their highest.

   ○ The amount of candy eaten by employees is only a small fraction of the candy sold by the company.

5. U.S. officials complain that the country's trade deficit with Japan is due to the fact that Japan's markets are not open enough to imports and investment. Japanese officials reply that the United States should concentrate on improving its school systems and investing more money in scientific research and worker training.

   It can be inferred from the statements above that the Japanese officials most probably hold which of the following opinions?

   ○ The United States should open its own markets to more imports and investment.

   ○ The trade deficit between the United States and Japan is more the result of poor American industrial performance than Japan's import restrictions.

   ○ The trade deficit between the United States and Japan is a result of Japan's closed markets.

   ○ U.S. school systems foster a mistrust of Japan that prevents U.S. businesspeople from negotiating intelligently with Japan.

   ○ Better education and worker training can help shrink the trade imbalance, but should not be counted on to close the gap entirely.

6. Children who attend private high schools may initially feel that they can succeed without doing the work required, but as they grow older they realize the necessity of serious study. Each year the overwhelming majority of students disciplined for plagiarism and cheating on their exams is found in the freshman class.

   The argument above would be most weakened if which of the following were true?

   - As they move up in grade, students learn how to cheat without being caught.
   - First-time offenders for plagiarism and cheating on exams are not disciplined.
   - The proctors for freshman exams are the least vigilant.
   - Acts of vandalism are most often committed by members of the sophomore class.
   - Public school students are no less likely than private school students to believe that they can succeed in life without working hard.

7. The conflict between an artist's work and the context in which it is placed is a traditional problem in aesthetics. Recent exhibits have given it a new urgency. Too often a painter's canvases have been hung in an improper context because the gallery managers have not understood what the painter envisioned as the work's proper environment.

   As an attempt to solve the problem described above, it would be most reasonable to

   - bring artists and gallery managers into closer contact, so as to increase each artist's input into the way the exhibit is held
   - provide brochures at the exhibit that describe the artist and how he or she intended the exhibit to look
   - redesign galleries so that their décor contains nothing that would distract the audience from the works themselves
   - provide a uniform environment for all the works in an exhibition so that they appear within the same context
   - instruct gallery managers in the fine points of aesthetic theory so that they will be able to tell what, if anything, a painting means

8. To improve the physical fitness of its students, School District 4 instituted a policy whereby students would be given extra credit in physical education for extracurricular athletic activities. School officials call the program a success, since participation in after-school sports has doubled since the program was instituted.

   Which of the following, if true, most seriously weakens the claim of the school officials?

   - Most students who joined after-school sports did so only to get extra credit.
   - Most children who are in poor physical condition cannot be persuaded to join after-school sports by such an incentive program.
   - Few students who joined after-school sports during the extra credit program will continue to play the sport after the school year ends.
   - Most of the new athletes are students who had never before participated in after-school sports.
   - Fitness tests show no significant improvement in the physical condition of students after they join after-school sports.

9. It takes four weeks for a team of five professional
    window washers working regular full-time hours
    to properly clean every window of the Empire State
    Building. The building's owner demands that all
    the windows always be clean. Yet even if the five
    washers work consistently throughout their regular
    work week, they will not be able to finish cleaning
    all the windows before some windows will again
    need cleaning.

    It can be correctly inferred on the basis of the
    statements above that which of the following must
    be true?

    ⬭ If an Empire State Building window is to be
       kept clean, it must be cleaned by a profes-
       sional window cleaner.

    ⬭ The owner's demand for proper cleaning of
       all the windows will never be fulfilled.

    ⬭ If a team of five window washers cleans all
       the Empire State Building's windows in less
       than four weeks, some of the windows will
       not be properly cleaned.

    ⬭ In order to ensure that all of the Empire State
       Building's windows are clean, the owner must
       have his window washers work overtime.

    ⬭ Some Empire State Building windows must
       be cleaned more frequently than once every
       four weeks if they are to be kept clean.

10. Cultural anthropologists who have been observing
    and interviewing customers in retail stores have
    announced a definitive theory to explain the effect
    that in-store product displays have on consumer
    purchasing behavior.

    Which of the following, if true, would be least
    likely to represent a benefit of the theory to
    retailers?

    ⬭ Retailers will be able to eliminate costly
       product displays that fail to increase sales.

    ⬭ Retailers will gain insight into how
       consumers determine whether or not to buy
       a particular product.

    ⬭ The new theory will make consumers aware
       of how product displays influence their
       purchasing decisions.

    ⬭ The new theory will determine what types of
       retail display gimmicks produce a negative
       reaction in consumers.

    ⬭ The new theory will explain why consumers
       often purchase at different stores goods that
       could be bought at just one store.

11. Archaeologists have recently found, in various grave sites in the Mexican state of Veracruz, small ceramic animals with attached wheels. At first, this find might seem to discredit the belief that the wheel and its uses were unknown in pre-Colombian culture. On reflection, however, it would seem that the discovery actually bears out this belief. To be familiar with these toys and yet not to apply the principle of the wheel to daily tasks such as carting, transportation, and pottery making must indicate a lack of understanding of the wheel and its potential benefits.

    Which of the following best expresses the argument made in the passage above?

    ○ If the pre-Colombian people of Veracruz had understood the principle of the wheel, they would not have attached wheels to ceramic animals.

    ○ If the pre-Colombian people of Veracruz had understood the principle of the wheel, they would have adapted it to everyday use.

    ○ If the pre-Colombian people of Veracruz had uses for the wheel in their everyday lives, they would have adapted the idea of the wheel from the wheeled ceramic figures.

    ○ The pre-Colombian people of Veracruz must have known of the wheel and its uses because they attached wheels to ceramic animals.

    ○ Since the pre-Colombian people of Veracruz did not know of the wheel or its uses, the ceramic animals found in the grave sites must be the remains of later cultures.

12. Doubling the cost of public transportation to compensate for money lost by declining ridership would be disastrous. The greater expense would only further discourage commuters who are already dissatisfied with the poor condition of buses and trains. If the fares are increased, many commuters will choose to drive their cars instead, causing pollution and traffic congestion. As a result, the city will lose money and become even more noisy and smog-filled than it is now.

    Which of the following is an assumption made in advancing the argument above?

    ○ Commuters who decide to drive instead of using public transportation will not share rides with one another.

    ○ Commuters will not park their cars in garages and thereby spend more money than they would by using buses or trains.

    ○ The condition of public transportation will not improve as a result of the fare increase.

    ○ Commuters who use their own cars currently outnumber those who use buses and trains.

    ○ A significant number of people who now use public transportation have cars or can easily obtain them.

13. The cost of transatlantic air fare has nearly doubled over the past five years, yet airlines are doing a booming business. Clearly, people today have more money to spend on vacations than they did five years ago.

    All of the following, if true, would weaken the argument above EXCEPT:

    ○ Most people buying transatlantic tickets today use them for business trips, so air fare is refunded by their companies.

    ○ There are fewer airlines in existence today than five years ago.

    ○ People are taking shorter vacations and staying in cheaper hotels than they used to.

    ○ Crossing the Atlantic by ship requires more time than most people can afford.

    ○ Domestic airline flights have seen a steady increase in passengers.

KAPLAN)

14. Truck driver: The gasoline tax is too high and it must be lowered. It has been raised every year for the past five years, while other sales taxes have not. If the government persists in unfairly penalizing truck drivers, our increased operating costs will either hurt consumers or put us out of business.

    State official: But your gasoline tax dollars maintain and improve the very roads you depend on. Without those additional revenues, road conditions would deteriorate, costing you and consumers much more in maintenance and repairs.

    If the statements made above are true, the best characterization of the logical relationship between the two arguments is that the state official's response

    ◯ points out that the truck driver's proposal will actually worsen the problem it is intended to solve

    ◯ is circular, assuming the truth of its conclusion in order to justify its conclusion

    ◯ points out that the truck driver is selfish because more people are aided by the gasoline tax than are penalized

    ◯ is merely an attempt to excuse the government's policies without providing any justification for those policies

    ◯ points to an inherent contradiction between the cause the truck driver cites and the effects the truck driver thinks will follow from the cause

15. Archaeologists recently unearthed a prehistoric statuette, portraying the figure of a woman, that had been carved from a mastodon bone. A team of researchers carefully studied the statuette, which they named the Venus of Orleans. Since it was similar in shape and design to another bone carving, the so-called Venus of Grenoble, they concluded that in all likelihood it was carved at the same time, about 70,000 years ago. Skeptics point out, however, that carbon-14 testing indicates that the recently discovered statuette is only about 50,000 years old.

    Which of the following, if true, would tend most to weaken the force of the skeptics' objection?

    ◯ Carbon-14 dating places the age of the Venus of Grenoble at 70,000 years.

    ◯ No other, similar, statuettes have been found at the site where the Venus of Orleans was unearthed.

    ◯ The carbon-14 dating process is unreliable for objects dating from before 60,000 B.C.

    ◯ The carbon-14 dating process has provided unreliable dates for many objects older than 100,000 years.

    ◯ Some speculation persists that the Venus of Orleans was carved out of the femur or thigh bone of a prehistoric ox.

16. The study of foreign languages is finally becoming a serious endeavor in U.S. education. The number of American college students enrolled in non-English language courses has increased by 20 percent over the past five years. Spanish, with over 500,000 students, is the most popular; its enrollment has increased by 30 percent. Meanwhile, enrollment in Japanese and Russian has nearly doubled, and now comprises 8 percent of total foreign language study. Clearly, there is now an increased interest in foreign language study. When these students join the workforce, they will enhance not only U.S. businesses' ability to compete internationally, but also our country's reputation abroad.

    The answer to which of the following questions would be LEAST relevant to evaluating the above claims?

    ◯ Do students enrolled in foreign language classes continue their studies long enough to attain competence in those languages?

    ◯ By what percentage has overall enrollment in U.S. colleges and universities increased over the past five years?

    ◯ Do a significant number of students of foreign languages go into professions in which the ability to speak other languages is useful?

    ◯ Has the study of "dead" languages like Latin and Ancient Greek increased at a similar rate to that of modern languages?

    ◯ How does the percentage increase in foreign language enrollment over the past five years compare to previous increases in enrollment?

ANSWERS AND EXPLANATIONS

1. D
2. D
3. C
4. B
5. B
6. A
7. A
8. E
9. E
10. C
11. B
12. E
13. E
14. A
15. C
16. D

1.   D

The Conclusion: Nonurban areas are now affected by air pollution.

The Evidence: An increase in the number of persons suffering from illnesses attributable to air pollution.

If more illnesses are now considered to be caused by air pollution, then it's possible for people who had been sick for what were considered other reasons to account for the increase in the number of people suffering from illnesses caused by air pollution. The general health of the population hasn't necessarily declined, just been reclassified, and so air pollution hasn't necessarily affected nonurban areas. The GMAT test makers are fond of this trick.

(A), "decreased air pollution in the cities," doesn't weaken an argument that says it's rising outside cities. (B) says fewer people are moving out of cities, and this has no clear effect. The new sufferers from air pollution would be nonurban, so the idea that not many urban dwellers die from air pollution, (C), won't weaken the argument. Antipollution measures, (E), are irrelevant. There could still be lots of pollution in nonurban areas, pollution that floated out from urban areas, for example.

2.   D

The Sugar Manufacturers' Conclusion: Low-calorie sweeteners aren't effective in helping people lose weight.

The Sugar Manufacturers' Evidence: Statistics show that although the consumption of these sweeteners has gone up, so has the percentage of obese people.

The manufacturers assume that the sweeteners are in some way responsible for the public's failure to lose weight. But if the consumers of the sweeteners aren't becoming more obese, then, despite the increase in the percentage of the public that is overweight, those using alternative sweeteners actually lost weight.

Another possible cause for weight gain, (A), weakens the argument, but it doesn't go as far as (D), which says that those who use the sweeteners have actually lost weight. (B) strengthens the manufacturers' claim, saying that some low-calorie sweeteners actually increase appetite. (C) tells us nothing about how effective low-calorie sweeteners may or may not be. And the sugar manufacturers' claim doesn't depend on an increase in the amount each user consumes, (E), rather than an increase in the number of users.

3. C

The Conclusion: There are new doubts as to the role of lotion M in the appearance of reaction O.

The Evidence: This is what we're looking for: what caused the doubts?

In (C), lotion M is absent, yet O has taken place with drug L. O in the absence of M suggests that M is superfluous and casts the doubt we need.

(A) has drug L plus lotion M resulting in reaction O, just as was always thought. (B), in which O is absent despite the use of L and M, and (E), in which reaction O goes away following the use of L and M, each cast doubt on the whole commonplace, not just lotion M. (D), in which L doesn't cause O in the absence of M, would cast doubt on L alone causing O .

4. B

The Conclusion: Candy manufacturers don't really lose thousands every year in potential sales through workers eating candy.

The Evidence: Workers eat the candy one piece at a time and wouldn't buy a whole box anyway.

The argument as stated assumes that the candy would, if not eaten, only be sold to the people who are eating it—the workers. We can undermine this assumption by pointing out that the candy could easily be sold to other people.

If the workers eat only candy that couldn't be sold, (A), then the manufacturers probably aren't losing potential sales. This is an *au contraire* choice. It doesn't matter how many workers are eating the candy, (C); what's important is how much is disappearing and whether it could be sold if it weren't being eaten. The issue of when the candy is eaten, (D), is irrelevant to whether the company is losing potential sales. Even if the eaten candy is a small fraction of the candy sold, (E), it could still represent a substantial loss of potential sales money.

5. B

The Conclusion: We need to infer a conclusion from the evidence provided.

The Evidence: The Japanese respond to a claim that their closed markets are responsible for the trade deficit with the claim that the United States needs to improve schools and to spend more money on research and training.

Inferably, the Japanese think that changes the United States should make would help shrink the deficit. So they likely believe the deficit exists because the U.S. industrial performance—a function of things like education, research, and training—is poor.

The Japanese don't address U.S. markets, (A); they focus on U.S. industrial performance. It is the U.S. officials' opinion, (C), that the deficit results from Japanese protectionism. The Japanese don't say what specifically is wrong with U.S. schools, (D), just that they need improvement. Neither have they implied, (E), that something in addition to improving industrial performance is necessary.

6. A

The Conclusion: Private high school kids start out willing to let academics "slide," but they learn the value of serious study as the years go by.

The Evidence: Most kids caught and punished for cheating are freshmen.

The assumption is that upperclassmen don't cheat as much, but if they learn how to cheat without getting caught, the link between evidence and conclusion is severed.

A policy of going easy on first offenders, (B), has no impact on the logic—the statistics remain the same. (C) could somewhat weaken the argument by implying that upperclassmen don't cheat as much as freshmen because upper-class proctors are more vigilant, but we're starting to argue on behalf of the choice. It could also strengthen the argument by implying that a higher percentage of upperclassmen who cheat get caught. Vandalism (D) has nothing to do with the matter at hand. Equally irrelevant is (E)'s distinction between private and public school students' attitudes towards life.

7. A

The Conclusion: Paintings are too often hung in inappropriate contexts.

The Evidence: (actually more of an explanation) Gallery managers don't know what context would be proper.

To solve the problem, we'd want to bring the managers and artists together so that the artist can have a say in how the paintings are hung. This eliminates the gallery managers' ignorance, which is the root cause of the problem.

(C) and (D) both play with the gallery's décor, but making it uniform or insignificant won't help if the artist has a particular decor in mind. (B)'s suggestion of brochures isn't good enough. Describing the appropriate environment isn't the same as providing it. And there's no reason to assume (E): that if a manager knows what the work means he'll be able to tell what context the painter had in mind.

8. E

The School Officials' Conclusion: A program intended to increase the physical fitness of students has been a great success.

The Evidence: Participation in after-school sports has doubled since the program began.

It's assumed that participation in after-school programs necessarily leads to better physical fitness. Denying this weakens the argument. Maybe the after-school sports are pool and bowling, which provide little physical conditioning.

The students' motivation, (A), is irrelevant; the end result of the program is what's important here. The school officials' claim concerns students in general, not just ones in poor condition, (B), so the program could still be a success even if the truly sickly don't join. How long students take part in after-school sports, (C), doesn't really matter. And (D)'s claim strengthens the argument by making it reasonable that the policy has encouraged the new athletes.

9. E

The Conclusion: Even if the five washers work consistently throughout the regular week, they won't finish cleaning before some windows again need cleaning.

The Evidence: It takes four weeks for the team of five washers to clean every window.

What can we conclude? If any given window can be revisited four weeks later, yet some of them already need cleaning, then some windows won't stay clean if attended to only once every four weeks. They get dirty more quickly than this.

(B), (C), and (D) are wrong because they ignore the possibility of two teams working, or of washers working overtime. There's no reason why the owner's demand couldn't be fulfilled, (B), by having 2 teams of 5 washers or by having one team work overtime. For all we know, one team working overtime could properly clean all the windows in less than 4 weeks, (C). Contrary to (D), it may be that

three teams of washers working part-time can accomplish the task. As for (A), no distinction between professional and amateur washers has been or can be made.

10. C

The Conclusion: A group of anthropologists claim to have formulated a "definitive" theory of consumer purchasing behavior.

The Evidence: There isn't any provided.

You need the choice that would be least likely to represent a benefit of the theory to retailers. This is an inference question, one where you will infer benefits of the theory. Clearly, if the theory makes consumers aware of how displays influence them, they will be less at the mercy of crafty retailers. This is a benefit to consumers, not retailers.

(A) and (D) point out that retailers will be able to use the new theory to display products to maximum advantage by cutting costs and pleasing customers. (B) names the overall benefit of the new theory: it will tell retailers why shoppers buy a particular product. And (E), if true, would help a retailer maximize the amount of shopping that customers do in her particular store.

11. B

The Conclusion: The pre-Colombian people of Veracruz must not have understood the principle and uses of the wheel.

The Evidence: Ceramic animals with attached wheels were found in Veracruz grave sites. Yet this culture did not use the wheel for tasks like carting, transportation, and pottery-making.

The author argues that these people didn't understand the wheel because they didn't employ it in their everyday activities. Thus, if these people had understood the uses of the wheel, they would have used it in their daily lives.

The author never hints that if they understood the wheel they wouldn't have used it on the animals, (A). Nor does the author argue that they didn't have uses for the wheel, (C); it's that they didn't understand the wheel enough to make use of it in their daily lives. As for (D), the author states the opposite, that they must not have known of the wheel's uses despite the wheels on the animals. (E) is way off topic—the author doesn't even hint that the animals came from a later culture.

12. E

The Conclusion: If the cost of public transportation is doubled, the city will lose money and become even more noisy and smog filled.

The Evidence: The added expense will deter commuters from using trains and buses—they will drive instead, resulting in pollution and congestion.

To state that the fare increase would have a major impact on the level of pollution and congestion by increasing the use of private cars, the author must assume that enough people have ready access to cars to make this impact.

People could, contrary to (A), share rides and still have a great negative impact on pollution and congestion, so long as the number of cars increases significantly. The amount of money commuters spend, (B), isn't the issue—the effect on the city is. Even if public transportation conditions did improve, (C), people would have already abandoned the commuter system. Nor does the author have to assume that drivers outnumber those in buses and trains, (D). The actual numbers aren't a part of this argument.

13. E

The Conclusion: People have more money to spend on their vacations.

The Evidence: Airlines are doing fine even though they're charging high fares to cross the Atlantic.

The idea that domestic flights are also booming doesn't sever the connection between booming business and vacation money—it shows more booming business.

The fact that most of the flights presented as evidence aren't bought by vacationers, (A), breaks the connection between booming business and vacation money. Airlines can do a booming business even if business as a whole is down, as long as, (B), there are fewer airlines. If people are skimping elsewhere, (C), then even if they're paying a lot for air fare, they needn't have more vacation money. And if in many cases people have no choice but to fly, (D), they must pay the higher fares no matter how little money they have.

14. A

The Truck Driver's Conclusion: The gas tax must be lowered.

The Truck Driver's Evidence: Increased costs will either put the truckers out of business or will hurt consumers.

The Official's Conclusion: The tax must remain.

The Official's Evidence: Highways will fall into disrepair without tax revenues, costing truckers and consumers even more.

The official wants the trucker to realize that cutting gas taxes won't help, but will likely raise costs for both industry and consumers. So she's arguing that the trucker's proposal, if carried out, will actually make matters worse.

(B)'s circular argument would be more or less a restatement of the conclusion—that's not what's happening here. The official doesn't accuse the trucker of selfishness, (C); moreover, the trucker also warns of the harm done to consumers by the gas tax. The official does provide justification of the tax policy, (D); the revenue pays for road upkeep. There's no inherent contradiction between high taxes and the destruction of the trucking industry, (E); nor does the official claim there is.

15. C

The Skeptics' Conclusion: The Venus of Orleans isn't 70,000 years old.

The Skeptics' Evidence: Carbon-14 testing indicates that the statue is only about 50,000 years old.

The skeptics contend that the 70,000 year dating is false. As evidence they present carbon-14 dating results that show the statuette to be only 50,000 years old. This argument is weakened if results from carbon-14 dating are unreliable when the object pre-dates 60,000 B.C. Basically, if the archaeologists are right, the skeptics' tests are worthless. So the issue is still open and the skeptics' evidence is greatly weakened.

(D) works along similar lines, but no one believes the statuette to be over 100,000 years old. (A) deals with the other statuette and, rather than casting doubt on its date, affirms it. The skeptics' argument doesn't rely on other statuettes having been found, (B), or on the material of which the statuette is composed, (E).

16. D

The Conclusion: Foreign language study is becoming a serious endeavor in American education. When foreign language students enter the workforce, they will help businesses to compete internationally and enhance the United States's reputation abroad.

The Evidence: The number of U.S. college students in language courses has increased 20 percent over the past five years.

Neither a no nor a yes answer to the question about dead languages would have any relevance whatsoever to the author's argument.

Let's see how answers to the others would affect the argument. If students only took brief courses, (A), they probably wouldn't enhance the United States' reputation or ability to compete. If overall enrollments are way up in the past five years, (B), then a 20 percent increase in the number of language students wouldn't have as great an impact or indicate a change in students' perception of foreign language study. If the students don't use the languages, (C), it can't help their employers or the country's reputation. And if this 20 percent increase is smaller than those in previous years, (E), the idea that language study is considered more seriously now is weakened.

1. A tariff against computers made in Country Z is
   needed to protect computer manufacturers in this
   country. With such a tariff, domestic computer
   manufacturers would see increased sales of their
   own products. And increased sales frequently lead
   to reduced prices.

   If the above statements are true, which of the
   following conclusions can most properly be drawn
   from them?

   ⚪ A tariff is a less drastic means of applying
   international economic pressure than an
   embargo.

   ⚪ A drop in computer prices is likely to create
   more jobs in the computer industry.

   ⚪ Domestic manufacturers will decrease
   computer production if a protective tariff is
   not established.

   ⚪ The lack of a protective tariff has hampered
   computer production in this country.

   ⚪ A tariff would probably lead to a drop in
   prices for buyers of domestically produced
   computers.

2. In recent years, attacks by Dobermans on small
   children have risen dramatically. Last year saw 35
   such attacks in the continental United States alone,
   an increase of almost 21 percent over the previous
   year's total. Clearly, then, it is unsafe to keep dogs
   as pets if one has small children in the house.

   The argument above depends upon which of the
   following assumptions?

   ⚪ No reasonable justification for these attacks
   by Dobermans on small children has been
   discovered.

   ⚪ Other household pets, such as cats, don't
   display the same violent tendencies that
   dogs do.

   ⚪ The number of attacks by Dobermans on
   small children will continue to rise in the
   coming years.

   ⚪ A large percentage of the attacks by
   Dobermans on small children could have
   been prevented by proper training.

   ⚪ The behavior toward small children exhibited
   by Dobermans is representative of that of
   dogs in general.

3. At Food World Supermarket, built in 1975, the number of successful thefts has risen dramatically in the past few months. Food World has a reliable electronic security system at all customer exit doors, and this system is always in operation. Therefore, the thefts must have been committed by people who used exits other than the regular customer exit doors.

Which of the following is an assumption that would make the conclusion above logically correct?

◯ If a surveillance system is installed in a supermarket, it is always equipped at every possible exit.

◯ If an employee so wishes, he is allowed to leave through an exit that is not monitored by surveillance equipment.

◯ If a store has a reliable security system, it is impossible to pass through the system undetected.

◯ If a supermarket was built before 1980, it often has exits that cannot be equipped with electronic surveillance.

◯ If a store has a reliable electronic security system but is still experiencing a rise in theft, it must be the case that the employees are stealing.

4. A complete ban on the sale of semiautomatic machine guns will not reduce the incidence of violent crime committed with these guns. People who want to commit violent crimes with these guns will still get them even if they are banned.

The argument above would be most weakened if which of the following statements were true?

◯ Banning semiautomatic machine guns will result in an increase in the number of other dangerous weapons purchased.

◯ People who do not want to break the law will not buy guns illegally.

◯ Fully automatic machine guns, presently banned, are much more difficult to obtain than other banned weapons, such as switchblade knives.

◯ Seeing semiautomatic machine guns legally displayed for sale tends to increase people's inclination to use those weapons to commit violent crimes.

◯ The number of accidental gun deaths is lowest in those states with the most restrictive gun control laws.

5. Magazine publishers claim that illegal photocopying of articles from their magazines costs them vast amounts of revenue every year. But most people who photocopy magazine articles are teachers using them in class. Given the economics of education, these teachers could not procure an original copy of the magazine for each student.

Which of the following is most probably the point towards which the author of the above passage is moving?

◯ Magazine publishers should provide free copies of their magazines to schools.

◯ Preventing illegal photocopying would have no effect on magazine sales.

◯ Teachers should be prevented from photocopying magazine articles for their students.

◯ Eliminating illegal photocopying would prevent the magazine publishers' loss of revenues.

◯ Illegal photocopying does not depress magazine sales as significantly as publishers believe.

6. The sanitation chief, hailing the success of her voluntary conservation program, reported that the amount of garbage produced per capita in the city decreased dramatically last year. But that statistic is deceptive. Last year the city incorporated three villages from the surrounding suburban area, increasing its population by almost 30 percent. It is this increase, rather than the conservation program, that explains the statistical drop.

   Which of the following, if true, would seriously weaken the author's objection to the sanitation chief's claim?

   ○ Because of differences between urban and suburban life, most suburban areas produce less garbage per capita than do urban areas.

   ○ The voluntary conservation program was not implemented in the three incorporated villages until very late last year.

   ○ The year before last, the three villages produced as many pounds of garbage per capita as did the city.

   ○ The statistics cited by the sanitation chief do not include commercial waste or garbage collected by private carters.

   ○ Due to a three-week strike, some of the garbage produced by the city during the year before last year was not counted in the statistics.

7. A spokesperson for the Reader's Book Club (RBC) recently hailed the club's free gift program as a big boost for sales. A year ago, RBC began offering a free gift to any member ordering five or more books in a single month. Since then, the number of members ordering five or more books at a time from RBC has risen by nearly 35 percent.

   Which of the following, if true, would most seriously weaken the spokesperson's assessment of the program's effect on sales?

   ○ The number of members ordering fewer than five books in a single month also rose in the last year.

   ○ Most members ordered the same number of books over the year but concentrated their orders in specific months.

   ○ The cost of providing free gifts nearly offset the increased revenue from higher sales.

   ○ Most other book clubs, many of which also sponsored free gift programs, saw a drop in sales last year.

   ○ The membership of the Reader's Book Club rose by more than 20 percent over the last year.

Questions 8-9 are based on the following:

The United States will soon begin spot-checking all shipments of imported coffee for tainting by sandfly larvae. Any coffee found to be so tainted will be destroyed. Officials predict that the spot checks will result in the destruction of approximately 10 percent of all coffee imported into this country. Even so, the checks will miss about half of the tainted coffee sent here, since it is estimated that 20 percent of all coffee worldwide is tainted by sandfly larvae.

8.   The author of the passage above is necessarily assuming which one of the following?

   ○ Spot inspections will not succeed in preventing unacceptable amounts of tainted coffee from entering the country.

   ○ Inspectors can detect sandfly larvae in only half of the tainted shipments they inspect.

   ○ The proportion of imported coffee tainted by sandfly larvae is representative of the proportion of coffee so tainted worldwide.

   ○ Spot-checking will mean that only 10 percent of all imported coffee will be inspected for tainting by sandfly larvae.

   ○ The 80 percent of imported coffee shipments that are not tainted by sandfly larvae should not be inspected.

9.   The information in the passage above best supports which of the following conclusions?

   ○ The amount of imported coffee available for consumption in the United States may soon decrease.

   ○ The United States should learn to rely more on domestically produced coffee.

   ○ The United States will eventually be forced to inspect all imported coffee for tainting by sandfly larvae.

   ○ Coffee producers worldwide will implement a more rigorous program of insect control.

   ○ The U.S. consumer will begin paying less for imported coffee in the future.

10.   The threatened prosecution of businesses flying 20 by 38 foot garrison flags, which are traditionally to be flown only on national holidays, instead of the smaller post flags, which can be flown at any time, is unconscionable. Legal technicalities of this sort should never restrict patriotic expression.

Which of the following, if true, would most weaken the argument above?

   ○ Many people find the garrison flags' size to be distracting and ill-suited to neighborhood aesthetics.

   ○ The businesses that are flying garrison flags are primarily using the oversized flags to attract customers.

   ○ The raising and lowering of different-sized flags on the correct days of the year is a laborious and time-consuming procedure.

   ○ The regulations that govern the correct display of the nation's flags are part of an old and time-honored tradition.

   ○ The symbolic significance of a flag's size is not generally understood by most of the customers patronizing these businesses.

11. Time and time again, it has been shown that students who attend colleges with low faculty/student ratios get the most well-rounded education. As a result, when my children are ready for college, I'll be sure they attend a school with a very small student population.

    Which of the following, if true, identifies the greatest flaw in the reasoning above?

    ◯ A low faculty/student ratio is the effect of a well-rounded education, not its source.

    ◯ Intelligence should be considered the result of childhood environment, not advanced education.

    ◯ A very small student population does not, by itself, ensure a low faculty/student ratio.

    ◯ Parental desires and preferences rarely determine a child's choice of a college or university.

    ◯ Students must take advantage of the low faculty/student ratio by intentionally choosing small classes

12. Sam: Statistics show that hospital patients who have no health insurance generally get fewer diagnostic procedures and leave the hospital sooner than do patients who are insured. People without insurance are obviously not being cared for properly.

    Dan: On the contrary, what your statistics show is that people insist on undergoing all sorts of unnecessary procedures when they know that someone else is footing the bill.

    Which of the following best describes Dan's response to Sam?

    ◯ He denies the truth of Sam's statistical evidence.

    ◯ He shows that Sam's argument is based on a logical fallacy.

    ◯ He provides counterevidence that contradicts that cited by Sam.

    ◯ He shows that Sam's argument is biased because of an unfair preconception.

    ◯ He provides an alternative explanation for the facts cited by Sam.

13. Though the number of nurses employed in the United States has risen over the past ten years, 15 percent of nursing positions in hospitals are vacant today. The situation will worsen unless hospitals improve working conditions and nursing schools attract students who have not traditionally been drawn to the profession. More scholarships and loans may make nursing education more affordable, and alternative routes to nursing may prompt adults interested in nursing to go back to studying in an undergraduate program.

    Which of the following can be logically inferred from the paragraph above?

    ◯ Nursing school recruitments are now at their lowest level in a decade.

    ◯ In the past ten years, the number of practicing hospital nurses has fallen.

    ◯ Financial considerations are the principal reason for the current nursing shortage.

    ◯ The supply of nurses has been rising, but not as fast as the demand for them.

    ◯ Working conditions in hospitals have become significantly worse in the past decade.

KAPLAN)

14. Cowonga lion cubs in the wild often engage in aggressive and even violent play with their siblings. This activity is apparently instigated by the parent lions. Cowonga lion cubs born in captivity, however, rarely engage in aggressive play. Zoologists have concluded that this form of play teaches the young lions the aggressive skills necessary for successful hunting in the wild, and that such play is not instigated in captivity because the development of hunting skills is unnecessary there.

The zoologists' conclusion would be most strengthened by demonstrating that

- ⃝ Cowonga lions raised in captivity are unable to hunt successfully in the wild
- ⃝ the skills developed from aggressive play are similar to those used for hunting in the wild
- ⃝ the young of other types of predatory animals also engage in aggressive play
- ⃝ parent lions that were raised in captivity do not instigate this play in their young
- ⃝ none of the Cowonga lions raised in the wild is incapable of hunting successfully

15. Which of the following best completes the passage below?

The question of whether a child's personality is the result of genetic material inherited from the parents or the nurturing and environment provided by the parents is a perennial subject of debate. While no one would deny that environment and upbringing play some limited, superficial role, the genetic traits the child inherits provide the basic blueprint for who, and what, the child becomes. After all, if one plants tomatoes, _____.

- ⃝ one must tend them carefully, in order to gather good vegetables
- ⃝ one had better choose the variety and location with equal care
- ⃝ one will eventually get tomatoes, but not necessarily good tomatoes
- ⃝ one must expect tomatoes to grow, not cucumbers or daffodils
- ⃝ one must be sure to tend them well, regardless of the quality of the seeds used

16. Zoologists have determined that the size of the litters produced by mating pairs of Beringer sloths is largely determined by the parent animals' diet. Sloths that feed primarily on catalpa trees tend to produce smaller numbers of offspring than do those that feed primarily on tulip trees. A new theory posits that the parent sloths choose their diet to achieve optimal population size for a given year, producing fewer offspring in dry years when food scarcity would threaten a large population.

    Which of the following, if true, would provide the strongest support for the theory that Beringer sloths choose their diets to suit the conditions of a given year?

    ⬭ In a forest dominated by catalpa trees, parent sloths ate far more tulip leaves than catalpa leaves in dry years.

    ⬭ In a forest dominated by tulip trees, parent sloths ate somewhat more tulip leaves than catalpa leaves in wet years.

    ⬭ The population of sloths in a particular area varied widely over several years during which precipitation remained relatively constant.

    ⬭ In a forest with roughly equal numbers of catalpa and tulip trees, parent sloths ate far more catalpa leaves than tulip leaves in dry years.

    ⬭ In a forest with roughly equal numbers of catalpa and tulip trees, parent sloths ate far more tulip leaves than catalpa leaves in dry years.

ANSWERS AND EXPLANATIONS

1. E
2. E
3. C
4. D
5. E
6. C
7. B
8. C
9. A
10. B
11. C
12. E
13. D
14. A
15. D
16. D

1. E

The Conclusion: A tariff should be imposed on Country Z's computers.

The Evidence: A tariff will increase sales of domestic computers. Increased sales often result in lower prices.

Basically, it's putting one and one together. If the tariff will increase sales and if increased sales often lower prices, then there's a good chance that the tariff will lower domestic computer prices.

Embargoes, (A), are outside the scope of the argument, which concerns the effects of a tariff, not alternatives to it. (B) mentions a possible effect of the tariff—reduced prices; unfortunately, though, there's no mention in the stimulus of this resulting in increased jobs. A tariff, we're told, will lead to increased production; that doesn't mean, though, that *no* tariff will force, (C), *reduced* production. (D) is an overstatement. The tariff will increase sales and probably production; that doesn't mean, however, that lack of a tariff has hampered production.

2. E

The Conclusion: It is unsafe to keep dogs as pets if one has small children in the house.

The Evidence: There were 35 attacks by Dobermans in the last year in the United States.

Pretty clearly, this is an Assumption question, so we are looking for the "missing link" in the argument. The evidence discusses attacks by Dobermans, but the conclusion is about dogs—all dogs. That's a big change of scope. The author must be thinking that all dogs behave as Dobermans do. So there's our prediction: "All dogs behave like Dobermans." That's exactly what (E) says, although of course the GMAT phrases it more densely. (Notice, though, how specific answer (E) is about the scope of the argument—dogs' behavior around small children!) The Denial Test would also work well here. If Dobermans' behavior toward children isn't typical of that of dogs in general, then the argument falls apart.

(A), whether the attacks were justified, is beside the point. Even if the kids were pulling the dogs' tails, the author's point that the dogs aren't safe still holds. Other pets are beyond the scope, so (B) is out. As for (C), the argument doesn't deal with the future, so the author needn't assume anything about it. And it certainly wouldn't weaken the argument if, contrary to (D), many of the attacks could not have been prevented, so (D) is not assumed.

3. C

The Conclusion: The thefts *must* (note that keyword) have been committed by people who used exits other than the regular customer exit doors.

The Evidence: The number of successful thefts has risen even though Food World has a reliable electronic security system at all customer exit doors.

In order to conclude that the thefts aren't taking place out the customer doors, the author must assume that the security system works. However, reliable doesn't necessarily mean infallible.

(A) plainly can't be assumed, since the author is concluding that the thefts took place at unequipped doors. (B) and (E) both play off the same red herring: employee theft. The issue is where the thefts are occurring, not who is committing them. The author seems to think that noncustomer exit doors are the problem, but there's no need to assume that these can't be equipped with a surveillance system (D).

4. D

The Conclusion: A ban on semiautomatic machine guns will not reduce the incidence of violent crime committed with these guns.

The Evidence: People who want to commit violent crimes with these guns will still get them.

There's not a whole lot of evidence here, just a couple of claims. To weaken the argument, we want to show that banning the guns will result in less criminal use of the guns. If much of the use isn't truly premeditated, but occurs to criminals when they see the guns displayed, then banning the guns (and their display) will result in less criminal use.

The author didn't argue that the ban would reduce crime, just the criminal use of these guns, so (A) attacks the wrong argument. (B) talks about law-abiding people, who aren't a part of the argument. The fact that some banned weapons are harder to get than others, (C), is irrelevant. Watch out for pointless comparisons—they are common wrong answers. Accidental deaths, (E), are also outside the scope.

5. E

The Conclusion: The stem tells us that the author is moving towards a point, so we read the stimulus with an eye towards an eventual conclusion that's not on the page.

The Evidence: Most people who photocopy magazine articles are teachers using them in class. These teachers could not afford a copy of the magazine for each student.

If the publishers claim illegal copying costs them, and the author responds that most copiers can't afford to buy the original issues, he's probably disputing the claim that copying costs publishers, (E). He's doing this by showing that the lost sales aren't really sales at all.

While he does take a "relax and calm down" attitude towards the publishers, he doesn't go so far as to tell them to give away free copies, (A). He argues that few copies represent lost sales, not that (B) none of them does. (C) and (D) can be dismissed because they run directly counter to the author's argument by presenting the illegal copying as a significant problem for publishers.

6. C

The Conclusion: The drop in per capita garbage is not due to the chief's conservation program.

The Evidence: The city incorporated three villages, whose extra residents accounted for the per capita drop.

Well, the author plainly believes (assumes) that the suburban villagers are deflating the per capita garbage figure, so he assumes that suburbanites produce less garbage. If, though, they produce every bit as much garbage, then the drop can't be due to their incorporation into the city and the statistics.

He assumes (A), so it strengthens rather than weakens his argument. (B) makes it less likely that the conservation program is responsible for the drop, which also strengthens his argument. As long as the same type of garbage is eliminated from both years' statistics, (D), the effect of this on the different arguments is anyone's guess—a clear sign of a wrong answer. More garbage the year before last year, (E), just increases the drop; it does not, however, affect the author's attempt to explain this drop.

7. B

The Conclusion: The free gift program increased sales.

The Evidence: The number of orders of five or more books has increased by 35 percent.

The representative argues from evidence of sales of five books or more to a conclusion about total sales. If the large sales have increased at the expense of other sales, then it's not necessarily the case that total sales have risen. People may be taking advantage of the offer without buying any more books.

If smaller orders are also up, (A), then the argument is strengthened. The argument concerns sales, not revenue, so (C) is off the point. If the argument concerned the competitiveness of RBC, then (D) might be relevant. As it stands, though, other clubs and their promotions have no effect on the representative's claims. And membership, (E), like revenues, is off the point. The representative hails the program as a success based on supposedly increased sales.

8. C

The Conclusion: The spot checks will miss half of the imported coffee tainted by sandfly larvae.

The Evidence: Only 10 percent of imported coffee will fail the spot checks, whereas 20 percent of coffee worldwide is tainted.

The evidence contains a figure for coffee worldwide; the conclusion, for coffee imported to the United States. Here we have a twist on a common GMAT theme. The argument isn't *based* on a sample; it *concludes* something about a sample (imported coffee) based on evidence about the whole (all coffee). The same key issue is at work, though: the sample must be representative. In order for the math to work, 20 percent of imported coffee (the same figure as for all coffee) must be tainted.

The author assumes that spot checks will detect some tainted coffee; there's no evidence, though, that this amount (10 percent) is unacceptable, (A). (B) is incorrect becuse it's not clear that they will miss half of the tainted coffee they inspect. These are spot checks; they may miss half the tainted coffee because they don't check that coffee. (D) misreads the numbers: it's not that 10 percent will be inspected, but that inspections will fail 10 percent. (E) is nonsensical. If inspectors knew which 80 percent was untainted, there would be no need for inspections.

9. A

Bearing in mind the situation described in the stimulus, we attack the choices, looking for one that seems likely. We don't look far. (A)'s claim that there may soon be less coffee is a likely outgrowth of the policy that's described. Spot checks will destroy 10 percent of imported coffee. While the amount of coffee imported may subsequently be increased, there is a good chance that, for some period of time, less coffee will be available.

The argument is descriptive, so (B)'s prescriptions about what should be done go awry. There's no support for the drastic conclusion, (C), that all coffee will have to be checked. Nor is there support for a conclusion, (D), about the reaction of coffee producers. Coffee prices, (E), like these other issues, are also unpredictable.

10. B

The Conclusion: Businesses flying garrison flags should not be prosecuted.

The Evidence: Legal technicalities should not prevent patriotic expression.

The author's argument depends upon the patriotism of the businesses flying these large flags. If, however, the businesses are not expressing patriotism, but merely touting their wares, the argument falls apart.

Aesthetic judgments, (A), are irrelevant; the author would merely argue that these, too, shouldn't be allowed to restrict patriotic expression. If switching flags is a big hassle, (C), then the author's argument is strengthened. (D) is similar to invoking aesthetics; the author would just argue that patriotism overrides tradition. (E) is as much an argument for the author; pointing out that the significance of the flags' size (which is the basis for the threatened prosecutions) is lost on most people.

11. C

The Conclusion: My child will get a well-rounded education at a school with a small student population.

The Evidence: Well-rounded education comes from schools with low student-to-faculty ratios.

We are asked to find a flaw, which means that our prediction will concern what's wrong with the argument already. We might paraphrase the argument like this: "The most well-rounded education comes from schools with low student-to-faculty ratios, so I will send my kids to colleges with low student populations." The author assumes that a low student population is the same thing as a low student/faculty ratio. That's an error—a school with a large student population could have a low student/faculty ratio by hiring lots of faculty. Similarly, a school with few students could have proportionally even fewer faculty, resulting in a high ratio. So our prediction would be something like this: "Having a low student population doesn't mean a school must have a low student/faculty ratio." That's exactly what (C) says, which is why it's the correct answer.

(A) claims that the author confuses cause and effect, but that isn't a big flaw here; even if (A) is right, the stimulus points out that the two are highly correlated, so the author's strategy would still likely work. (B) is out of scope, as *intelligence* and *well-rounded education* don't mean the same thing. (D) touches on the issue of whether the plan is practical, which is outside the scope of the argument. Nothing in the argument indicates whether this parent has influence. (E) is also outside of the scope because it addresses not college choice but what happens after admission.

12. E

Sam's Conclusion: The uninsured get poor hospital care.

Dan's Conclusion: The insured insist on unnecessary tests.

The Evidence: (for both) Hospital patients who have no health insurance generally get fewer diagnostic procedures and leave the hospital sooner than do patients who are insured.

As the breakdown above points out, the two agree on the facts, they just disagree on what the facts mean. Each has a different explanation for the discrepancy in hospital procedures. Dan, then, accepts the evidence but provides as a conclusion an alternative explanation for it.

Choices (A), (B), and (C) all have Dan disputing the evidence, or basis for Sam's argument. It's the interpretation that he disputes. He doesn't show a bias or preconception, (D).

13. D

The Conclusion: Unless steps are taken, the nursing shortage will worsen.

The Evidence: There's a 15 percent vacancy rate, which looks likely to worsen.

More than a straightforward argument, the stimulus is an exploration of the nursing shortage and approaches to handling it. Prephrasing here might get us the idea that working conditions aren't ideal or that there aren't enough students enrolling in nursing programs. As it turns out, though, it's simpler than that. If there are more nurses than ever, yet the shortage is worsening, then demand is rising faster than the supply.

There's no evidence that enrollments are actually down, (A), and we know that the number of nurses hasn't fallen, (B). Financial considerations, (C), seem to hurt nursing school enrollments, but that's a far cry from being "the principal

reason for the nursing shortage." The same reasoning eliminates (E): working conditions have something to do with the shortage, and they need improving, but we can't infer that they have worsened significantly.

14. A

The Zoologists' Conclusion: The play teaches the young lions the aggressive skills necessary for successful hunting in the wild.

Their Evidence: Cubs in the wild often engage in aggressive play with their siblings, play that is instigated by their parents. Cubs born in captivity, however, rarely engage in aggressive play.

There's cause and effect here. The zoologists believe that the play teaches hunting skills. Where there is need of the effect (hunting skills) there is the cause (play); where there is no need of the effect, the cause is lacking. That's a correlation, but the key issue remains: Does the play cause the hunting skills? The fact that lions raised in captivity, without the play, can't hunt tells us that without the alleged cause, there is no effect. This greatly strengthens the connection between the two.

The fact that the play and hunting are similar, (B), does little to show that the former leads to the latter; both could be effects of something more basic and instinctive. The behavior of other animals, (C), is beyond the scope of the zoologists' argument. Presumably, the parents raised in captivity, (D), are raising their young in captivity, so this adds nothing new. And the fact that wild lions learn to hunt, (E), has no effect on the hypothesis; the question is how they learned to hunt.

15. D

The Conclusion: Children's personalities are primarily the result of genetics.

The Evidence: Genetics provide the basic blueprint for who a child becomes.

There's not much evidence given (it's a restatement of the conclusion). The sentence with the blank is intended to provide more: an example or illustration, where tomatoes are compared to children. Since the author believes in the primacy of genetics, we need a completion, involving tomatoes, that illustrates this. If one plants tomatoes, then one will get tomatoes (it's genetic), not some other plant.

Careful tending, (A) and (E), parallels nurture or upbringing, which the author doesn't consider very important. Equal care devoted to variety and location, (B), would illustrate that both nature and nurture are equally important. (C), getting tomatoes but not necessarily good tomatoes, is close but no cigar. (D) does a better job of illustrating that certain outcomes are genetically impossible. Moreover, the issue of quality comes from nowhere, making this an incorrect GMAT argument completion.

16. D

The New Theory's Conclusion: Parent sloths choose their diet to achieve optimal population size for a given year by producing fewer offspring in dry years when food is scarce.

The Evidence: The size of the litters is largely determined by the parent animals' diet. Sloths that feed primarily on catalpa trees tend to produce smaller numbers of offspring than do those that feed primarily on tulip trees. With stimuli like this, it's often a good idea to jot down some shorthand describing what the theory says:

$$\text{dry} \rightarrow \text{scarce} \rightarrow \text{catalpa}$$
$$\text{wet} \rightarrow \text{not scarce} \rightarrow \text{tulip}$$

We want support. Nothing leaps to mind, so we look to the choices. Each describes a scenario; we need the one that "fits" the new theory. Sloths deliberately going for tulips over catalpa in dry years, (A), is contrary to the theory. (B) is in line with the theory—tulip leaves in wet years—yet because this forest was dominated by tulip trees, it could just be that the sloths ate most what they found most. (C) tells us nothing about diet and it's not obvious what it means, so it's out. (D), however, gives us what we want. Catalpa leaves in dry years is in line with the theory, and the trees are equally available. This makes it more likely that the sloths sought out the catalpa. Tulip leaves in dry years, (E), is directly counter to the theory.

PART FOUR

Putting It All Together

PRACTICE GMAT VERBAL SECTION

Here, at last, is your chance to see what an actual GMAT Verbal section feels like. The following practice Verbal section contains a typical mix of medium-to-hard GMAT Verbal questions. If you can answer most of these questions correctly under timed conditions, you can expect to do well on the real GMAT.

One thing, however, that we could not simulate in this book is the computer-adaptive nature of an actual GMAT. If you want that experience (and we recommend it strongly), we have two suggestions.

First, you can get your hands on some of Kaplan's great GMAT prep materials. One option is to pick up the latest edition of *Kaplan GMAT Premier*. It comes with a CD that contains four full-length, computer-adaptive GMATs, along with section-length practice quizzes.

You can also use the Kaplan GMAT Quiz Bank. You get more than 1,000 questions that you can access 24/7 from any Internet browser, each with comprehensive explanations. You can even customize your quizzes based on question type, content, and difficulty level. Take quizzes in Timed Mode to test your stamina or in Tutor Mode to see explanations as you work. Best of all, you also get detailed reports to track your progress. Visit **http://kaptest.com/GMAT** for more details on the Quiz Bank and for more on other online and classroom-based options.

Your other option is to get the *GMATprep*® software from the test maker's website, **mba.com**. It's free and contains two full-length CATs (detailed explanations of answers are not included) and a 15-question practice section for each question type, with answers and explanations. If you don't want to download the software over the Internet, you can have a CD-ROM version of the software sent to you free. If you choose to receive the software this way, you should allow up to two weeks for delivery within the United States and up to four weeks for delivery outside of the United States. You may wish to consider this timing when registering for your test.

How to Take This Practice Section

Before taking this practice section, find a quiet place where you can work uninterrupted for 75 minutes. Make sure you have a comfortable desk, a timer, a couple of pencils, and several sheets of scratch paper.

Make sure as well that you answer the questions in order. As you know, there's no skipping around on the actual GMAT.

You'll find the answer key and explanations following this section.

Good luck!

PRACTICE SECTION ANSWER SHEET

1. Ⓐ Ⓑ Ⓒ Ⓓ Ⓔ
2. Ⓐ Ⓑ Ⓒ Ⓓ Ⓔ
3. Ⓐ Ⓑ Ⓒ Ⓓ Ⓔ
4. Ⓐ Ⓑ Ⓒ Ⓓ Ⓔ
5. Ⓐ Ⓑ Ⓒ Ⓓ Ⓔ
6. Ⓐ Ⓑ Ⓒ Ⓓ Ⓔ
7. Ⓐ Ⓑ Ⓒ Ⓓ Ⓔ
8. Ⓐ Ⓑ Ⓒ Ⓓ Ⓔ
9. Ⓐ Ⓑ Ⓒ Ⓓ Ⓔ
10. Ⓐ Ⓑ Ⓒ Ⓓ Ⓔ
11. Ⓐ Ⓑ Ⓒ Ⓓ Ⓔ
12. Ⓐ Ⓑ Ⓒ Ⓓ Ⓔ
13. Ⓐ Ⓑ Ⓒ Ⓓ Ⓔ
14. Ⓐ Ⓑ Ⓒ Ⓓ Ⓔ

15. Ⓐ Ⓑ Ⓒ Ⓓ Ⓔ
16. Ⓐ Ⓑ Ⓒ Ⓓ Ⓔ
17. Ⓐ Ⓑ Ⓒ Ⓓ Ⓔ
18. Ⓐ Ⓑ Ⓒ Ⓓ Ⓔ
19. Ⓐ Ⓑ Ⓒ Ⓓ Ⓔ
20. Ⓐ Ⓑ Ⓒ Ⓓ Ⓔ
21. Ⓐ Ⓑ Ⓒ Ⓓ Ⓔ
22. Ⓐ Ⓑ Ⓒ Ⓓ Ⓔ
23. Ⓐ Ⓑ Ⓒ Ⓓ Ⓔ
24. Ⓐ Ⓑ Ⓒ Ⓓ Ⓔ
25. Ⓐ Ⓑ Ⓒ Ⓓ Ⓔ
26. Ⓐ Ⓑ Ⓒ Ⓓ Ⓔ
27. Ⓐ Ⓑ Ⓒ Ⓓ Ⓔ
28. Ⓐ Ⓑ Ⓒ Ⓓ Ⓔ

29. Ⓐ Ⓑ Ⓒ Ⓓ Ⓔ
30. Ⓐ Ⓑ Ⓒ Ⓓ Ⓔ
31. Ⓐ Ⓑ Ⓒ Ⓓ Ⓔ
32. Ⓐ Ⓑ Ⓒ Ⓓ Ⓔ
33. Ⓐ Ⓑ Ⓒ Ⓓ Ⓔ
34. Ⓐ Ⓑ Ⓒ Ⓓ Ⓔ
35. Ⓐ Ⓑ Ⓒ Ⓓ Ⓔ
36. Ⓐ Ⓑ Ⓒ Ⓓ Ⓔ
37. Ⓐ Ⓑ Ⓒ Ⓓ Ⓔ
38. Ⓐ Ⓑ Ⓒ Ⓓ Ⓔ
39. Ⓐ Ⓑ Ⓒ Ⓓ Ⓔ
40. Ⓐ Ⓑ Ⓒ Ⓓ Ⓔ
41. Ⓐ Ⓑ Ⓒ Ⓓ Ⓔ

1. Fossils found recently in Pakistan provide evidence <u>supporting the theory of land mammals returning to the water that later</u> evolved into modern whales.

   ⬭ supporting the theory of land mammals returning to the water that later

   ⬭ supporting the theory that land mammals, after returning to the water,

   ⬭ that supports the theory of land mammals that returned to the water and that later

   ⬭ in support of the theory that land mammals returned to the water and that they later

   ⬭ of support for the theory of land mammals that returned to the water and after

2. Although modern roller coasters have loops in which they turn upside-down, <u>old-fashioned roller coasters have more and longer straight drops</u>.

   ⬭ old-fashioned roller coasters have more and longer straight drops

   ⬭ the old-fashioned roller coaster has more and longer straight drops

   ⬭ whereas old-fashioned roller coasters have more and longer straight drops

   ⬭ old-fashioned roller coasters having more and longer straight drops

   ⬭ old-fashioned roller coasters drop longer and straighter

3. the governor's recent direct mail survey on the environment showed that 80 percent of those who responded, and thus allegedly the vast majority of the state's residents, support increased state spending for the environmentally safe disposal of solid waste. But we should expect that most of the people who respond to an environmental survey are in favor of spending money to protect the environment.

   Which of the following best expresses the author's point?

   ⬭ The survey was mailed only to those citizens who are environmentalists.

   ⬭ Most citizens are poor judges of how the state's revenues should be spent.

   ⬭ The survey failed because it neglected to ask citizens where the money for the increased spending would come from.

   ⬭ Those who responded to the survey are not truly representative of the state's residents.

   ⬭ The state does not need to spend more money to dispose of solid waste.

4. The dollar amount of federal tax revenues gained from personal income tax has increased markedly in recent years. Clearly, people are being more honest in declaring their annual earnings than they used to be.

   The argument above would be greatly weakened by each of the following EXCEPT:

   ⬭ Fewer income tax deductions are allowed now than in the past.

   ⬭ The nation's population has increased.

   ⬭ Tax revenue from of the corporate sector has decreased.

   ⬭ The average yearly income of the nation's residents has increased.

   ⬭ The rate of personal income taxation has increased.

GO ON TO THE NEXT PAGE ⟩

KAPLAN

Questions 5-7 refer to the following passage.

Line   Having rejected Catholicism, English society after the Protestant Reformation felt com-
pelled to impose new order on an uncertain
universe. Claiming knowledge of a divine
(5) plan that linked the celestial and natural
worlds into one "great chain of being," some
English thinkers depicted humans as the
highest link on the portion of the chain representing the natural world. Furthermore,
(10) they conceived of human society as a vertical series of political strata. One metaphor,
occurring in Shakespeare's *Coriolanus*, among
other places, likened society to the human
body. Queen Elizabeth I chided a recalcitrant
(15) Parliament by asserting that "the feet do not
rule the head." Edward Forset echoed this
assertion in 1606, when he elaborated a hierarchy in which the body was topped, literally
and morally, by the head and the soul. In
(20) Forset's scheme, both soul and monarchy
possessed "unity" or "indivisibility"; the soul
united and reigned over the physical body,
and the sovereign united and reigned over the
body politic. Popular acceptance of the idea of
(25) stability as God's will gave Elizabeth and her
immediate successors a potent, though short-
lived, ideological restraint on rebellious thought
and activity.

5.   The passage suggests that many English people saw
the idea of a new social order as

    ◯ necessary in order to fill a vacuum created by
the decline of the monarchy

    ◯ an idiosyncratic viewpoint advocated by a few
eccentric thinkers

    ◯ an amusing but not terribly urgent social
issue

    ◯ a disguised attempt by the Catholic Church
to restore its lost influence in English affairs

    ◯ unavoidable because an older order that had
provided them with structure and security no
longer existed

6.   The passage suggests that, in the years following
the Protestant Reformation, English monarchs
were able to maintain their political influence
primarily because

    ◯ popular opinion was tightly controlled by a
small group of thinkers

    ◯ English society accepted that a hierarchical
society was consistent with divine will

    ◯ monarchs accepted a social position basically
equal to that of most other people

    ◯ Parliament was politically passive and
offered no significant resistance

    ◯ English society traditionally supported a
strong monarchical authority

7.   Which of the following sentences would most
logically follow the last sentence of this passage?

    ◯ Subsequently, popular acceptance of a
divinely ordered social structure continued
to shape English politics for an unusually
lengthy period.

    ◯ However, because Forset's ideas were judged
to be too radical, they initially failed to make a
substantial impact on the balance of power in
English government.

    ◯ Forset's arguments for a strict, hierarchically
ordered society found especially enthusiastic
support among many members of the English
Parliament.

    ◯ This acceptance undoubtedly helped check
growing assertiveness of those social classes
that spoke through Parliament.

    ◯ Thus, freed of her problems with Parliament,
Elizabeth was able to focus on the threat to
social stability posed by Forset.

GO ON TO THE NEXT PAGE ▷

KAPLAN

8. When a movie that is panned by most film critics is a popular success, it is often taken as evidence of the poor taste of general audiences. But film critics belong to a fairly homogeneous class and their preferences are often rooted in the prejudices of that class. Their opinions are no more likely to be an unerring guide to quality than those of the average moviegoer.

    The passage above best supports which of the following conclusions?

    ◯ Judgments of film quality by professional film critics are usually incorrect.

    ◯ Judgments of quality applied to movies are meaningless.

    ◯ Film critics usually consider popular movies to be of poor quality.

    ◯ Professional critics generally agree on the quality of any given movie.

    ◯ When film critics and general audiences disagree about a movie's quality, the critics' opinion is not necessarily more accurate.

9. The State University debating club is always looking for money to renovate their headquarters in Stockton Hall. The latest plan is to contact alumni club members from the 1950s, 1960s, and 1970s and ask for contributions. Other such efforts have been tried in the past, however, and club headquarters are still in poor condition.

    If the author concludes that the debating club will not raise enough money to renovate their headquarters, which of the following best describes the way he supports his conclusion?

    ◯ He bases a conclusion on an analogy.

    ◯ He casts doubt on the reasoning ability of his opponents.

    ◯ He points out a logical fallacy.

    ◯ He bases a prediction on past experience.

    ◯ He disparages the motives of his opponents.

10. John F. Kennedy increased the participation of the United States in the war in Vietnam, <u>which Lyndon B. Johnson did</u> when he succeeded Kennedy.

    ◯ which Lyndon B. Johnson did

    ◯ which Lyndon B. Johnson was to be doing

    ◯ as Lyndon B. Johnson

    ◯ as did Lyndon B. Johnson

    ◯ as Lyndon B. Johnson did do

11. <u>The reason why Scipio Africanus wept after his defeat of Hannibal was because he knew</u> that, having attained this stunning victory, his fortunes could only turn for the worse.

    ◯ The reason why Scipio Africanus wept after his defeat of Hannibal was because he knew

    ◯ Scipio Africanus' weeping after his defeat of Hannibal was because he knew

    ◯ Scipio Africanus wept after his defeat of Hannibal because he knew

    ◯ The reason Scipio Africanus wept after his defeat of Hannibal was because he knew

    ◯ Scipio Africanus wept after his defeat of Hannibal, the reason being that he knew

12. The shipbuilding industry in eighteenth-century England created a need <u>that pine and flax from Russia be made into masts and sails</u>.

    ◯ that pine and flax from Russia be made into masts and sails

    ◯ for pine and flax from Russia that are made into masts and sails

    ◯ that there be a production of masts and sails out of pine and flax from Russia

    ◯ that masts and sails are made out of pine and flax from Russia

    ◯ for pine and flax from Russia to be made into masts and sails

GO ON TO THE NEXT PAGE ▷

KAPLAN)

Questions 13-16 refer to the following passage.

Line   Corporate managers often work in groups because of the complexity of strategic problems. A consensus-seeking group's effectiveness may be impaired, however, if the group
(5) values harmony over open evaluation of ideas. Consequently, some theorists advocate building decisional conflict into the group process. Doing so, they argue, should yield better decisions. While conflict potentially
(10) offers benefits, a group's effectiveness also depends on members' reactions to group experiences. Ideally, the group process wins the commitment of its members. The process, though, may generate so much divisiveness
(15) that implementation and future cooperation are undermined. Management groups thus face an apparent dilemma: Decisional conflict may yield better decisions at the risk of weakening managerial effectiveness. Conversely,
(20) the harmony that facilitates cooperation and implementation may come at the cost of inferior decisions.

Efforts to build conflict into group decision making have focused on two approaches,
(25) dialectical inquiry and devil's advocacy. Both work by dividing the group into two competing subgroups, relying on formal debate to prevent uncritical acceptance of the seemingly obvious, and continuing until participants
(30) agree on a decision. The approaches differ in the roles played by the subgroups. In dialectical inquiry, the subgroups present opposed sets of assumptions and recommendations, and debate until they reach agreement. In
(35) devil's advocacy, the second subgroup critiques the assumptions and recommendations of the first, but offers no alternative. The first subgroup revises its ideas and presents them for a second critique. The process con-
(40) tinues until the subgroups agree.

The varying roles of the subgroups have led to disagreement among theorists over the effectiveness of the approaches. Mason and Mitroff claim that devil's advocacy does not
(45) identify suitable alternatives, whereas dialectical inquiry's juxtaposition of opposed sets of ideas does so. Cosier, however, argues that dialectical inquiry adds potentially confusing steps to the process that would require exten-
(50) sive training, and may run counter to managers' accustomed ways of thinking; he also feels that this approach may lead to excessive compromise.

13. The author's primary purpose in the passage is to

  ○ emphasize the benefits of group decision making and reconcile two differing approaches

  ○ describe the benefits and risks of decisional conflict and alternative means of its use

  ○ defend an innovative method of group management against its critics

  ○ argue that group decision making is superior to any other decision-making approach

  ○ advocate one method of group decision making over another

14. It can be inferred from the passage that advocates of both the dialectical inquiry and devil's advocacy processes would agree with which of the following statements?

  ○ Superior decisions often reflect compromises made between opposing views.

  ○ Superior decisions stem from a consideration of opposing sets of proposals.

  ○ Managers should avoid changing their customary ways of thinking.

  ○ Formal debate can lead to a more thorough understanding of a problem.

  ○ Effective group management requires extensive training.

GO ON TO THE NEXT PAGE ⟩

KAPLAN

15. Which one of the following, if true, would counter Cosier's criticism of dialectical inquiry?

   ○ Frequent compromises among managers may lead to ill-advised actions.

   ○ Demanding that managers agree often weakens implementation of decisions.

   ○ Encouraging conflict among managers improves the quality of decisions.

   ○ Some managerial decisions must be made and implemented rapidly to be effective.

   ○ Managers willing to alter their accustomed modes of thinking often make better decisions.

16. Which of the following exemplifies the functioning of management groups, as those groups are described in the passage?

   ○ A citizens' group gathers to monitor the results of a closely contested election.

   ○ A special prosecutor's office organizes to investigate alleged misconduct on the part of government officials.

   ○ A committee of administrators forms to address the major problems of running a hospital.

   ○ A panel of experts assembles to study an issue of growing public concern.

   ○ A faculty committee forms to observe the search for a college president.

17. Manager: The success ratio for new businesses is lower than ever, with only 12 percent surviving the first two years. Furthermore, many businesses already operating are doing so at a loss, or with their lowest profit margin in decades. The blame must fall on the excessive demands of the workers. Profits drop in order to pay for new paint, radios, and artwork. We have lost sight of the fact that work is intended to be productive, not enjoyable.

Which of the following, if true, would most weaken the manager's argument?

   ○ Workers, whether they are performing productively or not, often have very difficult and highly taxing duties.

   ○ In most cases, improvements in the work environment increase productivity by increasing worker satisfaction.

   ○ The failure of many businesses in the past was due to exorbitant taxation rather than excessive demands of the workers.

   ○ The failure of a new business is not necessarily the same thing as the failure of an already existing business.

   ○ The failure of a new business is not necessarily the same thing as operating an already existing business without a profit.

18. The Republic of the Philippines encompasses more than seven thousand islands, two of them with two-thirds of its area.

   ○ two of them with two-thirds of its area

   ○ two-thirds of their area being in two of them

   ○ and its area is two-thirds in two islands

   ○ two of them have two-thirds of its area

   ○ which have two-thirds of its area in two of them

GO ON TO THE NEXT PAGE

KAPLAN

Questions 19-21 refer to the following passage.

Line   Scientists long believed that gradual changes in global climate caused the extinction of the dinosaurs. In 1979, however, a team from Berkeley discovered in Italy a layer
(5) of clay from about the time of the dinosaurs' disappearance, with an iridium level some thirty times greater than that of clays in adjacent strata. Since iridium settles fairly evenly over time and is extraterrestrial in origin, the
(10) researchers concluded that the high iridium level of this clay must have resulted from a sudden, catastrophic event. After finding similarly enriched marine rocks from the same period in Spain, Denmark, and New Zealand,
(15) the researchers calculated that some 500 billion tons of material settled on the earth in less than 150 years.

Scientists differ over the exact nature of the event. The possibility that a stellar explosion
(20) caused the deposition has been discounted, because certain radioactive isotopes are largely absent from the clay. If the material originated within the solar system, the earth must have collided with an astral body large
(25) enough to distribute the iridium-rich material around the globe. An asteroid of the required mass would have been approximately ten kilometers in diameter. A comet, being mostly ice, would have been twice as large.

(30)   There is no geological evidence of the impact of such massive objects, but Grieve argues that the clay layer could have settled as fallout after an atmospheric explosion. Kyte asserts that a comet, disrupted by the earth's
(35) gravitational field, would have produced a deluge of falling debris without creating major craters. The Berkeley group suggests that an asteroid may have landed in the sea.

Whatever the type of event, the Berkeley
(40) team argues that it disrupted the planetary ecology by suspending vast clouds of matter in the stratosphere. The effects of the impact would have increased as the blockage of sunlight impeded photosynthesis, causing a mas-
(45) sive disruption at the base of the global food chain.

19. The passage is primarily concerned with

○ summarizing and assessing differing theories

○ rebutting a traditional assumption

○ evaluating the results of a controversial methodology

○ suggesting a new course of investigation

○ discussing the implications of a discovery

20. According to the passage, scientists used the level of "certain radioactive isotopes" (line 21) in clay from Italy in order to

○ assess the validity of an older theory about the extinction of the dinosaur

○ estimate the approximate age of adjacent clay strata

○ determine whether or not iridium originates extraterrestrially

○ estimate the amount of fallout necessary to block sunlight

○ eliminate a possible theory as to the origin of the clay layer

GO ON TO THE NEXT PAGE

21. Judging from the information in the passage, the argument of the Berkeley group mentioned in the last paragraph would be most strengthened by

   ◯ a discovery of dinosaur fossils in strata older than the iridium-rich clay layer in Italy

   ◯ a drop in the number of plant fossils in strata above those studied in Italy

   ◯ a discovery of elevated levels of iridium in rocks above and below the clay strata in Spain

   ◯ the development of a consensus among scientists on the probability of a comet's impact with the earth

   ◯ a recalculation showing that the Italian clay layer was deposited over a period of several thousand years

22. Setting a distance record, in 1984 Joe Kittinger piloted his balloon from Maine to Italy, and he became the first balloonist to cross the Atlantic solo.

   ◯ Setting a distance record, in 1984 Joe Kittinger piloted his balloon from Maine to Italy, and he became the first balloonist to cross the Atlantic solo

   ◯ In 1984, Joe Kittinger, setting a distance record, piloted his balloon from Maine to Italy, and he became the first balloonist to cross the Atlantic solo

   ◯ In 1984, Joe Kittinger piloted his balloon from Maine to Italy, setting a distance record and becoming the first balloonist to cross the Atlantic solo

   ◯ Having been first to cross the Atlantic solo, and with a voyage from Maine to Italy, Joe Kittinger set a balloon distance record in 1984

   ◯ Joe Kittinger, in 1984, piloted his balloon from Maine to Italy, setting a new distance record, becoming the first balloonist to cross the Atlantic solo

23. Crises in international diplomacy <u>do not always result from malice; for nations, like individuals, can find</u> themselves locked into difficult positions, unable to back down.

   ◯ do not always result from malice; for nations, like individuals, can find

   ◯ does not always result from malice; nations, just as individuals, finding

   ◯ do not always result of malice; nations, such as individuals, can find

   ◯ aren't always the results of malice; nations in the same way that individuals can find

   ◯ aren't resulting always from malice; just like nations and individuals who can find

24. <u>Young female ballet dancers and gymnasts sometimes fail to maintain good eating habits caused by the desire to be as thin as possible.</u>

   ◯ Young female ballet dancers and gymnasts sometimes fail to maintain good eating habits caused by the desire to be as thin as possible

   ◯ Good eating habits sometimes fail to be maintained by young female ballet dancers and gymnasts caused by desiring to be as thin as possible

   ◯ Because they desire to be as thin as possible, good eating habits are sometimes not maintained by young female ballet dancers and gymnasts

   ◯ Good eating habits sometimes fail to be maintained by young female ballet dancers and gymnasts because they desire to be as thin as possible

   ◯ Young female dancers and gymnasts sometimes fail to maintain good eating habits because they desire to be as thin as possible

GO ON TO THE NEXT PAGE ▷

25. A talent agent analyzed her company's records in an attempt to determine why they were placing so few actors in roles. She attributed the company's poor performance to the fact that often the actors sent to an audition were completely inappropriate for the role.

    It can be concluded from the passage above that the agent believes that

    ◯ certain actors are inappropriate for certain roles

    ◯ the actors her company represents are not very good

    ◯ it is difficult to predict how appropriate an actor will be for a role

    ◯ her company does not send enough actors to audition for major roles

    ◯ directors often cast actors who are inappropriate for the role

26. Patient: Doctor, you decreased my Olanon from seven milligrams to two but you eliminated the Doril-T entirely. You said you prescribed the Doril-T in order to prevent possible side effects of the Olanon. Since I am still taking the Olanon, shouldn't I also be taking the Doril-T?

    Doctor: Since you did not experience any side effects from the seven milligrams of Olanon, there is no reason to fear side effects from two milligrams of Olanon.

    Which of the following identifies a problem in the doctor's reasoning?

    ◯ Medications cause side effects in proportion to the amount prescribed.

    ◯ Without Doril-T, a mere two milligrams of Olanon may prove insufficient.

    ◯ The Doril-T may have prevented side effects caused by the Olanon.

    ◯ Since no side effects were experienced from seven milligrams of Olanon, the new prescription should have called for a greater, not lesser, amount.

    ◯ The question as to why no Doril-T was prescribed is not addressed.

27. Analyst: This corporation is currently putting all its efforts into maximizing short-term profits. Whatever happened to our traditional philosophy of slow, steady growth and emphasis on long-term profitability? One aspect of the problem is seen in simple mathematics. Of our 57 district managers, only 7 have been with the corporation for five years or more. In addition, only 5 of our 16 vice presidents and only 2 of the 9 members of the board of directors have been with the corporation for five years.

    Which of the following conclusions does the author of this passage most probably want the reader to draw?

    ◯ The corporation needs to seek leadership from outside sources if it is to remain profitable in the long run.

    ◯ One of the reasons that the corporation's traditional financial goals have been ignored is that very few of its high-ranking employees have much experience with the corporation.

    ◯ The only reason that the corporation's traditional financial goals have been ignored is that very few of its high-ranking employees have much experience with the corporation.

    ◯ The corporation's traditional financial goals are outmoded.

    ◯ Even though the corporation's traditional financial goals are being ignored, company management has made great strides by bringing in leadership from outside sources.

GO ON TO THE NEXT PAGE ⇨

28. Hubert Humphrey's attempt in his campaign to dissociate <u>himself from the Johnson foreign policies was built around emphasis on Humphrey's Senate career.</u>

    ○ himself from the Johnson foreign policies was built around emphasis on Humphrey's Senate career

    ○ him from the Johnson foreign policies were built around emphasis on Humphrey's Senate career

    ○ him from the Johnson foreign policies was built around emphasis on Humphrey's Senate career

    ○ himself from the Johnson foreign policies were built around emphasis on Humphrey's Senate career

    ○ him from the Johnson foreign policies was built around emphasizing the Senate career of the candidate

29. Since conscious patients often died of shock on the operating table, <u>the invention of anesthesia was essential to the development of surgery as the invention of the propeller was to powered flight.</u>

    ○ the invention of anesthesia was essential to the development of surgery as the invention of the propeller was to powered flight

    ○ inventing anesthesia was as essential for the development of surgery as the invention of the propeller was for powered flight

    ○ the invention of anesthesia was as essential in the development of surgery much as the invention of the propeller had been for powered flight

    ○ the invention of anesthesia was as essential to the development of surgery as the invention of the propeller was to powered flight

    ○ the invention of anesthesia was essential to the development of surgery, so was the invention of the propeller essential to powered flight

30. New evidence suggests that women may react differently than men to high blood pressure, or hypertension. Women with hypertension are less likely to suffer from ensuing complications, such as heart attacks or strokes, and are less likely to die as a result. Women's higher estrogen levels may be related to this phenomenon: After menopause, when estrogen levels lower, women gradually become more and more susceptible to cardiovascular disease.

    Which of the following positions would be best supported by the statements in the passage above?

    ○ Very elderly women with high blood pressure are no less susceptible to complications than their male counterparts are.

    ○ When treating their female patients for hypertension, doctors should take into account whether or not the patient has gone through menopause.

    ○ Men with hypertension should receive immediate treatment, while women with high blood pressure may wait until their condition becomes severe.

    ○ Since women withstand high blood pressure more readily than men do, the benefits they receive from lowering it are relatively insignificant.

    ○ Women with very high blood pressure are as likely to suffer complications from their condition as are men with only slightly elevated blood pressure.

GO ON TO THE NEXT PAGE ▷

KAPLAN

31. Unlike football, which is played on a standardized field, <u>baseball fields vary considerably in both size and shape</u>.

   ○ baseball fields vary considerably in both size and shape

   ○ baseball fields vary considerably, in size as well as in shape

   ○ baseball is played on a field that varies considerably in both size and shape

   ○ baseball is played on fields that vary considerably in both size and shape

   ○ baseball is played on a field that varies considerably in size as well as in shape

32. <u>An important reason to be vaccinated would be that vaccination</u> prevents the spread of infectious diseases, such as cholera, typhoid, and typhus, that are prevalent in areas of the world that lack proper sanitation.

   ○ An important reason to be vaccinated would be that vaccination

   ○ Vaccination is important because it

   ○ An important reason to be vaccinated is because it

   ○ You should be vaccinated and this

   ○ An important reason to be vaccinated is that vaccination

Questions 33-36 refer to the following passage.

Line   A pioneering figure in modern sociology, French social theorist Emile Durkheim examined the role of societal cohesion on emotional well-being. Believing that scientific meth-
(5)   ods should be applied to the study of society, Durkheim studied the level of integration of various social formations and the impact that such cohesion has on individuals within the group. He postulated that social groups with
(10)   high levels of integration serve to buffer their members from frustrations and tragedies that could otherwise lead to desperation and self-destruction. Integration, in Durkheim's view, generally arises through shared activities and
(15)   values.

   Durkheim distinguished between *mechanical solidarity* and *organic solidarity* in classifying integrated groups. *Mechanical solidarity* dominates in groups in which individual
(20)   differences are minimized and group devotion to a common aim is high. Durkheim identified *mechanical solidarity* among groups with little division of labor and high rates of cultural similarity, such as among
(25)   more traditional and geographically isolated groups. *Organic solidarity*, in contrast, prevails in groups with high levels of individual differences, such as those with a highly specialized division of labor. In such groups,
(30)   individual differences are a powerful source of connection, rather than of division. Because people engage in highly differentiated ways of life, they are by necessity interdependent. In such societies, there is greater
(35)   freedom from some external controls, but such freedom occurs in concert with the interdependence of individuals, not in conflict with it.

GO ON TO THE NEXT PAGE ⇨

KAPLAN)

Durkheim realized that societies may take
(40) many forms and consequently that group
allegiance can manifest itself in a variety
of ways. In both types of societies outlined
above, however, Durkheim stressed that
adherence to a common set of assumptions
(45) about the world was a necessary prerequisite
for maintaining group integrity and avoiding
social decay.

33. The author is primarily concerned with

○ supporting a specific approach to the study of
the integration of social groups

○ comparing different ways that group
dynamics maintain allegiance among group
members

○ illustrating how a highly specialized division of labor can protect individuals from
depression

○ helping people determine what type of
society will best suit their emotional needs

○ contrasting a traditional view of a social
phenomenon with a more recent one

34. The passage contrasts *mechanical solidarity* and
organic solidarity along which of the following
parameters?

○ The degree to which each relies on objective
measures of group coherence

○ The manner and degree to which members
are linked to the central group

○ The means by which each allows members to
rebel against the group norm

○ The length of time that each has been used to
describe the structure of societies

○ The effectiveness of each in serving the interests of its members

35. It can be inferred from the passage that

○ as societies develop, they progress from
organic solidarity to *mechanical solidarity*

○ group integration enables societies to mask
internal differences to the external world

○ Durkheim preferred *organic solidarity* to
mechanical solidarity

○ individuals from societies with high degrees
of *organic solidarity* would be unable to
communicate effectively with individuals
from societies that rest on *mechanical
solidarity*

○ the presence of some type of group integration is more important for group
perpetuation than the specific form in which
it is manifest

36. The passage states that *organic solidarity*
predominates in societies with relatively high levels
of intragroup dissimilarity because

○ it enables individual differences to be
minimized

○ it causes societies to become more highly
specialized, thus aiding industrialization

○ individuals who engage in highly specialized
activities must rely on others to ensure that
their basic needs are met

○ these societies are at greater risk of being
affected by social stressors

○ these societies are more likely to engage in
shared activities and values

GO ON TO THE NEXT PAGE ⟩

KAPLAN)

37. The impact of the 1930s crisis on the different regions of Country X varied depending on the relationship of each region's economy to the international marketplace, with Region A most drastically affected. Interestingly, demand in foreign markets for Region A's tropical crops was only slightly affected by the drop in income levels after 1929; the same was true of foreign demand for the temperate-zone basic foodstuffs produced by Region B. However, Region B was better able to survive the crisis because it could adjust the supply of its crops. Since Region A could not, its economy was devastated by the slight decrease in foreign demand.

    Which one of the following provides the most reasonable explanation for the fact that Region A's economy was more drastically affected by the slight decrease in demand than was Region B's?

    ⬭ Tropical crops like those produced by Region A usually command higher prices on the world market than do basic foodstuffs like those produced by Region B.

    ⬭ Region B's economy was dependent on annual crops, the supply of which is easily adjusted because the plants are renewed each year, in contrast to the perennial crops grown in Region A.

    ⬭ Because tropical goods are generally bought by more affluent consumers, demand for these products rarely declines even when overall income levels drop.

    ⬭ The temperate-zone basic foodstuffs produced in Region B directly competed with similar crops produced by the countries that imported Region B's goods.

    ⬭ Because Region B's economy was dependent on the export of basic foodstuffs, there was only a slight decline in demand for its goods even after income levels dropped.

38. Through their selective funding of research projects, pharmaceutical companies exert too much influence upon medical research in universities. Only research proposals promising lucrative results are given serious consideration, and funding is usually awarded to scientists at large institutions who already have vast research experience. As a result, only larger universities will be able to continue developing adequate research facilities, and graduate students will learn that their future research must conform to the expectations of the corporation. Research will continue to be conducted at the expense of human welfare.

    The reasoning of the argument above depends upon which of the following assumptions?

    ⬭ As universities become primarily research institutions, teaching will be neglected.

    ⬭ Graduate students are not motivated by humane interests.

    ⬭ Smaller universities would be better suited to serve as product development laboratories for pharmaceutical companies.

    ⬭ Medical research should be funded by government-regulated foundations.

    ⬭ The interests of pharmaceutical companies and human welfare are usually incompatible in research.

GO ON TO THE NEXT PAGE ⟹

39. <u>Prosecutors use a reliable forensic method, graphology, in forgery cases, which may also be used by</u> employers to uncover clues to prospective employees' characters.

    ◯ Prosecutors use a reliable forensic method, graphology, in forgery cases, which may also be used by

    ◯ Prosecutors in forgery cases that have used graphology as a reliable forensic method and may also be used by

    ◯ Graphology, a reliable forensic method used by prosecutors in forgery cases, may also be used by

    ◯ As a reliable forensic method, prosecutors use graphology in forgery cases, which may also be used by

    ◯ Prosecutors which use graphology in forgery cases, a reliably forensic method may also be used by

40. Until recently, parents whose teenaged child had signed a purchase contract <u>without their written agreement were not</u> liable for the child's debt.

    ◯ without their written agreement were not

    ◯ that they do not agree in writing have not been

    ◯ and they had not agreed in writing had not been

    ◯ without them agreeing in writing had not been

    ◯ without their written agreement are not

41. The state legislature has proposed a law that requires all new cars sold in the state to be equipped with air bags for both front seat passengers. The auto industry has lobbied against the proposed law, pointing out that front seat air bags would prevent only a small percentage of serious injuries, since in most accidents, serious injuries are avoidable by the use of seat belts.

    Which of the following, if true, would most weaken the argument put forth by the auto industry?

    ◯ The government has a duty to protect the welfare of its citizens.

    ◯ The number of accidents per mile driven in the state is substantially higher than that for the rest of the nation.

    ◯ The cost of equipping automobiles with air bags will be passed on to the consumer in the form of higher prices.

    ◯ Most serious injuries occur when front seat passengers are not wearing their seat belts.

    ◯ Because the law would apply only to new cars, it would take nearly a decade for the majority of the state's cars to become equipped with air bags.

KAPLAN

ANSWERS AND EXPLANATIONS

1.	B	22.	C
2.	A	23.	A
3.	D	24.	E
4.	C	25.	A
5.	E	26.	C
6.	B	27.	B
7.	D	28.	A
8.	E	29.	D
9.	D	30.	B
10.	D	31.	D
11.	C	32.	B
12.	E	33.	B
13.	B	34.	B
14.	D	35.	E
15.	E	36.	C
16.	C	37.	B
17.	B	38.	E
18.	A	39.	C
19.	E	40.	A
20.	E	41.	D
21.	B		

1.   B

In (A), "the theory of land mammals returning" is awkward; "the theory that land mammals returned" is better. (C) and (E) make the same mistake as (A) with "theory of." (E) also talks about "evidence of support for the theory" when it should say "evidence in support of the theory." So (A), (C), and (E) all use incorrect prepositions. (D) has the unnecessary words "that they." (B) makes the sentence short and to the point.

2.   A

First, since the sentence starts with "although," "whereas" in (C) is redundant. Now we can concentrate on parallelism. The plural "modern roller coasters" should not be compared with the singular "the old-fashioned roller coaster," so (B) is wrong. Choice (D) leaves the sentence with no main verb. This brings us to (A) and (E). Choice (E) may not seem too bad, but (A), "have more and longer straight drops," is clearer than (E) and more strictly parallel to the first part of the sentence.

3.   D

The Conclusion: The governor's survey on solid waste disposal must have had skewed results.

The Evidence: Eighty percent of respondents support a rise in spending for environmentally safe disposal of solid waste.

The author assumes that most people who respond to this kind of survey will favor environmental safety—she's arguing that the respondents weren't representative of the population as a whole.

The author doesn't think that only environmentalists received the survey, (A), but that a disproportionate number of respondents are environmentalists. She isn't criticizing the judgment of "most citizens," (B). It's not that there's a problem with the survey itself, (C), but with the interpretation of the survey. And we don't know anything about the author's opinion on solid waste issues, (E).

4.   C

The Conclusion: People aren't cheating on their taxes as much as they used to.

The Evidence: The amount, in dollars, of taxes collected from personal income tax has gone up appreciably in recent years.

We're only concerned with revenue from the personal income tax, so any information about the corporate taxes is outside the realm of our interest.

All the wrong choices provide alternative explanations—explanations as to how we can have more tax dollars collected without people being more honest in reporting their incomes. Fewer deductions, (A), would probably cause people to pay more money in taxes. A population increase, (B), would produce more tax payers. If average income went up, (D), then average tax paid would go up as well. And if the tax rate rose, (E), the government would very likely collect more money.

PASSAGE 1—FORSET

Topic and Scope: A worldview prevalent in post-Reformation England.

Purpose and Main Idea: The author says that many English people after the Reformation conceived of the world as a system of hierarchies, in which the king's or queen's position as ruler is part of the natural order of things, and reflects God's plan.

Paragraph Structure: In a single paragraph, the author explains why early English Protestants hungered for order, and how the concept of order that some thinkers came up with coincided with the will of the British monarchs.

5.   E

(E) is a fairly direct paraphrase of the idea stated in the passage's opening sentence, with the added (but easy) inference that the Catholic Church formerly provided structure and stability to English society. There is nothing to suggest (A), that the monarchy was declining. Quite the contrary, according to the rest of the passage: Elizabeth and other monarchs managed quite well to maintain their grip on power, at least temporarily. The passage also implies something contrary to (B); rather than being seen as eccentric or peculiar, the "divinely inspired" hierarchical view of Forset and other thinkers won wide acceptance. Contrary to (C), the need for order was felt to be "compelling," as it's put in the first sentence. As for (D), there's no evidence for this idea. The passage mentions the Catholic Church simply as having been rejected, nothing more.

6.   B

This choice puts together the idea of hierarchy, as found in Forset and other thinkers, with the statement in the last sentence that people accepted stability as God's will. The implication is that Elizabeth and her successors maintained their influence and power because English society accepted the idea of a divinely prescribed social structure in which the monarch occupied the top of the social heap. Choice (A) exaggerates the role of the thinkers. Yes, they apparently had the ear of the public, but to say they were a small group that had tight, almost conspiratorial control is too extreme. It's inconsistent with the passage's tone. (C) puts things backwards; as the sentence about Elizabeth and Parliament make clear, the monarchs claimed a position far above that of most people. That same sentence also makes clear that Parliament, while apparently not mounting effective resistance to Elizabeth, was nonetheless "recalcitrant," not passive. Finally, (E) could be true, but there is nothing to suggest it in the passage; what the passage does do is tie Elizabeth's success to the idea of divine sanction for social hierarchy, and this should lead you back to correct choice (B).

7.   D

This choice is supported by two references in the passage. The first is the reference to a "recalcitrant Parliament"; the second is the veiled suggestion in the last sentence that there were restive elements in English society that had to be held down or kept in check by the monarchy, and that the English public's interim acceptance of a divine hierarchical scheme aided the monarchy in this situation. This choice completes the thought by adding the plausible idea that Parliament represented these rebellious interests. The other choices all fail, in one way or another, to follow the logic of the passage's ideas. Choice (A) contradicts the last sentence's suggestion that the monarchs' grip on power was short-lived. (B) contradicts the widespread acceptance and immediate influence of Forset's notions. (C) is inconsistent with the apparent opposition of Parliament to a political hierarchy in which the monarch was the unquestioned authority. (E), lastly, illogically pits Elizabeth against her staunch advocate, Forset. (In fact, though the passage doesn't mention it, Elizabeth was dead by the time Forset wrote his tract.)

8. E

The Conclusion: Critics' opinions aren't any more reliable than those of the average person.

The Evidence: Critics tend to have similar points of view that are rooted in the prejudices of their class.

The author seems to believe that critics' opinions aren't necessarily more significant than those of the average Joe, so (E), a restatement of the main idea, is easy to conclude. Their opinions are no more likely to be a guide to quality, so when they disagree with the public, they're no more likely to be right.

Though the author says that critics' opinions aren't more correct than those of average moviegoers, he doesn't imply that they're usually incorrect, (A). It's not that there are no right or wrong judgments about films, (B), but that critics don't always make the right judgments. We don't know how frequently critics dislike popular movies, (C), just that it's often assumed that they have valid reasons for doing so. And (D), that critics agree about any given movie, is too strong, since the author only says that their opinions tend to reflect certain class prejudices.

9. D

The Conclusion: (as stated in the stem) The club won't raise enough money from their plan to ask alumni for donations.

The Evidence: Similar plans have been tried in the past, and the clubhouse is still in bad shape.

The author is predicting that the plan won't work because it didn't work in the past.

An analogy, (A), would be a comparison, but there's no comparison made here. You may have thought of the argument as an analogy from past to future, but (D) is a much better description of this. The author has no opponents that we know about, so (B) and (E) are somewhat far-fetched. The author does point out past failures of alumni fund-raising, but there's no logical connection drawn by the club members between those attempts and this one, and so no fallacy, (C).

10. D

The second clause as it stands fails to clearly refer to the action of the first clause. It would be better to have said "which LBJ also did," but that still isn't correct. In this case, "as did" is proper, not "which did." (A) and (B) use the unidiomatic "which." (C) lacks a second verb. In (E), "do"

is redundant. (D) is correct because it repeats the verb: Kennedy increased, as did Johnson. "Did" correctly stands for the entire phrase "increased the participation of the United States in the war in Vietnam."

11. C

You should never say "the reason . . . was because." This rules out (A) and (D). A possessive form of a noun, like "Scipio Africanus'," cannot be the antecedent of a pronoun, so (B) is wrong. "The reason being" in (E) is unnecessarily wordy.

12. E

"Need for . . . to be" is one of those locutions that seems to pop up a lot on long and unwieldy sentence corrections. You can't say "a need that," so get rid of (A). A quick scan shows that (C) and (D) have the same problem as (A). They're just not idiomatically correct. (B) is illogical. The need isn't for pine and flax that "are made" into masts and sails. If the need had been for pine and flax in a ready-made form, then the correct way to say it would be "were made," not "are made," because we are talking about the past. The need was for pine and flax "to be made" into masts and sails, indicating what was to be done with the materials. That makes (E) the best choice. Even if you couldn't narrow it to one, knowledge of the idiom would allow you to eliminate three choices.

PASSAGE 2—GROUP MANAGEMENT

Topic and Scope: The value of group management; specifically, the benefits and risks of using decisional conflict in group management.

Purpose and Main Idea: Author agrees that building conflict into group management is good (it leads to better managerial decisions), but stresses that there are potential risks. Experts are divided over what form of decisional conflict is best (and least risky).

Paragraph Structure: Paragraph 1 acknowledges the value of group decision making and the use of decisional conflict, and identifies the risks, the "dilemma," involved in using decisional conflict: "Decisional conflict may yield better decisions at the risk of weakening managerial effectiveness. Conversely, the harmony that facilitates cooperation and implementation may come at the cost of inferior decisions."

Paragraph 2 identifies two methods of building conflict into group decisions (dialectical inquiry and devil's advocacy) and explains the similarities and differences. Paragraph 3 explains how experts disagree about which approach is better.

13. B

Choice (B) covers all the paragraphs. Paragraph 1 discusses the benefits and risks of decisional conflict, and paragraphs 2 and 3 focus on the two alternative approaches.

(A) ignores the discussion of the *risks* of decisional conflict. And the author never tries to "reconcile" the two approaches. The verb "defend" makes choice (C) suspect; the author never defends anything against critics. (D) doesn't work because the author never implies that group decision making is better than any other approach. As for (E), the author never indicates a preference for dialectical inquiry or devil's advocacy.

14. D

Paragraph 2 details similarities as well as differences between the two approaches. One similarity is that both rely on "formal debate," which clearly implies choice (D).

(A) is an irrelevant detail; the only mention of "compromise" is at the end of the passage where Cosier charges that dialectical inquiry could lead to compromises and inferior decisions. The problem with (B) is that only dialectical inquiry involves "opposing sets of proposals." (C) and (E), like (A), refer to irrelevant details in the last paragraph.

Note: Even without a line reference, the stem must steer you to paragraph 2. After a fast, *strategic* skimming of the passage, you should be equipped to recognize where the answer will be found.

15. E

You need the choice that's *inconsistent* with one of Cosier's criticisms, one of which is that dialectical inquiry "may run counter to managers' accustomed ways of thinking." (E) would cast doubt on this criticism: "Managers willing to alter their usual modes of thinking often make better decisions."

(A) doesn't work because it paraphrases—and therefore would support—one of Cosier's criticisms. With (B), Cosier implies nothing about "demanding that managers agree" about a decision. Choice (C) is a point that Cosier and everyone else connected with this passage would agree with. (D), like (B), is an irrelevant point; Cosier says nothing about the need for some decisions to be made rapidly.

16. C

Application questions like this one ask you to recognize a choice that's consistent with information in the passage. (C) parallels the passage's *basic idea* about management groups: The opening sentence states that "corporate managers often work in groups because of the complexity of strategic problems." In a similar way, in (C), "a committee of administrators forms to address the major problems of running a hospital." The hospital is a type of corporation, and its administrators work as a group to solve its problems.

None of the other choices supplies a parallel situation: monitoring election results, (A), investigating governmental misconduct, (B), studying an issue of public concern, (D), and observing a college presidential search, (E), are all different from running a corporation.

17. B

The Conclusion: Money spent to make the workplace more pleasant is the cause of stumbling and failing businesses.

The Evidence: New businesses almost always fail, and many established businesses show little or no profit. Workers want expensive perks like paint and radios.

The assumption here is that providing these niceties works only to the detriment or disadvantage of the businesses—that it's as simple as spending money and getting no return. We weaken the argument by denying this assumption, and showing that the perks increase productivity. In this case, the new paint, radios, and artwork might well be a wise investment.

Even if the workers work very hard, (A), it doesn't mean that they don't make excessive demands on their employers. It could be possible that in the past businesses went under for other reasons, (C), and yet still be true that they are now going under because of the perks. The author hasn't claimed that different types of businesses are the same thing, as in (D) and (E), but rather, that they're in trouble for the same reason.

18. A

The underlined part of the sentence is a modifying phrase; what's modified is "islands." Choice (D) gives us a run-on sentence. Choices (B) and (E) use pronouns in a confusing way. Choice (C) is just plain awkward.

PASSAGE 3—DINOSAUR EXTINCTION

Topic and Scope: The extinction of the dinosaur; specifically, recent findings suggest that the extinction was caused by "a sudden, catastrophic event" (paragraph 1).

Purpose and Main Idea: Author outlines new findings and theories that run counter to the old notion ("Scientists long believed . . . ," line 1) that the extinction resulted from gradual climate changes. Scientists differ about the exact type of event, but agree that a collision between earth and some kind of extraterrestrial body caused an environmental catastrophe that led to extinction.

Paragraph Structure: Paragraph 1: The opening two sentences are key; the discoveries in Italy led to a revision of the old view that the extinction resulted from gradual climate changes. The remainder of this paragraph—everything about iridium levels—is supporting detail. Skim confidently! Let the questions dictate a closer reading. Paragraph 2: The gist here is simply that "scientists differ over the exact nature of the event" (the opening line). All else should be skimmed. Paragraph 3: An objection is raised, then rebutted. Paragraph 4: The summary of what the Berkeley group believes, that the collision led to a massive disruption in the global food chain, which led to the demise of the dinosaurs.

19. E

Paragraph 1 discusses the discovery of high iridium levels in Italy and other locales, and the remaining paragraphs discuss the implications of that notable discovery. (E) expresses this in shorthand form.

(A) is too narrow. Paragraph 2 cites varying opinions, but that's the focus of one paragraph only. In (B), "rebutting" doesn't fit; it's too strong. It's true that the older belief about gradual climatic changes is outdated, but the passage's purpose isn't to "rebut." It's to describe new findings and their significance. Contrary to (C), the methodology of the Berkeley group is never described as "controversial." Nor does the passage "evaluate" the methodology. As for (D), the passage never suggests "a new course of investigation."

20. E

The point is clear from the cited sentence: The lack of the isotopes indicated to scientists that the iridium levels *did not* result from a stellar explosion. (E) is a clear paraphrase of that information.

The "older theory about the extinction of the dinosaur," choice (A), is an irrelevant detail from the previous paragraph. The passage says nothing about the isotope level being useful for dating purposes,(B). (C) misses the point. The question wasn't whether or not iridium originated extraterrestrially, but whether the specific source was an exploding star. The blockage of sunlight, (D), is another unrelated detail, from the final paragraph.

21. B

(B) jibes with information in the final paragraph. The Berkeley group believes that the main effect of the collision was the blockage of sunlight and a drop in photosynthesis. This would be reflected in a drop in plant fossils in strata younger than those studied in Italy.

Strata *older than* the iridium-rich level would not affect the argument of the Berkeley group, (A). The discovery of high iridium levels above and below the enriched clay layer, (C), would tend to raise questions about, not strengthen, the Berkeley group's findings. As for (D), the Berkeley group's argument is that an event *of some kind* led to a massive ecological disruption. Whether the collision involved an asteroid or a comet is secondary. Finally, a finding that the clay layer was deposited gradually, (E), would weaken the Berkeley group's thesis.

22. C

One way to start with this sentence is to try to figure out what's most important. Joe Kittinger seems to have done two equally important things: he set a distance record and he became the first balloonist to cross the Atlantic solo. Choice (C) puts these two achievements on an equal footing by expressing them both in participial phrases ("setting" and "becoming"). So does (E), but it omits the "and," which is necessary. Choices (A), (B), and (D) fail to make it clear that it was by piloting his balloon from Maine to Italy that Kittinger accomplished these two things.

23. A

First, "crises" is the plural form of "crisis," so (B), with the singular verb "does," is wrong. Next, "do not always result from malice" in (A) and "aren't always the results of malice" in (D) are both fine, but "do not always result of malice" in (C) is unidiomatic, and "aren't resulting always from malice" in (E) is awkward. Now let's look at the second part of the sentence. Remember that the part on each side of the semicolon must be an independent clause. All of the answer choices except (A) either fail to provide a main verb for the second clause, like (B), (D), and (E), or use unidiomatic expressions, like (B) and (C).

24. E

The problem here has to do with the placement of the modifier. What is caused by the desire to be as thin as possible? Not good eating habits, though that's the impression you could get from (A), and not the ballet dancers and gymnasts, though that's the impression you could get from (B). Eliminate both of these choices. And who or what desires to be as thin as possible? Again, not good eating habits, though you could get that impression from (C) or (D), both of which use the passive voice unnecessarily and indeed confusingly. The correct answer is (E), in which pronoun reference and the placement of modifiers are perfectly clear.

25. A

The Conclusion: Actors from the agency are being sent to audition for roles that are inappropriate for them.

The Evidence: Few actors from the agency are being placed in roles.

The agent must assume that certain actors are inappropriate for certain parts. If she didn't believe this, the argument would make no sense because it wouldn't be possible for an actor to audition for an inappropriate part.

The actors' talent (B) isn't questioned by the agent; she focuses on the types of roles. That it's hard to predict an actor's appropriateness, (C), needn't be assumed—it has no effect on the argument. She could, on the contrary, think it easy to judge a role's appropriateness, and just believe that her company employs incompetents. Major roles, (D), are outside the scope, since the agent doesn't mention them. And if it were true that directors often cast the wrong actors, (E), then the idea that the agency isn't doing well because it's doing just that—sending out the wrong actors—wouldn't wash.

26. C

The Doctor's Conclusion: The patient doesn't need to take Doril-T, the side-effect preventing drug.

The Doctor's Evidence: Since the patient didn't have side effects on 7 mg of Olanon, he won't have side effects on 2 mg.

What's the doctor missing here? The idea that the patient probably didn't have side effects on 7 mg because he was taking the Doril-T, the drug intended to prevent side effects. The doctor basically assumes that this drug had no effect, yet presents no evidence.

The doctor seems to believe, (A), that the smaller the amount taken, the less likelihood of side effects—so this isn't a flaw. We don't know and can't assume that the two drugs work together, (B), to produce the desired effect. Why would the doctor prescribe more Olanon, (D)? We're not doctors, so we can't argue this. And (E) is just plain false, since the doctor does describe why no Doril-T was prescribed—because the patient hasn't had side effects.

27. B

The Analyst's Conclusion: The company is moving away from its long-term growth commitment and putting all its eggs into the short-term profits basket.

Her Evidence: Few of the company's top managers have been with the company for more than five years.

What does the author want you to think about all of this? That these "newcomers" have caused the shift in emphasis, and thus, traditional values have been ignored. Otherwise, why argue for the shift in policy by pointing to the relatively short tenure of many of the top managers?

The author wouldn't advocate bringing in more newcomers, (A), since she thinks that they've caused all the trouble. We shouldn't go too far, however, by concluding that the newcomers are the only reason for the trouble, (C), especially since she refers to them as "one aspect of the problem." The author yearns for the traditional values, so she wouldn't want to convince us that they are outmoded, (D). And strong support for the company's hiring of newcomers, (E), is counter to the apparent feelings of our author.

28. A

This sentence talks about what Humphrey attempted to do to Humphrey, so we need the reflexive pronoun: "himself," not "him." We can rule out (B), (C), and (E). Now, "attempt," the noun, is singular, so it has to govern a singular verb: "was," not "were."

29. D

This sentence makes a comparison, so the correct answer will use the "as . . . as" formula. The first "as" is missing in (A). Choice (C) turns the second "as" into "much as," which spoils the construction. Choice (E) omits the "as . . . as" formula altogether, and creates a run-on sentence. You should also remember that the things being compared should be in parallel form, and this is not the case in (B).

30. B

The Conclusion: That's what we're looking for.

The Evidence: Women with high blood pressure are less likely to have heart attacks or strokes than are men with the same condition. This may be related to estrogen levels— after menopause, when estrogen is lowered, women are more likely to get cardiovascular disease.

What can we conclude? That doctors would be wise to take into account whether their female patients are pre- or post-menopausal, since estrogen levels will probably have an effect on their treatment needs. Perfectly reasonable.

We don't have any information that would allow us to conclude (A), that old women are as susceptible as old men, or that (E), women with very high blood pressure face the same risks as men with only slightly high blood pressure. In addition, we can't go so far as to claim that women can wait for treatment, (C). (D) is another distortion. Even though women are less likely to suffer complications from high blood pressure, we can't infer that they receive almost no benefit from lowering their high blood pressure.

31. D

Here's another comparison. Start by making sure that it's logical. Football can be compared with baseball, but not with baseball fields. This eliminates (A) and (B). And of course, a single field cannot vary in size and shape; it is different fields that vary. Since (D) uses the plural "fields," it is the correct answer.

32. B

Would be? No, it is; eliminate (A). "The reason . . . is because," in (C), is unidiomatic. In (D), there is no clear antecedent for "this." This brings us to (B) and (E). Choice (E) is unnecessarily long.

PASSAGE 4—DURKHEIM

Topic and Scope: Emile Durkheim's study of social cohesion in society.

Purpose and Main Idea: To describe two different ways that societies can maintain social integration among their members.

Paragraph Structure: The first paragraph introduces Durkheim and his study of social groups. The second paragraph discusses two ways societies can maintain social integration. The third paragraph offers a broader context for interpreting the evidence in the second paragraph.

33. B

The final paragraph gives you the key to answering this global question. The author is describing different ways that societies can function without choosing a side or advocating a specific position. You can rule out choice (A) immediately for its strong stand. Choice (C) distorts a detail beyond its acceptable scope. While the passage does discuss how social cohesion can function in societies with high degrees of labor specialization, this is not the author's main goal. Choice (D) takes a prescriptive stance, and the author never tells us how to live our lives. Finally, choice (E) makes a comparison that is not there. Both of the mechanisms for maintaining social solidarity were developed by Durkheim at the same time and are part of the same worldview, namely, his. The comparison between a traditional and a recent view is inapplicable here.

34. B

What is the crucial difference between *mechanical solidarity* and *organic solidarity*? The level of homogeneity in the group in which each functions. Neither one relies on any measure, objective or otherwise, of group coherence. Rather, they describe the way societies function naturally, ruling out choice (A). Choice (C) introduces the notion of rebellion, a concept that is not mentioned in the passage and, hence, cannot be correct. Choice (D) is wrong because the two types of solidarity were developed at the same time by Durkheim; we do not have a traditional view and a more recent view of the same phenomenon, but rather two different ways that societies can function within the same worldview. Choice (E) brings into question the effectiveness of each, and the last paragraph makes it clear that either one can serve its members' needs equally well.

35. E

In this inference question, you will need to think about the author's opinion as you approach the answer choices. Choice (A) is wrong because the author never discusses the two forms of *solidarity* as being related to each other, nor does he discuss the transformation of societies over time. Choice (B) is outside the scope, as the relationship of individual societies to the world at large is not an issue that concerns the author. Choice (C) makes a subjective statement about Durkheim that is never suggested by the passage. Choice (D) makes a comparison between the two types of social groups that is not supported by the passage. Choice (E), however, is basically stated verbatim in the final paragraph of the passage. The particular type of integration that exists within a given society is less important than that it is present in some form.

36. C

Look to the second paragraph, where *organic solidarity* is discussed, and you will see Durkheim's reasoning for why it exists in societies with high levels of heterogeneity. *Organic solidarity* prevails in societies with fewer similarities among members, because when a society is highly specialized, its members rely on each other out of necessity, as a way to ensure that everyone's needs are met. Reading through the answers, choice (C) should jump out at you as conveying this sentiment.

Choice (A) is *au contraire.* In societies in which *organic solidarity* dominates, individual differences are relatively high. Choice (B) implies a causal relationship between *organic solidarity* and the way a society is organized, but *organic solidarity* is simply a term to describe the way a society *is* functioning; it is not an active agent of anything. Choice (D) uses information that was never mentioned in the passage—namely, that some societies are more likely to be affected by social stressors. Finally, choice (E) misappropriates information from the section on societies in which *mechanical solidarity* dominates. Societies that operate by *organic solidarity*, by contrast, tend not to comprise members who lead highly similar lives.

37. B

Because the question stem says we are looking for an *explanation*, this is an Explain question.

The two facts presented in the stimulus are (1) demand for the crops produced by Region A and for those produced by Region B dropped only slightly and (2) Region B was better able to survive the crisis, while Region A's economy was devastated. Interestingly, the stimulus already seems to give part of the answer, signified by the keyword *because*—"[Region B] could adjust the supply of its crops." We might well predict that this ability will play an important part in the correct explanation.

(A) might seem to explain Region A's difficulty in an economic crisis. But the stimulus says that demand fell only slightly for Region A's foodstuffs and that the demand for Region B's dropped by the same amount. So (A) is irrelevant.

(B) shows us why Region B can adjust the supply of its crops and Region A cannot. Even if you don't know what *perennial* means, the answer choice explicitly says that such crops cannot be easily adjusted. It completes the explanation begun in the stimulus and is, therefore, the correct answer.

(C) explains why one might expect Region A to do well in an economic downturn, so it hardly constitutes an explanation for why it didn't. (D), if anything, would explain why Region B did poorly, not well. (E) is consistent with only part of the facts. It shows why Region B's demand didn't fall much, but we know that Region A's demand was affected similarly. So this answer doesn't explain the differing fortunes of the two region's economies.

38. E

We need an assumption, and if we compare evidence and conclusion (including the author's dire prediction), we find an element for which there's no evidence: the idea of "human welfare." The author must be assuming that the interests of these companies and human welfare are usually at odds in order to conclude that research conducted in the interests of the companies won't be compatible with human welfare.

The quality of university teaching, (A), has nothing to do with this argument. The author doesn't argue that grad students aren't interested in humane pursuits, (B), but rather that they must conform to the companies' expectations. That smaller universities are better for research from the companies' perspective, (C), is way off—the companies, we're told, are only funding the larger universities. And government-regulated foundations, (D), are outside the scope. The author may well believe that some other type of funding is needed, but this particular remedy is not required by the argument.

39. C

(A) and (D) make it seem as if it's forgery cases "which may be used by employers to uncover clues to prospective employees' characters." But the employers are really using graphology to do this. (C) clarifies the sentence. (B) is incomplete and nonsensical. (E) makes it sound as if forgery cases are a forensic method.

40. A

The nonunderlined verb "had signed" lets you know you're talking about the past. So (E)'s definitely out. The child didn't sign a "contract that they do not agree," so (B) can't be right. In (C) and (D), the phrases "and they had not agreed in writing," and "without them agreeing in writing," are unclear. They make it sound as if the parents need to agree with each other. In (A), "without their agreement" makes it clear that the parents are agreeing to the contract.

41. D

The Auto Industry's Conclusion: Putting air bags in cars won't make much difference in preventing injuries.

Its Evidence: In most accidents, injuries are avoidable through the use of seat belts.

In moving from evidence to conclusion, the auto industry is assuming that seat belts *do*, not just *can*, prevent most serious injuries. We break the link by showing that lots of injuries occur when people don't wear belts. So air bags will, in fact, prevent injuries because although the belts *would* work, they *aren't used*.

The industry could agree with (A)'s general principle that the government has to protect people without thereby weakening its argument. Evidence about this particular state, (B), is irrelevant to an argument about the protective power of air bags in general. The high cost of air bags, (C), would be more evidence for the auto industry's argument: assuming they won't prevent many injuries, why charge consumers for them? And (E)'s idea that it will take a long time for most cars to get air bags has no effect: this tells us that whether the bags are a good idea or not, it'll take a while to get it into practice.

PART FIVE

Analytical Writing Assessment

Chapter 6: **Analytical Writing Assessment (AWA) Strategies and Practice**

The AWA is the first task on the GMAT. After you are situated at your computer workstation, you will be presented with the two essay assignments: an Argument essay and an Issue essay. You will have 30 minutes to complete each.

For both essays, you will have to analyze a given topic and then type your essay into a simple word processing program. It allows you to do only basic functions:

- Insert text.
- Delete text.
- Cut and paste.
- Undo the previous action.
- Scroll up and down on the screen.

Spell-check and grammar-check functions are not available in the program, so you will have to check those things carefully yourself.

Thirty minutes is not enough time to produce the same kind of essay you'd write for a college class. Nor is it enough time to do a lot of trial and error as you type. It is, however, enough time to write a "strong first draft" if you plan it carefully, and that's what the essay graders are looking for.

The Argument essay always comes first, the Issue essay second. After the essays, you'll get an eight-minute break before the Quantitative section begins.

ESSAY FORMAT AND STRUCTURE

At the start of the AWA, you'll be given a brief tutorial on how to use the word processor. If you are concerned that you do not type very fast, you should spend some time practicing with full-page text documents between now and test day.

Analysis of an Argument Essay

The first assignment is the Argument essay. Your task is to assess the logic and use of evidence in an argument. It doesn't matter whether you agree or disagree with the argument's conclusion. Rather, you need to explain the ways in which the author has failed to fully support that conclusion.

Let's take a look at a sample prompt:

The following appeared in a memo from the CEO of Hula Burger, a chain of hamburger restaurants.

"Officials in the film industry report that over 60% of the films released last year targeted an age 8–12 audience. Moreover, sales data indicate that, nationally, hamburgers are the favorite food among this age group. Since a branch store of Whiz Vid Video Store opened in town last year, hamburger sales at our restaurant next door have been higher than at any other restaurant in our chain. Because the rental of movies seems to stimulate hamburger sales, the best way to increase our profits is to open new Hula Burger restaurants right nearby every Whiz Vid Store."

Discuss how well reasoned you find this argument. In your discussion, be sure to analyze the line of reasoning and the use of evidence in the argument. For example, you may need to consider what questionable assumptions underlie the thinking and what alternative explanations or counterexamples might weaken the conclusion. You can also discuss what sort of evidence would strengthen or refute the argument, what changes in the argument would make it more logically sound, and what, if anything, would help you better evaluate its conclusion.

Where are the holes in the argument? In what ways does it fail to be completely convincing? Why might the plan fail? Not only do you have to identify its major weaknesses, you must also explain them.

Analysis of an Issue Essay

For the Issue essay, you will be given a statement that expresses an opinion (sometimes two) about something. Your task is to communicate your views on the issue. Whether you agree or disagree with the opinion given in the essay prompt is irrelevant—there is no "right answer." What matters is how well how support your view.

Here's a sample Issue prompt:

"Everyone in the country over the age of 12 should be required to perform a minimum amount of public service. Such a required contribution would not only help society as a whole, but it would also add to the individual's character."

Discuss the extent to which you agree or disagree with the opinion stated above. Support your views with reasons and/or examples from your own experience, observations, or reading.

Although you must take a side (Should everyone—even children—be required to perform public service? Or not?), it doesn't matter which side you take. What matters is whether your argument is convincing. Can you come up with good reasons why your side is correct and explain your reasoning with relevant examples?

THE BASIC PRINCIPLES OF ANALYTICAL WRITING

You aren't just being evaluated on the strength of your ideas. Your score will also depend on how well you express them. If your writing style isn't clear, your ideas won't come across, no matter how brilliant they are.

Good essay writing isn't just grammatically correct. It is also clear and concise. The following principles will help you express your ideas in good GMAT style.

Your Control of Language Is Important

Writing that is grammatical, concise, direct, and persuasive displays the "superior control of language" (as the test makers term it) that earns top GMAT Analytical Writing scores. To achieve effective GMAT style in your essays, you should pay attention to the following points.

Grammar

Your writing must follow the same general rules of standard written English that are tested by Sentence Correction questions. If you're not confident of your mastery of grammar, review the Sentence Correction section.

Diction

Diction means word choice. Do you use the words *affect* and *effect* correctly? What about *its* and *it's*, *there* and *their*, *precede* and *proceed*, *principal* and *principle*, and *whose* and *who's*?

Syntax

Syntax refers to sentence structure. Do you construct your sentences so that your ideas are clear and understandable? Do you vary your sentence structure?

Keep Things Simple

Perhaps the single most important thing to bear in mind when writing a GMAT essay is to keep everything simple. This rule applies to word choice, sentence structure, and organization. If you obsess about how to spell an unusual word, you can lose your way. The more complicated your sentences are, the more likely they'll be plagued by errors. The more complex your organization gets, the more likely your argument will get bogged down in convoluted sentences that obscure your point.

Keep in mind that simple does not mean *simplistic*. A clear, straightforward approach can still be sophisticated and convey perceptive insights.

Minor Grammatical Flaws Won't Harm Your Score

Many test takers mistakenly believe they'll lose points over a few mechanical errors. That's not the case. GMAT essays should be final first drafts. This means that a couple of misplaced commas, misspellings, or other minor glitches aren't going to affect your score. Occasional mistakes of this type are acceptable. In fact, according to the scoring rubric, a top-scoring essay may well have a few minor grammatical flaws.

But if your essays are littered with misspellings and grammar mistakes, the graders may conclude that you have a serious communication problem.

So be concise, forceful, and correct. An effective essay wastes no words; makes its point in a clear, direct way; and conforms to the generally accepted rules of grammar and form.

Use a Logical Structure

Good essays have a straightforward, linear structure. The problem is that we rarely think in a straightforward, linear way. That's why it's so important to plan your response before you begin typing. If you write *while* planning, your essay will likely loop back on itself, contain redundancies, or fail to follow through on the ideas it sets up.

Logical structure consists of three things:

1. **Paragraph unity.** Paragraph unity means each paragraph discusses one thing and all the discussion of that one thing happens in that paragraph. Let's say that you're responding to the issue essay example we just saw and one of your points was that involuntary service might build resentment instead of character. The next paragraph should move on to another idea—perhaps something about the appropriateness of forcing a 12-year-old into work. If, in the middle of that next paragraph, you went back to your resentment point, you'd be violating paragraph unity.
2. **Train of thought.** This is similar to paragraph unity, but it applies to the whole essay. It's awkward to keep jumping back and forth between the different sides of an issue, for example. Lay out the support for one side fully, then address the other. Don't write another paragraph about a topic you've already discussed.
3. **Flow.** The basic idea of flow is that you should deliver on what you promise and not radically change the subject. If your intro says that you will mention reasons why Hula burgers might be less popular among the 8- to 12-year-old demographic than regular hamburgers are, you need to make sure that you actually do so. Similarly, avoid suddenly expanding the scope of the essay in the last sentence.

HOW THE AWA IS SCORED

Your essays will be graded on a scale from 0 to 6 (highest). You'll get one score, which will be an average of the scores that you receive for each of the two essays, rounded up to the nearest half point. Your essay will be graded by a human grader as well as a computerized essay grader (the IntelliMetric™ System). The two grade completely independently of each other—IntelliMetric™ isn't told the human's score, nor is the human told the computer's. If the two scores are identical, then that's your score.

If the scores differ by one point, those scores are averaged. If they disagree by more than one point, a second human will grade the essay to resolve any differences.

IntelliMetric™ was designed to make the same judgments that a good human grader would. In fact, part of the Graduate Management Admission Council's (GMAC's) argument for the validity of IntelliMetric™ is that its performance is indistinguishable from a human's. Still, you should remember that it is *not* a human and write accordingly.

Before you begin to write, outline your essay. Good organization always counted, and now it's more important than ever.

IntelliMetric's™ grading algorithm was designed using 400 officially graded essays for each prompt. That's a huge sample of responses, so don't worry about whether IM will understand your points—it's highly likely that someone out of those 400 responses had a similar idea. Computers are not good judges of humor or creativity. (The human judges don't reward those either. The standard is business writing, and you really shouldn't be making smart-alecky remarks in, say, an email to a CEO.)

The length of your essay is not a factor; the computer does not count the number of words in your response.

Use transitional phrases like *first, therefore, since,* and *for example* so that the computer can recognize structured arguments.

Avoid spelling and grammar errors. Though the IntelliMetric™ doesn't grade spelling per se, it might give you a lower score if it can't understand you or thinks you used the wrong words.

Here's what your essay will be graded on:

- **Quality of your reasoning.** For the Issue essay, how compelling were your reasons? On the Argument essay, did you discover the major weaknesses of the argument?
- **Organization.** Does your essay have good paragraph unity, structure, and flow?
- **Development.** It's not enough simply to assert good points. Do you explain them well? How relevant are the examples you provide?
- **Writing.** The GMAC calls this "control of the elements of standard written English." How well do you express your ideas?

Now let's take a more in-depth look at the scoring scale so you get a sense of what to aim for.

- **6: Outstanding.** Essays that earn the top score must be insightful, well developed, logically organized, and skillfully written. Among the words that the test maker uses to describe a 6 essay are *cogent, clear, effective,* and *insightful*.
- **5: Strong.** A 5 essay is well developed and well written but may not be as compellingly argued as a 6. There may also be more frequent or more serious writing errors than in a 6. The test maker describes a 5 as *generally thoughtful, sensible,* and *good*.

- **4: Adequate.** The important elements of the argument or issue are addressed but not explained robustly. The organization is good, but ideas may not be connected well. The writing may have some flaws but is generally acceptable. The test maker calls a 4 *competent, adequate, satisfactory,* and *reasonably clear.*

- **3: Limited.** A 3 response misses important elements of the Issue or Argument, has little or no development of its ideas, and doesn't clearly express its meaning. The test maker uses these words to describe a 3: *plainly flawed, tangential, irrelevant,* and *not clear.*

- **2: Seriously Flawed.** An essay scoring a 2 has some serious problems. It may not use any examples whatsoever or support its ideas in any way. Its writing will have many errors that interfere with the meaning of the sentences. An Issue essay that scores a 2 may well not develop a position on the issue, and an Argument essay that scores a 2 may be written like an Issue essay—substituting your own ideas for objective analysis. Here's how a 2 is described: *unclear, disorganized,* and *has serious and frequent problems.*

- **1: Fundamentally Deficient.** This score is rare. A 1 score is reserved for essays that provide little to no evidence of the ability to understand or analyze an issue or to develop ideas in any way. A 1 essay will have so many writing errors that the essay may be unintelligible. The test maker describes a 1 as *incoherent* and *having severe and persistent errors.*

- **0: No Score.** 0s aren't worse than 1s per se. They signify an attempt to avoid addressing the prompt at all, either by writing only random or repeating characters or by copying the prompt. You could also score a 0 by not writing in English or by addressing a completely different topic.

- **NR:** Blank. Speaks for itself. This is what you get if you write no essay at all. Most schools will not consider your GMAT score if your essay receives an NR. By skipping the essay, you give yourself an unfair advantage—everyone else wrote essays for an hour *before* the Quantitative and Verbal sections!

THE KAPLAN METHOD FOR ANALYTICAL WRITING

Here's the deal: You have a limited amount of time to show the business school admissions people that you can think logically and express yourself in clearly written English. They don't care how many syllables you can cram into a sentence or how fancy your phrases are. They care that you're making sense. Whatever you do, don't hide beneath a lot of hefty words and abstractions. Make sure that everything you say is clearly written and relevant to the topic. Get in there, state your main points, back them up, and get out.

Step 1: Take Apart the Issue/Argument

- Read it through to get a sense of the scope of the matter.
- In the Argument essay, identify the author's conclusion and the evidence used to support it.
- In the Issue essay, paraphrase both sides of the issue to define the two opinions clearly.

You can take about 2 minutes on this step.

Step 2: Select the Points You Will Make

- In the "Analysis of Argument" essay, identify all the important gaps between the evidence and the conclusion. Think of how you'll explain or illustrate those gaps and under what circumstances the author's assumptions would not hold true. Also, think about how the author could remedy these weaknesses.

- In the "Analysis of Issue" essay, think of the arguments and examples for *both* sides and decide which side you will support or the exact extent to which you agree with the stated position.

Step 2 should take about 5 minutes.

Step 3: Organize

- Outline your essay.
- Lead with your best arguments.
- Think about how the essay as a whole will flow.

If you decide on basic templates for your two essays before test day, this step will take less than 1 minute.

Step 4: Write Your Essay

- Be direct.
- Use paragraph breaks to make your essay easier to read.
- Use transitions to link related ideas; they will help your writing flow.
- Finish strongly.

You can afford no more than 20 minutes of typing. The other 10 minutes should be dedicated to planning and correcting.

Step 5: Proofread Your Work

- Save enough time to read through the entire essay—2 minutes as a minimum.
- Fix any spelling, grammar, syntax, or diction errors.
- Add any needed keywords to improve the flow of your ideas.
- Don't add any new ideas or change the structure of your essay. There just isn't time.

As explained before, the two essay types you'll write—Argument and Issue—require generally similar tasks. You must analyze a subject, take an informed position, and explain that position in writing. The two essay types, however, require different specific tasks.

BREAKDOWN: ANALYSIS OF AN ARGUMENT

The stimulus and question stem of an Analysis of an Argument topic should look something like this:

> "The problem of poorly trained teachers that has plagued the state public school system is bound to become a good deal less serious in the future. The state has initiated comprehensive guidelines that oblige state teachers to complete a number of required credits in education and educational psychology at the graduate level before being certified."

> Explain how logically persuasive you find this argument. In discussing your viewpoint, analyze the argument's line of reasoning and its use of evidence. Also explain what, if anything, would make the argument more valid and convincing or help you to better evaluate its conclusion.

The Stimulus

Analysis of an Argument topics that present an argument will probably remind you of Critical Reasoning questions. The basic idea is similar. Just as in Critical Reasoning, the writer tries to persuade you of something—her conclusion—by citing some evidence. So look for these two basic components of an argument: a conclusion and supporting evidence. You should read the arguments in the Analysis of an Argument topics in much the same way you read Critical Reasoning questions; be on the lookout for assumptions—the ways the writer makes the leap from evidence to conclusion.

The Question Stem

The question stem above instructs you to decide how convincing you find the argument, explain why, and discuss what might improve the argument. Unlike the Issue essay, there's a right answer here: the argument always has some problems. You want to focus your efforts on finding them, explaining them, and fixing them.

Exactly what are you being asked to do here?

> Explain how logically persuasive you find this argument. In discussing your viewpoint, analyze the argument's line of reasoning and its use of evidence.

Translation: Critique the argument. Discuss the ways in which it is not convincing: How and why might the evidence not fully support the conclusion?

> Also explain what, if anything, would make the argument more valid and convincing or help you to better evaluate its conclusion.

Translation: Spot weak links in the argument and offer constructive modifications that would strengthen them.

Let's use the Kaplan Method on the Analysis of an Argument topic we saw before:

> "The problem of poorly trained teachers that has plagued the state public school system is bound to become a good deal less serious in the future. The state has initiated comprehensive guidelines

that oblige state teachers to complete a number of required credits in education and educational psychology at the graduate level before being certified."

Explain how logically persuasive you find this argument. In discussing your viewpoint, analyze the argument's line of reasoning and its use of evidence. Also explain what, if anything, would make the argument more valid and convincing or help you to better evaluate its conclusion.

Step 1: Take Apart the Argument

First, identify the conclusion—the point the argument's trying to make. Here, the conclusion is this:

The problem of poorly trained teachers that has plagued the state public school system is bound to become a good deal less serious in the future.

Next, identify the evidence—the basis for the conclusion. Here, the evidence is the following:

The state has initiated comprehensive guidelines that oblige state teachers to complete a number of required credits in education and educational psychology at the graduate level before being certified.

Finally, sum up the argument in your own words:

The problem of badly trained teachers will become less serious because they'll be getting better training.

Step 2: Select the Points You Will Make

Now that you've found the conclusion and evidence, think about what assumptions the author is making or any reasoning flaws she commits. Also, think about any unaddressed questions that you feel would be relevant.

- She assumes that the courses will improve teachers' classroom performance.
- What about bad teachers who are already certified? Would they be required to retrain?
- Have currently bad teachers already had this training?
- Will this have any unintended negative consequences?

You also will need to explain how these assumptions could be false or how the questions reveal weaknesses in the author's argument. Add to your notes:

- She assumes that the courses will improve teachers' classroom performance. What if the problem is cultural? Or if it's a language barrier? Or if the teacher doesn't know the subject?
- What about bad teachers who are already certified? Would they be required to retrain? If not, those bad teachers would still be in the system.
- Have currently bad teachers already had this training? If so, this fact demonstrates that this training won't solve the problems.
- Will this have any unintended negative consequences? What does this training cost? If the state has to pay for it, will that mean less money available to the classroom? If teachers have to pay for it, then will good teachers leave the system?

KAPLAN

Then think about evidence that would make the argument stronger or more logically sound.

- Evidence verifying that the training will make teachers better
- Evidence that currently bad teachers have not already received this training and that they either will soon receive it or will be removed from the classroom
- Evidence that the cost of the training is not prohibitive

Step 3: Organize

Look over the notes you've jotted down. Select the strongest point to be first, the next-strongest to be second, and so on. Two criteria determine whether a point is strong. One is how well you can explain it. If, for example, you aren't sure how to explain potential negative consequences of an expensive training program, you should use that idea last—if at all. The other is how severe a problem the weakness poses to the argument's persuasiveness. If the training doesn't work, for example, the argument is in serious trouble!

Then decide how you'll arrange your points. There are several valid ways to organize an essay. You can discuss all of the problems and then move on to all of the needed solutions. Or you can discuss one problem and its solution, then move on to the next.

The following is an example of the latter approach:

¶ restate argument (conc: solve problem of poorly trained teachers; ev: courses in educational psychology)

¶ assumes courses = better performance. Culture? Language? Subject matter? Need ev. of relevance.

¶ assumes current bad teachers not already trained. If they have, training doesn't work. Need ev. of no training.

¶ assumes bad teachers will go if not trained. If not, will be bad until they retire. Need everyone to be trained or leave.

¶ assumes not too $. If too $, can cause problems. Need ev. of low $.

Step 4: Write Your Essay

Begin typing or writing your essay now. Keep in mind the basic principles of writing that we discussed earlier.

Keep your writing simple and clear. Choose words that you know how to use well. Avoid the temptation to make your writing "sound smarter" with overly complicated sentences or vocabulary that feels awkward.

Keep your eye on the clock and make sure that you don't run out of time to proofread. If you need to, leave out your last point or two. (Make sure that you include at least two points.) Let's pretend that the writer of the following essay had only four minutes left on the clock after the fourth paragraph. She wisely chooses neither to rush through her final paragraph nor to skip proofreading. Instead, she leaves out her point about cost.

The writer concludes that the present problem of poorly trained teachers will become less severe in the future because of required credits in education and psychology. However, the conclusion relies on assumptions for which there is no clear evidence.

The writer assumes that the required courses will make better teachers. In fact, the courses might be entirely irrelevant to the teachers' failings. If, for example, the prevalent problem is cultural and linguistic gaps between teacher and student, graduate-level courses that do not address these specific issues probably won't do much good. The courses also would not be heplful for a teacher who did not know their subject matter. The argument that the courses will improve teachers would be strengthened if the writer provided evidence that the training will be relevant to the problems.

In addition, the writer assumes that currently poor teachers have not already had this training. In fact, the writer doesn't mention whether or not some or all of the poor teachers have had similar training. The argument would be strengthened considerably if the writer provided evidence that currently poor teachers have not had training comparable to the new requirements.

Finally, the writer assumes that poor teachers currently working will either stop teaching in the future or will have received training. The writer provides no evidence, though, to indicate that this is the case. As the argument stands, it's highly possible that only brand-new teachers will be receiving the training and the bright future to which the writer refers is decades away. Only if the writer provides evidence that all teachers in the system will receive training—and will then change there teaching methods accordingly—does the argument hold.

Step 5: Proofread Your Work

Save a few minutes to go back over your essay and catch any obvious errors. Look over the previous essay. It has at least four grammar errors and is missing at least one keyword. By leaving herself ample proofreading time, our author will be able to find them.

- ¶1—no errors
- ¶2
    - Add a keyword to the beginning of the paragraph. Since it is the first assumption discussed, "The writer assumes . . ." should be changed to "First, the writer assumes . . ."
    - The second-to-last sentence has some problems: The courses also would not be heplful for a teacher who did not know their subject matter. For one thing, "heplful" should be "helpful." For another "a teacher" is singular, but "their" is plural. Let's change "a teacher" to "teachers."
- ¶3—no errors
- ¶4
    - There's an awkward phrase about halfway through: "only brand-new teachers will be receiving the training." There's no need for anything but simple future tense: "only brand-new teachers will receive the training."
    - In the last sentence, "there teaching methods" should be "their teaching methods."

The best way to improve your writing and proofreading skills is to practice. Write some practice essays using the prompts provided by the test maker at **mba.com** or in the *Official Guide to GMAT Review*. These prompts—from the pool from which the computer selects students' essay problems—are the actual ones that the GMAT tests.

BREAKDOWN: ANALYSIS OF AN ISSUE

The stimulus and question stem of an Analysis of an Issue topic will look something like this:

> Many assert that individuals allowed to work flexible schedules at home will be both more productive and happier than colleagues working under more traditional arrangements. But others assert that the close supervision of an office workplace is necessary to ensure productivity and quality control and to maintain morale.
>
> Which argument do you find more compelling, the case for flexible work conditions or the opposing viewpoint? Explain your position using relevant reasons or examples drawn from your own experience, observations, or reading.

The Stimulus

In this example, the stimulus consists of a few sentences that discuss two points of view on a general issue. Sometimes the stimulus is a single sentence. You don't need prior knowledge of any specific subject matter to discuss the issue.

The first sentence or two introduce the general issue and express one point of view. Sometimes, a keyword—here, it's the word *but*—will signal the introduction of the contrasting point of view. In other cases, the contrasting viewpoint will not be explicitly stated. In those cases, you must deduce what that opposing view is.

The Question Stem

The stem asks you which of the two viewpoints you find more convincing and instructs you to explain your position using reasons or examples. Though the specific wording will vary for each question, the basic task will be essentially the same.

Exactly what are you being asked to do here?

Which argument do you find more compelling, the case for flexible work conditions or the opposing viewpoint?

Translation: There are two conflicting viewpoints here. Take one side or the other.

Explain your position using relevant reasons or examples drawn from your own experience, observations, or reading.

Translation: Argue your position, using specific examples. Support your points with evidence.

Not all Issue essay topics will look exactly like our example. Some may present only one sentence in which the two conflicting viewpoints are not specified, as in this instance:

Allowing individuals to work flexible schedules is an idea that makes sense.

Notice that this is just a reworking of our original topic. Here, the two viewpoints are implicit, so your task includes a little digging: What are the two viewpoints? From here, your basic task is the same. Explain what the issue is and make a case for one opinion on that issue.

Now let's use the Kaplan Method on this Analysis of an Issue topic:

Many assert that individuals allowed to work flexible schedules at home will be both more productive and happier than colleagues working under more traditional arrangements. But others assert that the close supervision of an office workplace is necessary to ensure productivity and quality control and to maintain morale.

Which argument do you find more compelling, the case for flexible work conditions or the opposing viewpoint? Explain your position using relevant reasons or examples drawn from your own experience, observations, or reading.

Step 1: Take Apart the Issue

This prompt gave us two opinions on an issue, though some prompts will only give us one. Regardless of how the Issue prompt is written, we should begin by summarizing *both* sides of the debate. Here, we can paraphrase the two sides as "Flexible schedules make workers happier and more productive," versus "Traditional, supervised workplaces make people happier and more productive."

Step 2: Select the Points You Will Make

So which side do you take? Remember, this isn't about showing the admissions people what your politics are—it's about showing you can formulate an argument and write it down. Think through the pros and cons of each side and choose the side for which you have more relevant things to say. For this topic, that process might go something like this.

Arguments for flexible schedules:

- People feel more valued, work better.
- Fewer absences.
- People feel happier if they don't have to commute.

Arguments for traditional workplace:

- People less likely to waste time if boss is there.
- People need to feel part of a team.
- More quality control possible.
- More resources available.

You should add to your list of reasons any support or examples you can think of.

Arguments for flexible schedules:

- People feel more valued, work better—???
- Fewer absences—can work from home if sick.
- People feel happier if they don't have to commute—ex: LA commute.

Arguments for traditional workplace:

- People less likely to waste time if boss is there.
- People need to feel part of a team—isolation vs. friendship.
- More quality control possible—boss can check in on work.
- More resources available—technical & staff.

In this example, the writer could think of more supporting details for the reasons on the "traditional workplace" side, so that is the viewpoint she will argue. It would have been great if she knew of a business that had abandoned telecommuting in favor of a traditional office environment; she could have used that as a good illustration of her reasoning. But even without that, she can write a strong essay.

Her final step is to plan a rebuttal of the opposing side: Difficult commutes can be eased in other ways, such as by staggered work schedules and subsidized mass transit costs.

Step 3: Organize

Your first paragraph should always restate the issue. A common mistake is to present only your own side, but strong authors will define both positions clearly. Once the debate has been framed, then you can define the position you hold—and therefore, implicitly, the position you disagree with.

Now it's time to arrange your points in order. It's best to start with your most compelling point. If you need to drop a point for time, let it be your weakest. Finish by addressing and rebutting an argument from the other side.

Here's how this author might organize her points. Noting that "the boss" showed up in two different points, she rolls those two points into one. That way she avoids seeming redundant.

¶ frame the issue—home versus office. Happier & more productive at office.

¶ team spirit—friendships vs. isolation.

¶ more resources = higher productivity. Technical & staff resources.

¶ boss can supervise—less wasted time, more quality control.

¶ OTHER SIDE: home = no painful commute. REBUTTAL: staggered shifts; share mass transit cos.

Step 4: Write Your Essay

Remember that your main goal is to communicate your ideas clearly. Don't try to impress the grader with academic-sounding rhetoric. It's also wise to avoid strident rhetoric—let the quality of your ideas do the convincing.

Keep your eye on the clock and make sure that you don't run out of time to proofread. If you need to, drop one of your supporting arguments. You need at least two supporting arguments, and you need to address the other side.

Here's how this essay might be written:

Many companies face the decision to either allow employees flexible work schedules or to maintain traditional work environments. I will show that workers are happier and more productive in a traditional office environment.

A main reason that people are happier in traditional offices is the team spirit and personal satisfaction that come from working in a group. People who spend their workday at home are more likely to feel isolated from the company and divorced from the final product. Additionally, people who work in an office environment are also more likely to form close friendships with co-workers than those who are rarely in the office, which fosters greater happiness and stability within the company.

The bottom line for businesses is, of course, productivity, and there are several reasons why the traditional workplace promotes greater productivity than work at home. One reason is the increased resources the workplace provides. An office space is more likely to have better technical resources than a home work space. Also, the company staff provides problem-solving resources to which a home worker would not have direct access.

Traditional work space is far better from a managerial standpoint, as well. An office environment makes for easier supervision and quality control. Managers can make sure employees aren't wasting time or doing shoddy work. Also, a manager can more quickly spot and fix problems if they are occurring in the office, increasing productivity significantly.

Working from home does have its benefits, of course. Rush-hour traffic can make for a very difficult commute, whereas those who work from home need not commute at all. However, there are ways that an employer can address those concerns without giving up the benefits that a traditional workplace provides. For example, the cost of mass transit could be partially reimbursed, which would not only save employees the stress of driving in rush hour but would also improve morale. Also, work shifts can be staggered, allowing some employees to periodically avoid rush hour altogether. All in all, it is clear that there are greater advantages to the traditional work environment. The traditional office space allows for workers to be happier and more productive than those who work at home.

Step 5: Proofread Your Work

Be sure to save at least two minutes to check your writing. Read through the sample essay above, looking for writing that could be improved. There are five style errors and two grammar errors:

- ¶1
  - Use of the first person is often weak style. "I will show . . ." could be changed to "A close examination of the issue reveals . . ."
- ¶2
  - This sentence has plenty of errors:
    - Additionally, *people who work in* an office environment are also more likely to form *close friendships with co-workers than those who are* rarely in the office, which fosters greater happiness and stability within the company.

  "Additionally" and "also" are redundant. "Office environment" is also redundant—an office is an environment. The comparison is slightly off—"more *likely to form* . . . than *those who*." It's better to compare action to action. And let's see if we can avoid saying "office" twice in the same sentence.

There's a modification error at the end—the use of "which" means that we are describing the word immediately before the comma, but plainly the author meant not to describe "office" but "the forming of close friendships."

- Additionally, people who work in an office are more likely to form close friendships with co-workers than are those who work from home, an occurrence that fosters greater happiness and stability within the company.

- ¶3—No errors.

- ¶4—No errors.

- ¶5

   - "Work from home" comes just a little bit after "working from home." Vary word choice a little. Replace "those who work from home" with "those with home offices."

GMAT STYLE CHECKLIST

- **Cut the fat:**
   - Cut out words, phrases, and sentences that don't add any information or serve a purpose.
   - Watch out for repetitive phrases such as "refer back" or "serious crisis."
   - Don't use conjunctions to join sentences that would be more effective as separate sentences.

- **Be forceful:**
   - Avoid jargon and pompous language; it won't impress anybody. For example, "a waste of time and money" is better than "a pointless expenditure of temporal and financial resources."
   - Avoid clichés and overused terms or phrases (for example, "beyond the shadow of a doubt").
   - Don't be vague. Avoid generalizations and abstractions when more specific words would be clearer.
   - Don't use weak sentence openings. Be wary of sentences that begin with "there is" or "there are." For example, "There are some ways that this sentence is awkward," should be rewritten as "This sentence is awkward in some ways."
   - Don't refer to yourself needlessly. Avoid pointless phrases like "in my personal opinion"; even phrases such as "I agree" or "I think" are considered stylistically weak.
   - Don't be monotonous: vary sentence length and style.
   - Use transitions to connect sentences and make your essay easy to follow.

- **Be correct:**
   - Stick to the rules of standard written English.

PRACTICE ESSAYS

Directions: Write an essay on each of the topics below. The writing should be concise, forceful, and grammatically correct. After you have finished, proofread to catch any errors. Allow yourself 30 minutes to complete each essay.

Argument Essay

The following appeared in a memo from the regional manager of Luxe Spa, a chain of high-end salons.

"Over 75% of households in Parksboro have Jacuzzi bathtubs. In addition, the average family income in Parksboro is 50% higher than the national average, and a local store reports record-high sales of the most costly brands of hair and body care products. With so much being spent on personal care, Parksboro will be a profitable location for a new Luxe Spa—a salon that offers premium services at prices that are above average."

Discuss how well reasoned you find this argument. In your discussion, be sure to analyze the line of reasoning and the use of evidence in the argument. For example, you may need to consider what questionable assumptions underlie the thinking and what alternative explanations or counterexamples might weaken the conclusion. You can also discuss what sort of evidence would strengthen or refute the argument, what changes in the argument would make it more logically sound, and what, if anything, would help you better evaluate its conclusion.

Issue Essay

"The invention of the Internet has created more problems than it has solved. Most people would have a higher quality of life had the Internet never been invented."

From your perspective, is this an accurate observation? Why or why not? Explain, using reasons and/or examples from your experience, observations, and reading.

After writing your essays, compare them to the sample responses that follow. Don't focus on their length, as word count is not part of the grading rubric. Rather, focus on how logical the structures are and how each essay makes its points in a clear and straightforward style.

Argument Essay

Though it might seem at first glance that the regional manager of Luxe Spa has good reasons for suggesting that Parksboro would be a profitable place for a new spa, a closer examination of the arguments presented reveals numerous examples of leaps of faith, poor reasoning, and ill-defined terminology. In order to better support her claim, the manager would need to show a correlation between the figures she cites in reference to Parksboro's residents and a willingness to spend money at a spa with high prices.

The manager quotes specific statistics about the percentage of residents with Jacuzzis and the average income in Parksboro. She then uses these figures as evidence to support her argument. However, neither of these statistics as presented does much to bolster her claim. Just because 75% of homes have Jacuzzis doesn't mean those homeowners are more likely to go to a pricey spa. For instance, the presence of Jacuzzis in their houses may indicate a preference for pampering themselves at home. Parksboro could also be a planned development in the suburbs where all the houses are designed with Jacuzzis. If this is the case, than the mere ownership of a certain kind of bathtub should hardly be taken as a clear indication of a person's inclination to go to a spa. In addition, the fact that Parksboro's average family income is 50% higher than the national average is not enough on its own to predict the success or failure of a spa in the region. Parksboro may have a very small population, for instance, or a small number of wealthy people counterbalanced by a number of medium- to low-income families. We simply cannot tell from the information provided. In addition, the failure of the manager to provide the national average family income for comparison makes it unclear if earning 50% more would allow for a luxurious lifestyle or not.

The mention of a local store's record-high sales of expensive personal care items similarly provides scant evidence to support the manager's assertions. We are given no indication of what constitutes "record-high" sales for this particular store or what "most costly" means in this context. Perhaps this store usually sells very few personal care products and had one unusual month. Even if this one store sold a high volume of hair- and body-care products, it may not be representative of the Parksboro market as a whole. And perhaps "most costly" refers only to the most costly brands available in Parksboro, not to the most costly brands nationwide. The manager needs to provide much more specific information about residents' spending habits in order to provide compelling evidence that personal care ranks high among their priorities.

To make the case that Parksboro would be a profitable location for Luxe Spa, the regional manager should try to show that people there have a surplus of income and a tendency to spend it on indulging in spa treatments. Although an attempt is made to make this very argument, the lack of supporting information provided weakens rather than strengthens the memo. Information such as whether there are other high-end spas in the area and the presence of tourism in the town could also have been introduced as reinforcement. As it stands, Luxe Spa would be ill-advised to open a location in Parksboro based solely on the evidence provided here.

Issue Essay

The emergence of the Internet in the 1990s fundamentally changed the way people exchange information. With this dynamic web of technology, people across the world are immediately connected to information—and each other—through the quick click of a button, and normal business operations for major corporations were radically altered. It's true that this industry has had a bumpy beginning—for instance, its spectacular economic meltdown in the late nineties and the advent of file sharing are just a few of the issues raised by the Internet. But while the Internet has created more than its fair share of moral and financial issues for today's consumer, it's unreasonable to assume that the Internet has produced more problems than benefits.

As with any new technology, the Internet opened up infinite avenues allowing businesses to streamline operations. Delivery of information is instantaneous. Communication by email eliminates high phone and paper costs and contributes to overall efficiency, saving time that would have been spent mailing documents or holding a long conversation on the phone. Web-enabling transactions—whether buying products for a major corporation or downloading an application to a university—can cut costs in the millions of dollars. A recent article in the magazine Fast Company tells how Jonathan Ayers, CEO of Carrier Corp. (the world's largest manufacturer of air conditioners), used the Web to cut costs of over $100 million. In short, the Internet allows companies to execute business quicker and cheaper, which leads to customer satisfaction—and profitability.

One of the larger challenges posed by the Internet has to do with intellectual property and copyrighting. Napster was the first to realize a major benefit of the Internet: file sharing. Started in a dorm room, the company's software enabled users to swap digitized music files—for free. Eventually, the software put a significant dent in music sales, becoming a constant worry for music executives and artists alike. However, this isn't the first time the entertainment industry has faced this concern; VHS and audio tape recorders posed the same threat in the seventies and eighties. Companies like Napster and LimeWire simply pushed the entertainment industry to find creative solutions to the copyright issues—creating jobs as they solved the problem. For instance, Apple's iTunes, an online music store where each song costs $0.99, made $70 million in its first year.

From a morality standpoint, the Internet has been fertile ground for pornography as well as a virtual stomping ground for child molesters.

Psychologists say that the Internet promotes molesting and porn-viewing habits because of the relative anonymity provided by the medium. But, like everything else, porn and child molesters developed these practices around the advancements of technology and society. They were around long before the Internet. Is it fair to say that the invention of the printing press promoted pornography and sexual abuse?

The economy certainly suffered a great deal in 1999 and 2000, as the world saw the fast-rising dot-com industry implode, causing a depression that was exacerbated by the tragic events of 9/11. The implosion was not due to the technology of the Internet; rather, it was due to distorted, impractical attitudes and unsound business decisions. Wealth was concentrated in shares of stock that were unrealistically inflated, and as long as the stock prices were high, analysts, investors, and even federal regulators took a lax attitude towards business models and company practices. Therefore, the dot-com bust can be attributed to a lapse in human judgment rather than the existence of the Internet.

Finally, the consumer benefits of the Internet can't be ignored. Small businesses are better able to promote themselves and can introduce their products to a far-reaching audience of consumers. The Internet has simplified and improved things like travel reservations, communication, and customer service. For example, customers of shipping companies like FedEx or UPS are able to track packages online, rather than making a phone call that eventually leads to a ten-minute wait on hold.

The very definition of *technology* is the application of scientific knowledge in industry or business. A new idea begets other new ideas, and along with them comes a period of adjustment, both for industries and for society. The introduction of the Internet opened up a new world of communication, allowing for business to advance, just as the invention of the car, electricity, and the printing press did for past generations. To eschew new technology because of some of its negative characteristics is to deny the progression of society.

PART SIX

Appendixes

Appendix 1: **Grammar Reference Guide**

SENTENCE STRUCTURE

Understanding the basic rules of sentence structure enables you to spot the classic GMAT errors quickly. The fundamental principles described here will play a role in nearly every Sentence Correction item you see, whether in the original version or among some of the answer choices. Especially if English is not your native language, be sure to know this basic material.

Run-on Sentences

When a sentence consists of more than one clause (a group of words that contains a subject and a verb), those clauses must be joined properly. It is never acceptable to hook two clauses together with a comma, as the "sentence" below does. That's called a **run-on sentence**.

Wrong:	Nietzsche moved to Basel in 1869, he planned to teach classical philology.

There are a number of acceptable ways to fix a run-on.

Correct:	Nietzsche moved to Basel in 1869; he planned to teach classical philology.
Also Correct:	Nietzsche planned to teach classical philology; therefore, he moved to Basel in 1869.
Also Correct:	Nietzsche moved to Basel in 1869, and he planned to teach classical philology. (The word *and*, like *or*, *for*, *but*, *nor*, so, and *yet*, is what's called a *coordinating conjunction*.)
Also Correct:	Because Nietzsche planned to teach classical philology, he moved to Basel in 1869. (The word *because*, like *although*, *if*, *though*, etc., is what's called a *subordinating conjunction*.)
Also Correct:	Nietzsche, who planned to teach classical philology, moved to Basel in 1869. (The word *who*, like *which*, *where*, *whom*, *that*, and *whose*, is what's called a *relative pronoun*.)

KAPLAN

Sentence Fragments

Every sentence must contain at least one complete independent clause. If there is no independent clause at all, or if what's supposed to be the independent clause is incomplete, you've got a **sentence fragment**.

Wrong:	While most people, who have worked hard for many years, have not managed to save any money, although they are trying to be more frugal now.

This sentence fragment consists of nothing but subordinate clauses. One of the subordinate clauses must be made into an independent clause.

Correct:	Most people, who have worked hard for many years, have not managed to save any money, although they are trying to be more frugal now.
Also Correct:	While most people, who have worked hard for many years, have not managed to save any money, they are trying to be more frugal now.

SUBJECT-VERB AGREEMENT

Remember, in English, a subject and its verb must **agree** in number and person. **Number** refers to whether a subject (or a verb) is singular or plural. **Person** refers to first person (*I*, *we*), second person (*you*), and third person (*he, she, it, one, they*).

Intervening Phrases

When the subject of a sentence is followed by a phrase (a group of words that does not have a subject and verb) or relative clause, the words are not part of the subject. They simply add information about that subject.

Learn to recognize groups of words that can come between the subject and verb!

1. **Relative clauses**, which contain important information about the subject of another clause, are very often placed in between a subject and verb. (The previous sentence contains a relative clause.)

Wrong:	John Clare, *who during the mid-nineteenth century wrote many fine poems on rural themes*, were confined for decades to an insane asylum.

The subject is *John Clare*, which is singular, but the verb is *were*, which is plural. The fact that the relative clause ends with a plural noun (*themes*) is supposed to distract you from the fact that the subject and verb don't agree.

Correct:	John Clare, who during the mid-nineteenth century wrote many fine poems on rural themes, *was* confined for decades to an insane asylum.

2. **Appositives** often come between a subject and a verb. Appositives are nouns, pronouns, or noun phrases that are placed next to nouns to describe them further.

Wrong: John Smith, *the man who led British expeditions to several American sites*, have left several written accounts of dramatic events there.

Correct: John Smith, the man who led British expeditions to several American sites, *has* left several written accounts of dramatic events there.

Relative clauses and appositives are sometimes set off from the rest of the sentence by commas. When this is the case, it's a dead giveaway that those words are not part of the subject. That makes checking for subject-verb agreement much easier; just ignore the words set off by commas and concentrate on the subject and the verb.

3. The **prepositional phrase** is an all-time favorite.

Wrong: Wild animals *in jungles all over the world* is endangered.

Correct: Wild animals in jungles all over the world *are* endangered.

Prepositional phrases, and some relative clauses and appositives, are not set off by commas. It's harder to recognize intervening phrases and clauses when they're not set off by commas, but if you remember to check each sentence carefully for such things, you'll be able to pick them out anyway.

Compound Subjects

When two nouns or groups of nouns are joined by *and*, they're called a **compound subject** and are therefore plural.

Correct: *Ontario and Quebec* contain about two thirds of the population of Canada.

Some connecting phrases may look as though they should make a group of words into a compound subject—but they don't result in a compound subject.

Wrong: George Bernard Shaw, as well as Mahatma Gandhi and River Phoenix, were vegetarians.

And is the only connecting word that results in a compound and plural subject. The following words and phrases do not create compound subjects:

along with	*as well as*
together with	*besides*
in addition to	

Correct: *George Bernard Shaw*, as well as Mahatma Gandhi and River Phoenix, *was* a vegetarian.

| Wrong: | Neither Thomas Jefferson nor Alexander Hamilton were supportive of Aaron Burr's political ambitions. |

When words in the subject position are connected by *either . . . or* or *neither . . . nor*, the verb agrees with the last word in the pair. If the last word is singular, the verb must be singular. If the last word is plural, the verb must be plural.

| Correct: | Neither Thomas Jefferson nor *Alexander Hamilton was* supportive of Aaron Burr's political ambitions. |
| Correct: | Neither Thomas Jefferson nor *the Federalists were* supportive of Aaron Burr's political ambitions. |

Both . . . and is the only pair that always results in a plural subject.

| Correct: | *Both* Thomas Jefferson *and* Alexander Hamilton *were* unsupportive of Aaron Burr's political ambitions. |

Unusual Sentence Patterns

When you're checking for subject-verb disagreement, remember that the subject doesn't always appear before the verb.

| Wrong: | Dominating the New York skyline is the Empire State Building and the Chrysler Building. |

The subject of this sentence is a compound subject, *the Empire State Building and the Chrysler Building*. The verb should be plural.

| Correct: | Dominating the New York skyline *are* the Empire State Building and the Chrysler Building. |

Subjects That Are Not Nouns or Pronouns

An entire clause can serve as the subject of a sentence. When used as subject, a clause always takes a singular verb:

Whether the economy will improve in the near future *is* a matter of great concern.

Infinitives and gerunds can be used as subjects. Remember that they're singular subjects:

To err is human.

Rollerblading is dangerous.

See the section on verbs for more on infinitives and gerunds.

MODIFICATION

Adjectives and adverbs aren't the only sentence elements whose job it is to modify. Phrases and even relative clauses can act as modifiers in a sentence. The following sentence contains several types of modifiers:

> Waiting to regain enough strength to eat, a cheetah, which expends most of its energy in the chase, must rest beside its prey.

Waiting to regain enough strength to eat is a phrase that describes the cheetah, as does the relative clause *which expends most of its energy in the chase*. The phrase *beside its prey* modifies the verb *rest*.

English depends heavily on word order to establish modifying relationships. When a sentence's modifiers violate the conventions of word order, confusion often results.

Introductory Modifiers

Wrong: Sifting the sand of a river bed, gold was discovered by prospectors in California in 1848.

A modifying phrase that begins a sentence refers to the noun or pronoun immediately following the phrase. But if we apply that rule here, the sentence says that the *gold was sifting sand*. See the problem? The author presumably meant to say that the prospectors were sifting sand. There are several ways to correct the sentence so that it expresses the intended meaning.

Correct: Sifting the sand in a river bed, prospectors discovered gold in California in 1848.

Also Correct: Prospectors, sifting the sand in a river bed, discovered gold in California in 1848.

Also Correct: Gold was discovered by prospectors, who were sifting the sand in a river bed, in California in 1848.

In all three cases the phrase or clause directly precedes or follows the noun it describes.

Dangling Modifiers

A modifying phrase or clause should clearly refer to a particular word in the sentence. A modifying phrase or clause that does not sensibly refer to any word in the sentence is called a **dangling modifier.** The most common sort of dangler is an introductory modifying phrase that's followed by a word it can't logically refer to.

Wrong: Desiring to free his readers from superstition, the theories of Epicurus are expounded in Lucretius's poem *De rerum natura*.

The problem with this sentence is that the phrase that begins the sentence seems to modify the noun following it: *theories*. In fact, there is really nowhere the modifier can be put to make it work properly, and no noun to which it can reasonably refer (*Lucretius's*, the possessive, is functioning as an adjective modifying *poem*). Get rid of dangling constructions by clarifying the modification relationship or by making the dangler into a subordinate clause.

Correct: Desiring to free his readers from superstition, Lucretius expounded the theories of Epicurus in his poem *De rerum natura*.

Now the phrase *desiring to free his readers from superstition* clearly refers to the proper noun *Lucretius*.

Other Modifiers

In correcting some misplaced introductory modifiers, we move the modifier to a position inside the sentence rather than at the beginning. This is perfectly acceptable, but just remember that modifying phrases inside a sentence can also be misplaced.

Wrong: That night they sat discussing when the cow might calve in the kitchen.

The problem here is the phrase *in the kitchen*, which seems to refer to where the cow might have her calf. What the author probably meant to say is the following correct sentence:

Correct: That night they sat in the kitchen discussing when the cow might calve.

This sentence is correct because the phrase comes directly after the word it modifies: the verb *sat*.

Wrong: As a young man, the French novelist Gustave Flaubert traveled in Egypt, which was a fascinating experience.

It's not that *Egypt* itself was a fascinating experience, but that traveling there was fascinating.

Correct: Traveling in Egypt as a young man was a fascinating experience for the French novelist Gustave Flaubert.

PRONOUNS

When doing Sentence Correction questions, always try to locate the antecedent of a pronoun (that is, the word to which the pronoun refers). Most of the pronoun problems you'll encounter on the test result from a problem in the relationship of the pronoun and its antecedent.

Pronoun Reference

In GMAT English, a pronoun must refer clearly to one and only one antecedent.

1. Watch out for sentences in which pronouns refer to indefinite antecedents, paying particular attention to the pronoun *they*. (Avoid references to some vague *they*.)

Wrong:	They serve meals on many of the buses that run from Santiago to Antofagasta. (Who are *they*?)
Better:	Meals are served on many of the buses that run from Santiago to Antofagasta.

In the preceding sentence, it's acceptable to use the passive voice because you don't know who is doing the action. Also note that it's quite all right to use *it* like this:

> *It* seldom rains in Death Valley.

2. Sometimes a sentence is structured so that a pronoun can refer to more than one thing, and as a result the reader doesn't know what the author intended.

Wrong:	Pennsylvania Governor William Keith encouraged the young Benjamin Franklin to open his own printing shop because he perceived that the quality of printing in Philadelphia was poor. (*Which* man perceived that the quality of printing in Philadelphia was poor?)

Pronouns are assumed to refer to the nearest reasonable antecedent. Nonetheless, it is best to avoid structural ambiguity of the sort that occurs in this sentence.

Better:	Because *he* perceived that the quality of printing in Philadelphia was poor, Pennsylvania Governor *William Keith* encouraged the young Benjamin Franklin to open his own printing shop. (*Keith* perceived that the quality of printing was poor.)
Better:	Because the young *Benjamin Franklin* perceived that the quality of printing in Philadelphia was poor, Pennsylvania Governor William Keith encouraged *him* to open *his* own printing shop. (In this version, *Franklin* is the one who perceived that the printing was poor.)

3. Sometimes it's easy to see what the author meant to use for the antecedent, but when you examine the sentence more closely that antecedent is nowhere to be found. Correct the problem either by replacing the pronoun with a noun or by providing a clear antecedent.

Poor:	The proslavery writer A. C. C. Thompson questioned Frederick Douglass's authorship of *The Narrative*, claiming that he was too uneducated to have written such an eloquent book.

What's the antecedent of *he*? It should be the noun *Frederick Douglass*, but the sentence contains only the possessive form *Douglass's*. As a rule, avoid using a possessive form as the antecedent of a personal pronoun.

Better:	The proslavery writer A. C. C. Thompson questioned whether Frederick Douglass actually wrote *The Narrative*, claiming that *he* was too uneducated to have written such an eloquent book.

Oddball Problems

Here are two oddball pronoun reference problems to watch out for:

DO SO

Wrong:	It is common for a native New Yorker who has never driven a car to move to another part of the country and have to learn to do it.
Better:	It is common for a native New Yorker who has never driven a car to move to another part of the country and have to learn to *do so*.

ONE AND *YOU*

When we give advice to others or make general statements, we often use the pronouns *one* and *you*. "You should brush your teeth every day." "One never knows what to do in a situation like that."

It is never acceptable to mix *one* and *you*, or *one* and *yours*, or *you* and *one's* in a sentence together.

Wrong:	One shouldn't eat a high-fat diet and avoid exercise, and then be surprised when you gain weight.
Correct:	*One* shouldn't eat a high-fat diet and avoid exercise, and then be surprised when *one* gains weight.
Also Correct:	*You* shouldn't eat a high-fat diet and avoid exercise, and then be surprised when *you* gain weight.

Also, never use *one* or *one's* to refer to any antecedent except *one*.

Wrong:	A person should leave a light on in an empty house if one wants to give the impression that someone is at home.
Correct:	A *person* should leave a light on in an empty house if *he or she* wants to give the impression that someone is at home.
Also Correct:	*One* should leave a light on in an empty house if *one* wants to give the impression that someone is at home.
Also Correct:	*One* should leave a light on in an empty house if *he or she* wants to give the impression that someone is at home.

Pronoun Agreement

Always use singular pronouns to refer to singular entities and plural pronouns to refer to plural entities. First, identify the antecedent of a given pronoun, and don't allow yourself to be distracted by a phrase that comes between the two. The GMAT will frequently try to confuse you by inserting a phrase containing plural nouns between a pronoun and its singular antecedent, or vice versa.

Wrong:	A cactus will flower in spite of the fact that they receive little water.
Correct:	A *cactus* will flower in spite of the fact that *it* receives little water.

Wrong:	The number of people with college degrees is many times what they were last summer.
Correct:	The *number* of people with college degrees is many times what *it* was last summer.

Note: The number is always singular. (The number of cookies he ate *was* impressive.) *A number* is always plural. (A number of turkeys *were* gathered outside the shed.)

Pronoun Case

One type of pronoun problem you can't catch by looking at the relationship between a pronoun and its antecedent is wrong case.

	Subjective Case	Objective Case
First Person:	*I, we*	*me, us*
Second Person:	*you*	*you*
Third Person:	*he, she, it, they, one*	*him, her, it, them, one*
Relative Pronouns:	*who, that, which*	*whom, that, which*

When to Use Subjective Case Pronouns

1. Use the subjective case for the subject of a sentence:
    She is falling asleep.

2. Use the subjective case after forms of *to be*:
    It is *I.*

3. Use the subjective case in comparisons between the subjects of understood verbs:
    Gary is taller than *I* (am tall).

When to Use Objective Case Pronouns

1. Use the objective case for the object of a verb:
    I called *him.*

2. Use the objective case for the object of a preposition:
    I laughed at *her.*

3. Use the objective case after infinitives and gerunds:
    Asking *him* to go was a big mistake.

4. Use the objective case in comparisons between objects of understood verbs:
    She calls you more than (she calls) *me.*

There probably won't be many times when you are in doubt as to which case of a pronoun is correct. However, the following hints may prove helpful:

When two or more nouns or pronouns are functioning the same way in a sentence, determine the correct case of any pronoun by considering it separately:

Beatrice and (*I* or *me*) are going home early.

Without *Beatrice*, should the sentence read: *Me am going home early* or *I am going home early*? *I am going*, of course, so *Beatrice and I are going home early*.

A common mistake in the use of relative pronouns is using *who* (subject case) when *whom* (object case) is needed, or vice versa. If you tend to confuse the two, try the following system.

Scholars have disagreed over (*who* or *whom*) is most likely to have written *A Yorkshire Tragedy*, but some early sources attribute it to Shakespeare.

1. Isolate the relative pronoun in its own clause: *whom is most likely to have written* A Yorkshire Tragedy.
2. Ask yourself the question: Who or whom wrote *A Yorkshire Tragedy*?
3. Answer with an ordinary personal pronoun: *He* did. (If you are a native speaker of English, your ear undoubtedly tells you that *him did* is wrong.)
4. Since *he* is in the subjective case, we need the subjective case relative pronoun: *who*. Therefore this sentence should read:

Scholars have disagreed over *who* is most likely to have written *A Yorkshire Tragedy*, but some early sources attribute it to Shakespeare.

VERBS

Here are some important terms and concepts to review before you read this section:

Verb: A word that expresses an action or a state of being.

Verbal: A word that is formed from a verb but is not functioning as a verb. There are three kinds of verbals: *participles*, *gerunds*, and *infinitives*.

It is important to realize that a verbal is not a verb, because a sentence must contain a verb, and a verbal won't do. A group of words containing a verbal but lacking a verb is not a sentence.

Participle: Usually ends in *-ing* or *-ed*. It is used as an adjective in a sentence:

Let *sleeping* dogs lie.
It is difficult to calm a *frightened* child.
Peering into his microscope, Robert Koch saw the tuberculosis bacilli.

Gerund: Always ends in *-ing*. It is used in a sentence as a noun:

Skiing can be dangerous.
Raising a family is a serious task.
I was surprised at his *acting* like such a coward.

Note from the third sentence that a noun or pronoun that comes before a gerund is in the possessive form: *his*, not *him*.

Infinitive: The basic form of a verb, generally preceded by *to*. It is usually used as a noun, but may be used as an adjective or an adverb.

> Winston Churchill liked *to paint*. (Infinitive used as a noun.)
> The will *to conquer* is crucial. (Infinitive used as an adjective—modifies the *will*.)
> Students in imperial China studied the Confucian classics *to excel* on civil service exams. (Infinitive used as an adverb—modifies *studied*.)

Verb Tense

On the GMAT, you'll find items that are wrong because a verb is in the wrong tense. To spot this kind of problem, you need to be familiar with both the way each tense is used individually and the ways the tenses are used together.

Present Tense

Use the present tense to describe a state or action occurring in the present time:

> Congress *is* debating health policy this session.

Use the present tense to describe habitual action:

> Many Americans *jog* every day.

Use the present tense to describe "general truths"—things that are always true:

> The earth *is* round and *rotates* on its axis.

Past Tense

Use the simple past tense to describe an event or state that took place at a specific time in the past, and is now over and done with:

> Hundreds of people *died* when the *Titanic* sank.
> Few people *bought* new cars last year.

There are two other ways to express past action:

> Bread *used to* cost a few cents per loaf.
> George Bush *did promise* not to raise taxes.

Future Tense

Use the future tense for intended actions or actions expected in the future:

> The twenty-second century *will begin* in the year 2101.

We often express future actions with the expression *to be going to:*

> I *am going to move* to another apartment as soon as possible.

The simple present tense is also used to speak of future events. This is called the **anticipatory future.** We often use the anticipatory future with verbs of motion, such as *come, go, arrive, depart,* and *leave*:

The senator *is leaving* for Europe tomorrow.

We also use the anticipatory future in two-clause sentences when one verb is in the regular future tense:

The disputants will announce the new truce as soon as they *agree* on its terms.

Present Perfect Tense

Use the present perfect tense for actions and states that started in the past and continue up to and into the present time:

Hawaii *has been* a state since 1959.

Use the present perfect for actions and states that happen a number of times in the past and may happen again in the future:

Italy *has had* many changes in government since World War II.

Use the present perfect for something that happened at an unspecified time in the past. Notice the difference in meaning between the two sample sentences below:

Present Perfect: Susan Sontag *has written* a critical essay about Leni Riefenstahl. (We have no idea when—we just know she wrote it.)

Simple Past: Susan Sontag *wrote* a critical essay about Leni Riefenstahl in 1974. (We use the simple past because we're specifying when Sontag wrote the essay.)

Past Perfect Tense

The past perfect tense is used to represent past actions or states that were completed before other past actions or states. The more recent past event is expressed in the simple past, and the earlier past event is expressed in the past perfect:

After he came to America, Vladimir Nabokov translated novels that *he had* written in Russian while he was living in Europe.

Note the difference in meaning between these two sentences:

The Civil War *had ended* when Lincoln was shot. = *The war was over by the time of Lincoln's death.*
The Civil War *ended* when Lincoln was shot. = *The war ended when Lincoln died.*

Future Perfect Tense

Use the future perfect tense for a future state or event that will take place before another future event:

By the time the next election is held, the candidates *will have debated* at least once. (Note that the present tense form [anticipatory future] is used in the first clause.)

Sequence of Tenses

When a sentence has two or more verbs in it, you should always check to see whether the tenses of those verbs correctly indicate the order in which things happened. As a general rule, if two things happened at the same time, the verbs should be in the same tense.

Wrong: Just as the sun rose, the rooster crows.

Rose is past tense and *crows* is present tense, but the words *just as* indicate that both things happened at the same time. The verbs should be in the same tense.

Correct: Just as the sun *rose*, the rooster *crowed*.

Also Correct: Just as the sun *rises*, the rooster *crows*.

When we're talking about the past or the future, we often want to indicate that one thing happened or will happen before another. That's where the past perfect and the future perfect come in.

Use the past perfect for the earlier of two past events, and the simple past for the later event.

Wrong: Mozart finished about two thirds of the Requiem when he died.

Putting both verbs of the sentence in the simple past tense makes it sound as if Mozart wrote two thirds of the Requiem after dying. If we put the first verb into the past perfect, though, the sentence makes much more sense.

Correct: Mozart *had finished* about two thirds of the Requiem when he *died*.

Note: Occasionally, the GMAT won't use the past perfect for the earlier event. They'll use a word like *before* or *after* to make the sequence of events clear. You should always look for the past perfect, but if it's not there, you can settle for the simple past with a time word such as *before* or *after*.

Use the future perfect for the earlier of two future events.

Wrong: By the time I write to Leo he will probably move.

The point the author is trying to get across is not that Leo will move when he gets the letter, but that by the time the letter arrives he'll be living somewhere else.

Correct: By the time I write to Leo, he *will* probably *have moved*.

When you use a participial phrase in a sentence, the action or the situation that phrase describes is assumed to take place at the same time as the action or state described by the verb of the sentence.

Wrong: *Being* a French colony, Senegal is a Francophone nation.

This implies that Senegal is still a French colony. We can make the information in the participial phrase refer to an earlier time than does the verb by changing the regular participle to what's called a **perfect participle.** The way to do it is to use *having + the past participle*.

Correct: *Having been a French colony*, Senegal is a Francophone nation.

You can do the same thing with infinitives by replacing the regular infinitive with *to have + the past participle:*

> I'm glad *to meet* you. (I'm glad to be in the process of meeting you right now.)
> I'm glad *to have met* you. (I'm glad now that I met you earlier today, last week, or whenever.)

Subjunctive Mood

On the GMAT you may come across an item that tests your knowledge of the subjunctive. Subjunctive verb forms are used in two ways.

The subjunctive form *were* is used in statements that express a wish or situations that are contrary to fact:

> I wish I *were* a rich man. (But I'm not.)
> If I *were* you, I wouldn't do that. (But I'm not you.)

The **subjunctive of requirement** is used after verbs such as *ask, demand, insist,* and *suggest*—or after expressions of requirement, suggestion, or demand. A subjunctive verb of requirement is in the base form of the verb: the infinitive without *to:*

> Airlines insist that each passenger *pass* through a metal detector.
> It's extremely important that silicon chips *be made* in a dust-free environment.

Conditional Sentences

Conditional sentences are if-then statements:

> *If* you go, *then* I'll go, too.

Note that many conditional sentences imply rather than state the word then, and this is also correct usage:

> *If* you go, I'll go too.

We use conditional sentences when we want to speculate about the results of a particular situation. There are three types of conditional sentences.

Statements of Fact: There is a real possibility that the situation described in the *if* clause really happened, or is happening, or will happen:

> If Vladimir Putin resigns, there will be unrest in Russia.
> If John Milton met Galileo, they probably discussed astronomy.

Contrary to Fact: The situation in the *if* clause never happened, so what is said in the *then* clause is pure speculation:

> Blaise Pascal wrote that if Cleopatra's nose had been shorter, the face of the world would have changed.
> Alexander the Great said, "If I were not Alexander, I would want to be Diogenes."

Future Speculation: Some conditional sentences speculate about the future, but with the idea that the situation in the *if* clause is extremely unlikely to happen:

> If Shakespeare's manuscripts were to be discovered, the texts of some of his plays would be less uncertain.

PARALLELISM

Remember, when you express a number of ideas of equal importance and function in the same sentence, you should always be careful to make them all the same grammatical form (that is, all nouns, all adjectives, all gerunds, all clauses, or whatever). That's called **parallel structure** or **parallelism.**

Coordinate Ideas

Coordinate ideas occur in pairs or in series, and they are linked by conjunctions such as *and*, *but*, *or*, and *nor*, or, in certain instances, by linking verbs such as *is*.

Wrong:	To earn credits, an American college student can take up folk dancing, ballet, or study belly dancing.
Correct:	To earn credits, an American college student can take up *folk dancing*, *ballet*, or *belly dancing*.

Note that once you begin repeating a word in a series like the following, you must follow through:

Wrong:	A wage earner might invest her money in stocks, in bonds, or real estate.
Correct:	A wage earner might invest her money *in* stocks, *in* bonds, or *in* real estate.
Also Correct:	A wage earner might invest her money *in* stocks, bonds, or real estate.

This principle applies equally to prepositions (*in*, *on*, *by*, *with*, etc.), articles (*the*, *a*, *an*), helping verbs (*had*, *has*, *would*, etc.), and possessive pronouns (*his*, *her*, etc.). You must either repeat the preposition, helping verb, or whatever, in front of each element in the series, or include it only in front of the first item in the series.

Correlative Constructions

There is a group of words in English that are called **correlative conjunctions.** They are used to relate two ideas in some way. Here's a list of them:

> *both . . . and*
>
> *either . . . or*
>
> *neither . . . nor*
>
> *not only . . . but (also)*

You should always be careful to place correlative conjunctions immediately before the terms they're coordinating.

Wrong: Isaac Newton not only studied physics but also theology.

The problem here is that the author intends to coordinate the two nouns *physics* and *theology*, but makes the mistake of putting the verb of the sentence (*studied*) after the first element of the construction (*not only*), and in so doing destroys the parallelism. Note that the solution to an error like this is usually to move one of the conjunctions.

Correct: Isaac Newton studied not only *physics* but also *theology*.

Compared or Contrasted Ideas

Frequently, two or more ideas are compared or contrasted within the same sentence. Compared or contrasted ideas should be presented in the same grammatical form.

Certain phrases should clue you in that the sentence contains ideas that should be presented in parallel form. These phrases include *as . . . as* and *more (or less)* x *than* y.

Wrong: Skiing is as strenuous as to run.
Correct: *Skiing* is as strenuous as *running*.
Wrong: Skiing is less dangerous than to rappel down a cliff.
Correct: *To ski* is less dangerous than *to rappel* down a cliff.

To Be

In certain cases, sentences with forms of *to be* must be expressed in parallel form.

Wrong: To drive while intoxicated is risking grave injury and criminal charges.

When an infinitive is the subject of *to be*, don't use a gerund after the verb, and vice versa. Pair infinitives with infinitives and gerunds with gerunds.

Correct: *To drive* while intoxicated is *to risk* grave injury and criminal charges.

Note that we wouldn't change both words to gerunds in this sentence because it wouldn't sound idiomatic.

COMPARISONS

On the GMAT, you will see a number of sentences that make comparisons. A sentence that makes a comparison must do two things: It must be clear about what is being compared, and it must compare things that logically can be compared. A sentence that makes an unclear or illogical comparison is grammatically unacceptable. When you see a comparative expression such as *like, as, more than, unlike, less than, similar to,* or *different from,* it should remind you to ask yourself two questions about the comparison in the sentence: Is it clear? Is it logical?

Unclear Comparisons

Sometimes it isn't clear what the author is trying to compare.

Wrong: Byron admired Dryden more than Wordsworth.

There are two ways to interpret this sentence: that Dryden meant more to Byron than Wordsworth did, or that Byron thought more highly of Dryden than Wordsworth did. Whichever meaning you choose, the problem can be cleared up by adding more words to the sentence.

Correct: Byron admired Dryden more than *he did* Wordsworth.

Also Correct: Byron admired Dryden more than *Wordsworth did*.

Illogical Comparisons

Sometimes what the author meant to say is clear enough, but what the author meant to say is not what he ended up saying.

Wrong: The peaches here are riper than any other fruitstand.

This sentence is comparing *peaches* to *fruitstands*, even though that's clearly not the intention of the author. We can correct it so that we're comparing peaches to peaches by inserting the phrase *those at*.

Correct: The peaches here are riper than *those at* any other fruitstand.

Now the pronoun *those* is standing in for *peaches*, so the sentence is accurately comparing things that can be reasonably compared: the peaches here and some other peaches.

Incomplete comparisons like this one are normally corrected by inserting a phrase like *those of, those in, those at, that of, that in*, and *that at*.

Incomplete comparisons can also be corrected by use of the possessive.

Wrong: Many critics considered Enrico Caruso's voice better than any other tenor. (This is comparing a voice to a person.)

Correct: Many critics considered Enrico Caruso's voice better than *any other tenor's*. (Note that this is a shortened version of: *Many critics considered Enrico Caruso's voice better than any other tenor's voice*.)

The second sort of incomplete comparison occurs when one thing is being compared to a group it is a part of. This error is corrected by inserting either the word *other* or the word *else*.

Wrong: Astaire danced better than any man in the world.

This is wrong because he couldn't have danced better than himself.

Correct: Astaire danced better than any *other* man in the world.

Comparative Forms

The comparative form is used when comparing only two members of a class, and the superlative for three or more.

Loretta's grass grows *more vigorously* than Jim's.
Loretta's grass grows the *most vigorously* of any in the neighborhood.

Of Buchanan and Lincoln, the *latter* was *taller*.
Of McKinley, Roosevelt, and Taft, the *last* was *heaviest*.

Idiom

Sometimes the right way to say something isn't a matter of grammar but is a matter of **idiom**: an accepted, set phrase or usage that's right for no other reason than that's just the way we say it.

Most of what we call "idioms" are pairs of words that are used together to convey a particular meaning, and many "idiom errors" result from substituting an unacceptable word—usually a preposition—for a word that is always part of the idiom.

Wrong: Brigitte Bardot has joined an organization that is concerned in preventing cruelty to animals.

The adjective *concerned* is followed by either *about* or *with*, either of which would be idiomatic here. But the expression *concerned in* simply isn't idiomatic—we just don't say it that way.

Correct: Brigitte Bardot has joined an organization that is *concerned with* preventing cruelty to animals.

Also Correct: Brigitte Bardot has joined an organization that is *concerned about* preventing cruelty to animals.

There are so many possible idiom errors of this kind that we can't list them all. The most frequently tested errors, however, are contained in appendix 3 of this book, Common GMAT Idioms.

ELLIPSIS

An **ellipsis** is the omission from a sentence of words that are clearly understood. Ellipsis is perfectly acceptable as long as it's done properly—in fact, we do it all the time. Not many people would make a statement like:

I've seen more movies this year than you have seen movies this year.

Instead, we would automatically shorten the statement to the much more concise and natural sounding:

I've seen more movies this year than you have.

In the following sentence, ellipsis is properly used:

The Spectator was written by Addison and Steele.

This is a shorter way of saying:

The Spectator was written by Addison and by Steele.

It's all right to leave the second *by* out of the sentence because the same preposition appears before *Addison* and before *Steele*, so you need to use it only once.

Now watch what happens when ellipsis is improperly used.

Wrong: Ezra Pound was interested but not very knowledgeable about economics.

This is wrong because the preposition that's needed after the word *interested* (*in*) is not the same as the preposition that follows the word *knowledgeable* (*about*).

Correct: Ezra Pound was *interested in* but not very *knowledgeable about* economics.

Wrong: London always has and always will be the capital of the United Kingdom.

This is wrong because the verb form that's needed after *has* is not the same as the one that's needed after *will*, so both must be included.

Correct: London *always has been* and *always will be* the capital of the United Kingdom.

Negatives

You will probably run across at least one item that tests your ability to recognize the difference between idiomatic and unidiomatic ways to express negative ideas. You already know that a double negative is a no-no in standard written English. You wouldn't have any trouble realizing that a sentence such as "I don't want no help" is unacceptable. But the incorrect negatives you will probably see on the exam won't be quite that obvious.

The obviously negative words are *neither, nobody, nor, nowhere, never, none, not, no one,* and *nothing.* But don't forget that *barely, rarely, without, hardly, seldom,* and *scarcely* are also grammatically negative.

In Sentence Correction, you'll find problems with these words where sentences connect two or three negative ideas. Read through the following example sentences carefully:

There were *neither* threats *nor* bombing campaigns.
There were *no* threats *or* bombing campaigns.
There were *no* threats *and no* bombing campaigns.
There were *no* threats, *nor* were there bombing campaigns.

These are the most common idiomatic ways to join two negative ideas. If you can remember these patterns, you can probably eliminate many wrong answers, because they in some way violate these idiomatic patterns.

Wrong:	When Walt Whitman's family moved to Brooklyn, there were no bridges nor tunnels across the East River.

The phrase *no bridges nor tunnels* is just not idiomatic—it contains a double negative. The sentence can be rewritten to correct the problem in several ways.

Correct:	There were *no bridges or tunnels* across the East River.
Also Correct:	There were *neither bridges nor tunnels* across the East River.
Also Correct:	There were *no bridges and no tunnels* across the East River.

Another situation in which negatives can cause problems is in a series. Words like *no*, *not*, and *without* must follow the same rules as prepositions, articles, helping verbs, and the like.

Wrong:	After the floods in the Midwest, many farmers were left without homes, businesses, and huge bills to replace all they had lost.

When a preposition, such as *without* in this sentence, is used in front of only the first member of a series, it's taken to refer to all three members of the series. Here, that causes the sentence to say that the farmers were left without homes, without businesses, and without huge bills to replace what they had lost, which makes no sense. There are several ways to rewrite the sentence so that it makes sense.

Correct:	After the floods in the Midwest, many farmers were left *without* homes, *without* businesses, and *with* huge bills to replace all they had lost.
Also Correct:	After the floods in the Midwest, many farmers were left *with no* homes, *with no* businesses, and *with* huge bills to replace all they had lost.
Also Correct:	After the floods in the Midwest, many farmers were left *with no* homes, *no* businesses, and huge bills to replace all they had lost.

Appendix 2: **Guide to Usage and Style**

In part five, we discussed how to analyze a GMAT essay topic, organize your thoughts, and outline an essay. Once you have an overall idea of what you want to say in your essay, you can start thinking about how to say it. This appendix emphasizes the skills you need for the second stage of the writing process: producing clearly developed and well-organized essays. The best strategy is to study this section and tackle the exercises in short, manageable blocks, interspersed with the study of other subjects in preparation for the GMAT.

Perhaps the single most important thing to bear in mind when writing essays is this: *Keep it simple*. This applies to word choice, sentence structure, and argument. Obsession about how to spell a word correctly can throw off your flow of thought. The more complicated (and wordy) your sentences, the more likely they will contain errors. The more convoluted your argument, the more likely you will get bogged down in convoluted sentence structure. Yet recall that simple does *not* mean simplistic. A clear, straightforward approach can be sophisticated.

Many students mistakenly believe that their essays will be "downgraded" by such mechanical errors as misplaced commas, poor choice of words, misspellings, faulty grammar, and so on. Occasional problems of this type will not significantly affect your GMAT essay score. The test readers understand that you are writing first-draft essays. They will *not* be looking to take points off for such errors, unless you make them repeatedly. If an essay is littered with misspellings, incorrect usage, and the like, then a more serious communication problem is indicated.

Bottom line: Don't worry excessively about writing mechanics, but do try to train yourself out of poor habits and do proofread your essays for obvious errors. Your objective in taking the GMAT is admission to business school. To achieve that objective, give the business schools what they want. They do not expect eloquence in a 30-minute assignment, but they do want to see effective writing.

KAPLAN

To write an effective essay, there are three things you need to do:

1. **Be concise.**
2. **Be forceful.**
3. **Be correct.**

An effective essay is concise; it wastes no words. An effective essay is forceful; it makes its point. And an effective essay is correct; it conforms to the generally accepted rules of grammar and form.

The following pages break down the three broad objectives of concision, forcefulness, and correctness into 16 specific principles. Don't panic! Many of them will already be familiar to you. And, besides, you will have many chances to practice in the exercises we provide.

Principles 1 through 4 aim primarily at the first objective: concise writing; principles 5 through 10 aim primarily at the second objective: forceful writing; and principles 11 through 16 aim primarily at the third objective: grammatically correct writing. (For a thorough understanding of the third of these objectives, though, you should consult appendix 1, Grammar Reference Guide.) In this appendix, we concentrate on principles that are rarely tested in Sentence Correction, but become important when you do your writing. Each principle is illustrated by exercises. (Answers to these exercises are at the end of this section.)

The principles of concise and forceful writing are generally not as rigid as the principles of grammatically correct writing. Concision and forcefulness are matters of art and personal style as well as common sense and tradition. But if you are going to disregard a principle, we hope you will do so out of educated choice. On the GMAT Analytical Writing Assessment, sticking closely to the principles of standard English writing should produce a concise, forceful, and correct essay.

BE CONCISE

The first four principles of good writing relate to the goal of expressing your points clearly in as few words as possible. Each principle represents a specific way to tighten up your writing.

Principle 1: Avoid Wordiness

Do not use several words when one will do. Wordy phrases are like junk food: they add only fat, not muscle. Many people make the mistake of writing phrases such as *at the present time* or *at this point in time* instead of the simpler *now*, or *take into consideration* instead of simply *consider*, in an attempt to make their prose seem more scholarly or more formal. It does not work. Instead, their prose ends up seeming inflated and pretentious. Don't waste your words or your time.

Wordy:	I am of the opinion that the aforementioned managers should be advised that they will be evaluated with regard to the utilization of responsive organizational software for the purpose of devising a responsive network of customers.
Concise:	We should tell the managers that we will evaluate their use of flexible computerized databases to develop a customer network.

Exercise 1: Wordy Phrases

Improve the following sentences by omitting or replacing wordy phrases.

1. In view of the fact that John has prepared with much care for this presentation, it would be a good idea to award him with the project.

   _____

2. The airline has a problem with always having arrivals that come at least an hour late, despite the fact that the leaders of the airline promise that promptness is a goal which has a high priority for all the employees involved.

   _____

3. In spite of the fact that she only has a little bit of experience in photography right now, she will probably do well in the future because she has a great deal of motivation to succeed in her chosen profession.

   _____

4. Accuracy is a subject that has great importance to English teachers and company presidents alike.

   _____

5. The reason why humans kill each other is that they experience fear of those whom they do not understand.

   _____

Principle 2: Don't Be Redundant

Redundancy means that the writer needlessly repeats an idea. It's redundant to speak of "a beginner lacking experience." The word *beginner* implies lack of experience by itself. You can eliminate redundant words or phrases without changing the meaning of the sentence. Watch out for words that add nothing to the sense of the sentence.

Here are some common redundancies:

Redundant	Concise
refer back	*refer*
few in number	*few*
small-sized	*small*
grouped together	*grouped*
end result	*result*

Redundancy often results from carelessness, but you can easily eliminate redundant elements when proofreading.

Exercise 2: Redundancy

Repair the following sentences by crossing out or rephrasing redundant elements.

1. All these problems have combined together to create a serious crisis.

   _____

2. A staff that large in size needs an effective supervisor who can get the job done.

   _____

3. He knows how to follow directions and he knows how to do what he is told.

   _____

4. The recently observed trend of spending on credit has created a middle class that is poorer and more impoverished than ever before.

   _____

5. Those who can follow directions are few in number.

   _____

Principle 3: Avoid Needless Qualification

Since the object of your essay is to convince your reader, you will want to adopt a reasonable tone. There will likely be no single, clear-cut "answer" to the essay topic, so don't overstate your case. Occasional use of such qualifiers as *fairly*, *rather*, *somewhat*, and *relatively*, and of such expressions as *seems to be*, *a little*, and *a certain amount of* will let the reader know you are reasonable, but overusing such modifiers weakens your argument. Excessive qualification makes you sound hesitant. Like wordy phrases, qualifiers can add bulk without adding substance.

Wordy: This rather serious breach of etiquette may possibly shake the very foundations of the corporate world.

Concise: This serious breach of etiquette may shake the foundations of the corporate world.

Just as bad is the overuse of the word *very*. Some writers use this intensifying adverb before almost every adjective in an attempt to be more forceful. If you need to add emphasis, look for a stronger adjective (or verb).

Weak: Novak is a very good pianist.

Strong: Novak is a virtuoso pianist.

                    or

               Novak plays beautifully.

And don't try to qualify words that are already absolute.

Wrong	Correct
more unique	*unique*
the very worst	*the worst*
completely full	*full*

Exercise 3: Excessive Qualification

Practice achieving concision by eliminating needless qualification in the sentences below.

1. She is a fairly excellent teacher.

_____

2. Ferrara seems to be sort of a slow worker.

_____

3. You yourself are the very best person to decide what you should do for a living.

_____

4. Needless to say, children should be taught to cooperate at home and in school.

_____

5. The travel agent does not recommend the trip to Tripoli, since it is possible that one may be hurt.

_____

Principle 4: Do Not Write Sentences Just to Fill Up Space

This principle suggests several things:

- Don't write a sentence that gets you nowhere.
- Don't ask a question only to answer it.
- Don't merely copy the essay's directions.
- Don't write a whole sentence only to announce that you're changing the subject.

If you have something to say, say it without preamble. If you need to smooth over a change of subject, do so with a transitional word or phrase, rather than with a meaningless sentence. If your proofreading reveals unintentional wasted sentences, neatly cross them out.

Wordy:	Which idea of the author's is more in line with what I believe? This is a very interesting . . . .
Concise:	The author's beliefs are similar to mine.

The author of the wordy example above is just wasting words and time. Get to the point quickly and stay there. Simplicity and clarity win points.

Exercise 4: Unnecessary Sentences

Rewrite each of these multiple-sentence statements as one concise sentence.

1. What's the purpose of getting rid of the chemical pollutants in water? People cannot safely consume water that contains chemical pollutants.

   _____

2. I do not believe those who argue that some of Shakespeare's plays were written by others. There is no evidence that other people had a hand in writing Shakespeare's plays.

   _____

3. Which point of view is closest to my own? This is a good question. I agree with those who say that the United States should send soldiers to areas of conflict.

   _____

4. Frank Lloyd Wright was a famous architect. He was renowned for his ability to design buildings that blend into their surroundings.

   _____

5. A lot of people find math a difficult subject to master. They have trouble with math because it requires very precise thinking skills.

   _____

BE FORCEFUL

The next group of principles aim at the goal of producing forceful writing. If you follow these principles, your writing will be much more convincing to the reader.

Principle 5: Avoid Needless Self-Reference

Avoid such unnecessary phrases as "I believe," "I feel," and "in my opinion." There is no need to remind your reader that what you are writing is your opinion.

Weak: I am of the opinion that air pollution is a more serious problem than the government has led us to believe.

Forceful: Air pollution is a more serious problem than the government has led us to believe.

Self-reference is another form of qualifying what you say—a very obvious form. One or two self-references in an essay might be appropriate, just as the use of qualifiers like *probably* and *perhaps* can be effective if you practice using them *sparingly*. Practice is the only sure way to improve your writing.

Exercise 5: Needless Self-Reference

Eliminate needless self-references in these sentences.

1. I do not think this argument can be generalized to most business owners.

   _____

2. My own experience shows me that food is the best social lubricant.

   _____

3. Although I am no expert, I do not think privacy should be valued more than social concerns.

   _____

4. My guess is that most people want to do good work, but many are bored or frustrated with their jobs.

   _____

5. I must emphasize that I am not saying the author does not have a point.

   _____

Principle 6: Use the Active Voice

Using the passive voice is a way to avoid accountability. Put verbs in the active voice whenever possible. In the active voice, the subject performs the action (e.g., we write essays). In the passive voice, the subject is the receiver of the action and the performer of the action is often only implied (e.g., essays are written).

You should avoid the passive voice *EXCEPT* in the following cases:

- When you do not know who performed the action: *The letter was opened before I received it.* (Here the subject *the letter* is the receiver of the action; the performer of the action is unknown.)
- When you prefer not to refer directly to the person who performs the action: *An error has been made in computing this data.*

Passive: The estimate of this year's tax revenues was prepared by the General Accounting Office.

Active: The General Accounting Office prepared the estimate of this year's tax revenues.

Exercise 6: Undesirable Passives

Replace passive voice with active wherever possible.

1. The politician's standing in the polls has been hurt by recent allegations of corruption.

   _____

2. The bill was passed in time, but it was not signed by the president until the time for action had passed.

   _____

KAPLAN

3. Advice is usually requested by those who need it least; it is not sought out by the truly lost and ignorant.

_____

4. The minutes of the City Council meeting should be taken by the city clerk.

_____

5. The report was compiled by a number of field anthropologists and marriage experts.

_____

Principle 7: Avoid Weak Openings

Try not to begin a sentence with _there is_, _there are_, or _it is_. These roundabout expressions usually indicate that you are trying to distance yourself from the position you are taking.

Exercise 7: Weak Openings

Rewrite these sentences to eliminate weak openings.

1. It would be unwise for businesses to ignore the illiteracy problem.

_____

2. It would be of no use to fight a drug war without waging a battle against demand for illicit substances.

_____

3. There are many strong points in the candidate's favor; intelligence, unfortunately, is not among them.

_____

4. It has been decided that we, as a society, can tolerate homelessness.

_____

5. There seems to be little doubt that Americans like watching television better than conversing.

_____

Principle 8: Avoid Needlessly Vague Language

Don't just ramble on when you're writing your GMAT essays. Choose specific, descriptive words. Vague language weakens your writing because it forces the reader to guess what you mean instead of concentrating fully on your ideas and style. The essay topics you're given aren't going to be obscure. You will be able to come up with specific examples and concrete information about the topics. Your argument will be more forceful if you stick to this information.

Weak:	Brown is highly educated.
Forceful:	Brown has a master's degree in business administration.
Weak:	She is a great communicator.
Forceful:	She speaks persuasively.

Notice that sometimes, to be more specific and concrete, you will have to use more words than you might with vague language. This principle is not in conflict with the general objective of concision. Being concise may mean eliminating unnecessary words. Avoiding vagueness may mean adding necessary words.

Exercise 8: Needlessly Vague Language

Rewrite these sentences to replace vague language with specific, concrete language.

1. Water is transformed into steam when the former is heated up to 100 °C.

   _____

2. The diplomat was required to execute an agreement that stipulated that he would live in whatever country the federal government thought necessary.

   _____

3. The principal told John that he should not even think about coming back to school until he changed his ways.

   _____

4. The police detective had to seek the permission of the lawyer to question the suspect.

   _____

5. Thousands of species of animals were destroyed when the last ice age occurred.

   _____

Principle 9: Avoid Clichés

Clichés are overused expressions, expressions that may once have seemed colorful and powerful but are now dull and worn out. Time pressure and anxiety may make you lose focus; that's when clichés may slip into your writing. A reliance on clichés will suggest you are a lazy thinker. Keep them out of your essay.

Weak:	Performance in a crisis is the acid test for a leader.
Forceful:	Performance in a crisis is the best indicator of a leader's abilities.

Putting a cliché in quotation marks in order to indicate your distance from the cliché does not strengthen the sentence. If anything, it just makes weak writing more noticeable. Notice whether you use clichés. If you do, ask yourself if you could substitute more specific language for the cliché.

Exercise 9: Clichés

Make the following sentences more forceful by replacing clichés.

1. Beyond the shadow of a doubt Jefferson was a great leader.

   _____

2. Trying to find the employee responsible for this embarrassing information leak is like trying to find a needle in a haystack.

   _____

3. The military is putting all its eggs in one basket by relying so heavily on nuclear missiles for the nation's defense.

   _____

4. Older doctors should be required to update their techniques, but you can't teach an old dog new tricks.

   _____

5. A ballpark estimate of the number of fans in the stadium would be 120,000.

   _____

Principle 10: Avoid Jargon

Jargon includes two categories of words that you should avoid. First is the specialized vocabulary of a group, such as that used by doctors, lawyers, or baseball coaches. Second is the overly inflated and complex language that burdens many students' essays. You will not impress anyone with big words that do not fit the tone or context of your essay, especially if you misuse them.

If you are not certain of a word's meaning or appropriateness, leave it out. An appropriate word, even a simple one, will add impact to your argument. As you come across words you are unsure of, ask yourself, "Would a reader in a different field be able to understand exactly what I mean from the words I've chosen?" "Is there any way I can say the same thing more simply?"

Weak:	The international banks are cognizant of the new law's significance.
Forceful:	The international banks are aware of the new law's significance.
Wrong:	The new law would negatively impact each of the nations involved.
Correct:	The new law would hurt each of the nations involved. (*Impact* is also used to mean *affect* or *benefit*.)

The following are commonly used jargon words:

prioritize	*parameter*
optimize	*time frame*
utilize	*input/output*
finalize	*maximize*
designate	*facilitate*
bottom line	

Exercise 10: Jargon

Replace the jargon in the following sentences with more appropriate language.

1. We anticipate utilizing hundreds of paper clips in the foreseeable future.

   _____

2. Education-wise, our schoolchildren have been neglected.

   _____

3. Foreign diplomats should always interface with local leaders.

   _____

4. There is considerable evidentiary support for the assertion that Vienna sausages are good for you.

   _____

5. In the case of the recent railway disaster, it is clear that governmental regulatory agencies obfuscated in the preparation of materials for release to the public through both the electronic and print media.

   _____

BE CORRECT

Correctness is perhaps the most difficult objective for writers to achieve. The complex rules of standard English usage can leave you feeling unsure of your writing and more than a bit confused. But remember, the most important lesson you can take from this section is how to organize your thoughts into a strong, well-supported argument. Style and grammar are important but secondary concerns. Your readers will *not* mark you down for occasional errors common to first-draft writing. So just think of this section, together with the Grammar Reference Guide, as helping you to improve the details of good writing. If it begins to overwhelm you, stop and take a break. You need time to absorb this information.

Do the exercises and then compare your answers to ours. Make sure you understand what the error was in each sentence. Use what you learn in this section to help you proofread your practice essays; later, return to your practice essays and edit them. Better yet, ask a friend to edit them, paying special attention to correctness.

Principle 11: Avoid Slang and Colloquialisms

Conversational speech is filled with slang and colloquial expressions. However, you should avoid slang on the GMAT Analytical Writing Assessment. Slang terms and colloquialisms can be confusing to the reader, since these expressions are not universally understood. Even worse, such informal writing may give readers the impression that you are poorly educated or arrogant.

Inappropriate:	He is really into gardening.
Correct:	He enjoys gardening.
Inappropriate:	She plays a wicked game of tennis.
Correct:	She excels in tennis.
Inappropriate:	Myra has got to go to Memphis for a week.
Correct:	Myra must go to Memphis for a week.
Inappropriate:	Joan has been doing science for eight years now.
Correct:	Joan has been a scientist for eight years now.

With a little thought, you will find the right word. Using informal language is risky. Play it safe by sticking to standard usage.

Exercise 11: Slang and Colloquialisms

Replace the informal elements of the following sentences with more appropriate terms.

1. Cynthia Larson sure knows her stuff.

   _____

2. Normal human beings can't cope with repeated humiliation.

   _____

3. If you want a good cheesecake, you must make a top-notch crust.

   _____

4. International organizations should try and cooperate on global issues like hunger.

   _____

5. The environmentalists aren't in it for the prestige; they really care about protecting the yellow-throated hornswoggler.

   _____

Principle 12: Use Commas Correctly

When using the comma, follow these rules:

A. Use commas to separate items in a series. If more than two items are listed in a series, they should be separated by commas; the final comma—the one that precedes the word *and*—is optional. Never use a comma *AFTER* the word *and*.

Correct:	My recipe for buttermilk biscuits contains flour, baking soda, salt, shortening, and buttermilk.
Correct:	My recipe for chocolate cake contains flour, baking soda, sugar, eggs, milk and chocolate.

B. Do not place commas before the first element of a series or after the last element.

Wrong:	My investment adviser recommended that I construct a portfolio of, stocks, bonds, commodities futures, and precious metals.
Wrong:	The elephants, tigers, and dancing bears, were the highlights of the circus.

C. Use commas to separate two or more adjectives before a noun; do not use a comma after the last adjective in the series.

Wrong:	I can't believe you sat through that long, dull, uninspired, movie three times.
Correct:	I can't believe you sat through that long, dull, uninspired movie three times.

D. Use commas to set off parenthetical clauses and phrases. (A parenthetical expression is one that is not necessary to the main idea of the sentence.)

Correct:	Gordon, who is a writer by profession, bakes an excellent cheesecake.

The main idea is that Gordon bakes an excellent cheesecake. The intervening clause merely serves to identify Gordon; thus it should be set off with commas.

Correct:	The newspaper that has the most insipid editorials is the *Daily Times*.
Correct:	The newspaper, which has the most insipid editorials of any I have read, won numerous awards last week.

In the first of these examples, the clause beginning with *that* defines which paper the author is discussing. In the second example, the main point is that the newspaper won numerous awards, and the intervening clause beginning with *which* identifies the paper.

E. Use commas after introductory participial or prepositional phrases.

Correct:	Having watered his petunias every day during the drought, Harold was very disappointed when his garden was destroyed by insects.
Correct:	After the banquet, Harold and Martha went dancing.

F. Use commas to separate independent clauses (clauses that could stand alone as complete sentences) connected by coordinate conjunctions such as *and, but, not, yet,* and the like.

Correct:	Susan's old car has been belching blue smoke from the tailpipe for two weeks, but it has not broken down yet.

Note: Make sure the comma separates two *independent* clauses, joined by a conjunction. It is incorrect to use a comma to separate the two parts of a compound verb.

Wrong: Barbara went to the grocery store, and bought two quarts of milk.

Exercise 12: Commas

Correct the punctuation errors in the following sentences.

1. It takes a friendly energetic person to be a successful salesman.

   _____

2. I was shocked to discover that a large, modern, glass-sheathed, office building had replaced my old school.

   _____

3. The country club, a cluster of ivy-covered whitewashed buildings was the site of the president's first speech.

   _____

4. Pushing through the panicked crowd the security guards frantically searched for the suspect.

   _____

5. Despite careful analysis of the advantages and disadvantages of each proposal Harry found it hard to reach a decision.

   _____

Principle 13: Use Semicolons Correctly

When using a semicolon, follow these rules:

A. Use a semicolon *instead of* a coordinate conjunction such as *and*, *or*, or *but* to link two closely related independent clauses.

Wrong: Whooping cranes are an endangered species; and they are unlikely to survive if
                       we continue to pollute.

Correct: Whooping cranes are an endangered species; there are only fifty whooping
                       cranes in New Jersey today.

Correct: Whooping cranes are an endangered species, and they are unlikely to survive if
                       we continue to pollute.

B. Use a semicolon between independent clauses connected by words like *therefore*, *nevertheless*, and *moreover*.

Correct: Farm prices have been falling rapidly for two years; nevertheless, the traditional
                       American farm is not in danger of disappearing.

Exercise 13: Semicolons

Correct the punctuation errors in the following sentences.

1. Morgan has five years' experience in karate; but Thompson has even more.

———

2. Very few students wanted to take the class in physics, only the professor's kindness kept it from being canceled.

———

3. You should always be prepared when you go on a camping trip, however you must avoid carrying unnecessary weight.

———

Principle 14: Use Colons Correctly

When using a colon, follow these rules:

A. In formal writing, the colon is used only as a means of signaling that what follows is a list, definition, explanation, or concise summary of what has gone before. The colon usually follows an independent clause, and it will frequently be accompanied by a reinforcing expression like *the following*, *as follows*, or *namely*, or by an explicit demonstrative like *this*.

Correct:	Your instructions are as follows: read the passage carefully, answer the questions on the last page, and turn over your answer sheet.
Correct:	This is what I found in the refrigerator: a moldy lime, half a bottle of stale soda, and a jar of peanut butter.
Correct:	The biggest problem with America today is apathy: the corrosive element that will destroy our democracy.

B. Be careful not to put a colon between a verb and its direct object.

Wrong:	I want: a slice of pizza and a small green salad.
Correct:	This is what I want: a slice of pizza and a small green salad. (The colon serves to announce that a list is forthcoming.)
Correct:	I don't want much for lunch: just a slice of pizza and a small green salad. (Here what follows the colon defines what "don't want much" means.)

C. Context will occasionally make clear that a second independent clause is closely linked to its predecessor, even without an explicit expression like those used above. Here, too, a colon is appropriate, although a period will always be correct also.

Correct:	We were aghast: the "charming country inn" that had been advertised in such glowing terms proved to be a leaking cabin full of mosquitoes.
Correct:	We were aghast. The "charming country inn" that had been advertised in such glowing terms proved to be a leaking cabin full of mosquitoes.

Exercise 14: Colons

Edit these sentences so they use colons correctly.

1. I am sick and tired of: your whining, your complaining, your nagging, your teasing, and, most of all, your barbed comments.

   _____

2. The chef has created a masterpiece, the pasta is delicate yet firm, the mustard greens are fresh, and the medallions of veal are melting in my mouth.

   _____

3. In order to write a good essay, you must: practice, get plenty of sleep, and eat a good breakfast.

   _____

Principle 15: Use Hyphens and Dashes Correctly

When using a hyphen or a dash, follow these rules:

A. Use the hyphen with the compound numbers twenty-one through ninety-nine, and with fractions used as adjectives.

Correct:	Sixty-five students constituted a majority.
Correct:	A two-thirds vote was necessary to carry the measure.
Wrong:	Only two-thirds of the students passed the final exam.

B. Use the hyphen with the prefixes *ex*, *all*, and *self* and with the suffix *elect*.

Correct:	The constitution protects against self-incrimination.
Correct:	The president-elect was invited to chair the meeting.

C. Use the hyphen with a compound adjective when it comes before the word it modifies, but not when it comes after the word it modifies.

Correct:	The no-holds-barred argument continued into the night.
Correct:	The argument continued with no holds barred.

D. Use the hyphen with any prefix used before a proper noun or adjective.

Correct:	They believed that his activities were un-American.

E. Use a hyphen to separate component parts of a word in order to avoid confusion with other words or to avoid the use of a double vowel.

Correct:	The sculptor was able to re-form the clay after the dog knocked over the bust.
Correct:	They had to be re-introduced, since it had been so long since they last met.

F. Use the dash to indicate an abrupt change of thought. In general, however, formal writing is best when you think out what you want to say in advance and avoid abrupt changes of thought.

Correct: To get a high score—and who doesn't want to get a high score?—you need to devote yourself to prolonged and concentrated study.

Exercise 15: Hyphens and Dashes

Edit these sentences so they use hyphens and dashes correctly.

1. The child was able to count from one to ninety nine.

   _____

2. The adults only movie was banned from commercial TV.

   _____

3. It was the first time she had seen a movie that was for adults-only.

   _____

4. A two thirds majority would be needed to pass the budget reforms.

   _____

5. The house, and it was the most dilapidated house that I had ever seen was a bargain because the land was so valuable.

   _____

Principle 16: Use the Apostrophe Correctly

When using an apostrophe, follow these rules:

A. Use the apostrophe with contracted forms of verbs to indicate that one or more letters have been eliminated in writing. But try to avoid contractions altogether on the GMAT. (See also Principle 11: Avoid Slang and Colloquialisms.)

Full Forms:

you are	*it is*	*you have*	*the boy is*
Harry has	*we would*	*was not*	

Contracted:

you're	*it's*	*you've*	*the boy's*
Harry's	*we'd*	*wasn't*	

One of the most common errors involving use of the apostrophe is using it in the contraction *you're* or *it's* to indicate the possessive form of *you* or *it*. When you write *you're*, ask yourself whether you mean *you are*. If not, the correct word is *your*. Similarly, are you sure you mean *it is* or *it has*? If not, use the possessive form *its*. You spell *his* or *hers* without an apostrophe, so you should spell *its* without an apostrophe.

Incorrect:	You're chest of drawers is ugly.
Incorrect:	The dog hurt it's paw.
Correct:	Your chest of drawers is ugly.
Correct:	The dog hurt its paw.

B. Use the apostrophe to indicate the possessive form of a noun.

Not Possessive:

the boy   *Harry*   *the children*   *the boys*

Possessive Form:

the boy's   *Harry's*   *the children's*   *the boys'*

Correct:	Ms. Fox's office is on the first floor. (One person possesses the office.)
Correct:	The Foxes' apartment has a wonderful view. (There are several people named Fox living in the same apartment. First you must form the plural, then add the apostrophe to indicate possession.)

C. The apostrophe is used to indicate possession only with nouns; in the case of pronouns, there are separate possessives for each person and number.

my, mine   *our, ours*
your, yours   *your, yours*
his, his   *their, theirs*
her, hers
its its

The exception is the neutral "one," which forms its possessive by adding an apostrophe and an *s*.

Exercise 16: Apostrophes

Edit these sentences so they use apostrophes correctly.

1. The presidents limousine had a flat tire.

_____

2. You're tickets for the show will be at the box office.

_____

3. The opportunity to change ones lifestyle does not come often.

_____

4. The desks' surface was immaculate, but it's drawers were messy.

_____

5. The cat on the bed is hers'.

_____

Answers to Exercises

Answers to Exercise 1: Wordy Phrases

1. Since John has prepared for this presentation so carefully, we should award him the project.
2. Flights are always at least an hour late on this airline, though its leaders promise that promptness is a high priority for all its employees.
3. Although she is inexperienced in photography, she will probably succeed because she is motivated.
4. Accuracy is important to English teachers and company presidents alike.
5. Humans kill each other because they fear those whom they do not understand.

Answers to Exercise 2: Redundancy

1. All these problems have combined to create a crisis.
2. A staff that large needs an effective supervisor.
3. He knows how to follow directions.
4. The recent trend of spending on credit has created a poorer middle class.
5. Few people can follow directions.

Answers to Exercise 3: Excessive Qualification

1. She is a good teacher.
2. Ferrara is a slow worker.
3. You are the best person to decide what you should do for a living.
4. Children should be taught to cooperate at home and in school. (If there's no need to say it, don't!)
5. The travel agent said not to go to Tripoli, since one may be hurt. (Saying *it is possible that one may be hurt* is an example of redundant qualification, since both *possible* and *may* indicate uncertainty.)

Answers to Exercise 4: Unnecessary Sentences

1. People cannot safely consume water that contains chemical pollutants.
2. No present evidence suggests that Shakespeare's plays were written by others.
3. The United States should send soldiers to areas of conflict.
4. The architect Frank Lloyd Wright was famous for his ability to design buildings that blend into their surroundings.
5. A lot of people find math a difficult subject because it requires very precise thinking skills.

Answers to Exercise 5: Needless Self-Reference

1. This argument cannot be generalized to most business owners.
2. Food is the best social lubricant.
3. Privacy should not be valued more than social concerns.
4. Most people want to do good work, but many are bored or frustrated with their jobs.
5. The author has a point.

Answers to Exercise 6: Undesirable Passives

1. Recent allegations of corruption have hurt the politician's standing in the polls.
2. Congress passed the bill in time, but the president did not sign it until the time for action had passed.
3. Those who need advice least usually request it; the truly lost and ignorant do not seek it.
4. The city clerk should take the minutes of the City Council meeting.
5. A number of field anthropologists and marriage experts compiled the report.

Answers to Exercise 7: Weak Openings

1. Businesses ignore the illiteracy problem at their own peril.
2. The government cannot fight a drug war effectively without waging a battle against demand for illicit substances.
3. The candidate has many strong points; intelligence, unfortunately, is not among them.
4. We, as a society, have decided to tolerate homelessness.
5. Americans must like watching television better than conversing.

Answers to Exercise 8: Needlessly Vague Language

1. When water is heated to 100 °C, it turns into steam.
2. The diplomat had to agree to live wherever the government sent him.
3. The principal told John not to return to school until he was ready to behave.
4. The police detective had to ask the lawyer for permission to question the suspect.
5. The last ice age destroyed thousands of animal species.

Answers to Exercise 9: Clichés

1. Jefferson was a great leader.
2. Trying to find the employee responsible for this embarrassing information leak may be impossible.
3. The military should diversify its defense rather than rely so heavily on nuclear missiles.
4. Older doctors should be required to update their techniques, but many seem resistant to changes in technology.
5. I estimate that 120,000 fans were in the stadium. (Even when a cliché is used in its original context, it sounds old.)

Answers to Exercise 10: Jargon

1. We expect to use hundreds of paper clips in the next two months.
2. Our schoolchildren's education has been neglected.
3. Foreign diplomats should always talk to local leaders.
4. Recent studies suggest that Vienna sausages are good for you.
5. Government regulatory agencies lied in their press releases about the recent railway disaster.

Answers to Exercise 11: Slang and Colloquialisms

1. Cynthia Larson is an expert.
2. Normal human beings cannot tolerate repeated humiliation.
3. If you want a good cheesecake, you must make a superb crust.
4. International organizations should try to cooperate on global issues like hunger.
5. The environmentalists are not involved in the project for prestige; they truly care about protecting the yellow-throated hornswoggler.

Answers for Exercise 12: Commas

1. It takes a friendly, energetic person to be a successful salesman.
2. I was shocked to discover that a large, modern, glass-sheathed office building had replaced my old school.
3. The country club, a cluster of ivy-covered whitewashed buildings, was the site of the president's first speech.
4. Pushing through the panicked crowd, the security guards frantically searched for the suspect.
5. Despite careful analysis of the advantages and disadvantages of each proposal, Harry found it hard to reach a decision.

Answers for Exercise 13: Semicolons

1. Morgan has five years' experience in karate; Thompson has even more.
2. Very few students wanted to take the class in physics; only the professor's kindness kept it from being canceled.
3. You should always be prepared when you go on a camping trip; however, you must avoid carrying unnecessary weight.

Answers to Exercise 14: Colons

1. I am sick and tired of the following: your whining, your complaining, your nagging, your teasing, and, most of all, your barbed comments.
2. The chef has created a masterpiece: the pasta is delicate yet firm, the mustard greens are fresh, and the medallions of veal are melting in my mouth.
3. In order to write a good essay, you must do the following: practice, get plenty of sleep, and eat a good breakfast.

Answers to Exercise 15: Hyphens and Dashes

1. The child was able to count from one to ninety-nine.
2. The adults-only movie was banned from commercial TV.
3. It was the first time she had seen a movie that was for adults only.
4. A two-thirds majority would be needed to pass the budget reforms.
5. The house—and it was the most dilapidated house that I had ever seen—was a bargain because the land was so valuable.

Answers to Exercise 16: Apostrophes

1. The president's limousine had a flat tire.
2. Your tickets for the show will be at the box office.
3. The opportunity to change one's lifestyle does not come often.
4. The desk's surface was immaculate, but its drawers were messy.
5. The cat on the bed is hers.

Appendix 3: **Common GMAT Idioms**

Note: All of the following have been known to appear on more than one GMAT. Entries with double ellipses (such as **between . . . and . . .**) indicate that the idiom also sets up a parallelism (between A and B).

able to (ability to)

No one has been *able to* prove that the person who wrote Shakespeare's plays was named Shakespeare.

among versus between

Use *between* when referring to two items or groups, *among* when referring to three or more.

Don't make me choose *between* Tweedledum and Tweedledee.

Among all five candidates, he's by far the best qualified.

amount versus number

Use *amount* when referring to an uncountable quantity, like soup or love, and *number* when referring to countable things, like jelly beans or people.

The *amount* of work you put into your studies will affect the *number* of points you will add to your GMAT score.

as versus like

Use *like* to compare nouns; use *as* to compare actions—in other words, use *as* when what follows is a clause.

Like fine wine, fruitcake tastes better after it has aged.

Dogs don't scratch up furniture, *as* cats often do.

as . . . as

She actually is *as* naïve *as* she appears.

associate with

Many people *associate* the smell of vinegar *with* coloring Easter Eggs.

at least as . . . as

The Eiffel Tower is *at least as* tall *as* the Statue of Liberty.

attribute to

I *attribute* his success *to* having good friends in high places.

believe to be

The expert *believes* the painting *to be* a fraud.

between . . . and . . .

You must decide *between* wealth *and* fame.

both versus each

Use *both* when pointing out similarities; use *each* when pointing out differences. Note that *each* is always singular.

Although *both* cooks enjoy making goulash, *each* has a different take on this classic dish.

both . . . and . . .

He is *both* an artist *and* a rogue.

compare to versus compare with

On the GMAT, *compare with* is the generally preferred form. Use *compare to* to point out an abstract or figurative likeness, and *compare with* to consider likenesses and differences in general.

Shall I *compare* thee *to* a summer's day?
Compared with a summer's day, it's cold outside.

connection between

I saw little *connection between* her words and her deeds.

consequence of

One *consequence of* the Supreme Court decision was increased public distrust in the judicial system.

consider

I *consider* you a very good friend.

Note: Although *consider to be* is also correct, it will never be correct on the GMAT.

continue to

Do not *continue to* deny the obvious.

contrast with

I like to *contrast* my plaid pants *with* a lovely paisley jacket.

credit with

> James Joyce is often *credited with* the invention of the literary form called stream of consciousness.

debate over

This idiom only applies when *debate* is used as a noun.

> They held a lively *debate over* whom to throw off the island.

decide to

> She *decided to* go to the party after all.

define as

> My dictionary *defines* a clause *as* group of words containing a subject and a verb.

different from

> John Major's policies were not very *different from* those of Margaret Thatcher.

difficult to

> It's *difficult to* disagree with such a persuasive argument.

dispute over

This idiom applies only when *dispute* is used as a noun.

> The *dispute over* how to read the punchcards was never properly resolved.

distinguish between . . . and . . .

> Some colorblind people cannot *distinguish between* red *and* green.

distinguish . . . from . . .

> Other colorblind people find it difficult to *distinguish* blue *from* purple.

double versus **twice** (**triple** versus **three times**, etc.)

On the GMAT, *double* (*triple, quadruple*, etc.) is only used as a verb; when making a comparison, the preferred form is *twice* (*three times*, etc.).

> He promised to *double* the company's profits in less than a year.
> I ate *twice* as much as you did.

each (See **both** versus **each** above.)

each other versus **one another**

In GMAT English, *each other* is used to refer to two things, and *one another* is used for three or more.

> Those two theories contradict *each other*.

> Those three theories contradict *one another*.

either . . . or . . .

Today I will *either* look for a job *or* watch the Boston marathon on TV.

-er than

Winston Churchill was a bet*ter* dancer *than* Neville Chamberlain ever was.

extent to which

You should appreciate the *extent to which* the same idioms repeatedly appear on the GMAT.

estimate to be

The oldest cave paintings known to exist are *estimated to be* over 50,000 years old.

fewer versus less

Use *fewer* to describe countable things, like jelly beans or people, and *less* to describe an uncountable quantity, like soup or love. (See **amount** versus **number** above.)

I ate *fewer* hotdogs and *less* potato salad than I did at last year's picnic.

forbid to

I was *forbidden to* discuss politics at the dinner table.

from . . . to . . .

From the Redwood forest *to* the Gulf Stream waters, this land was made for you and me.

just as . . . so too . . .

Just as sand flows through an hourglass, *so too* flow the days of our lives.

if versus whether

If you're ever given a choice on the GMAT, choose *whether*. The actual rule states that whenever you're discussing a choice between alternatives, you should use *whether* (as in *whether or not* to do something) rather than *if*. On the GMAT, *if* is reserved for conditional "if-then" statements.

Let me know *if* I behave inappropriately in front of the royal family. (Translation: I may or may not behave inappropriately, but if I do, I should be informed).

Tell me *whether* I behaved inappropriately in front of the royal family. (Translation: Either I behaved inappropriately or I didn't; tell me the truth.)

in danger of

Conservationists fear that the West Indian manatee is *in danger of* becoming extinct.

less (See **fewer** versus **less** above.)

like versus such as

If you're ever given a choice on the GMAT, choose *such as*. The GMAT writers prefer *such as* to *like* when what follows are examples; to these writers *like* means "similar to."

I prefer salty snacks *such as* potato chips to sweet snacks *such as* candy bars.

I've never met anyone *like* him before.

likely to

You're *likely to* do well on the GMAT verbal section.

link to

Exposure to classical music has been *linked to* improved performance on mathematical aptitude tests.

model after

Louisiana's legal system is *modeled after* the Napoleonic Code.

more than

I was *more* prepared this time *than* I was the last time I took the test.

native

Use *native to*, meaning "indigenous to," when discussing plants, animals, and the like. Use *a native of* when discussing people and where they were born.

The sugar maple is *native to* Canada.

Brendan Fraser is *a native of* Canada.

neither . . . nor . . .

Note that when a sentence has a *neither . . . nor . . .* subject, whatever follows *nor* determines whether the verb is singular or plural. (The same thing is true of *either . . . or . . .* subjects.)

Neither the players *nor* the coach was surprised by the team's victory.

not . . . but [rather, merely] . . .

It's *not* a bother *but rather* an honor to serve you.

not only . . . but also . . .

I am *not only* charming *but also* modest to a fault.

not so . . . as

It's *not so* bad *as* it seems.

not so much . . . as . . .

The company's recent success is due *not so much* to better management *as* to an improved economy.

number (See **amount** versus **number** above.)

Also note that on the GMAT *the number of* will always be singular, while *a number of* will always be plural.

The number of stars in our galaxy *is* huge.

A number of guests *are* waiting in the foyer.

one another (See **each other** versus **one another** above.)

opposition to

There has been far less *opposition* in the United States than in Europe *to* the use of genetically modified foods.

perceive as

I didn't mean for my comments to be *perceived as* criticism.

prohibit from

People are *prohibited from* entering the park after 10 P.M.

range from . . . to . . .

Scores on the GMAT *range from* 200 *to* 800.

regard as

I *regard* him *as* little more than a common criminal.

require to

The laws in many states *require* couples *to* have their blood tested before getting married.

resistance to

Stress can lower one's *resistance to* cold and flu viruses.

same as

I got the *same* score *as* he did.

seem to

He *seemed to* be at a loss for words.

so . . . as to be . . .

My new game app is *so* entertaining *as to be* genuinely addictive.

so . . . that

In fact, it's *so* addictive *that* I spend several hours every day playing it.

such as (See **like** versus **such as** above.)

superior to

Superman's powers are clearly *superior to* those of Batman.

target at

I sometimes suspect that beer ads are *targeted at* morons.

the -er . . . the -er . . .

The bigg*er* they come, *the* hard*er* they fall, or so I have heard.

try to

Try to write a short story based on your travel experiences.

twice (See **double** versus **twice** above.)

use as

Lacking cooking implements, we *used* one of the car's hubcaps *as* a makeshift pan.

view as

Many *view* the former publishing magnate *as* a con artist extraordinaire.

whether (See **if** versus **whether** above.)

worry about

There's no need to *worry about* idioms on the GMAT; just study the ones you don't recognize.

Idioms Quiz

1. Richard Gere portrays not only an officer (and also, and as well, but also) a gentleman in this film.

2. I respect Geri Halliwell, aka Ginger Spice, both as an entertainer (and also, and as, but also as) a humanitarian.

3. I must have either Twinkies™ (or else, or, and) Ding Dongs™ for lunch.

4. You must decide (between, among) the hot and sour soup (or, and) the egg drop soup.

5. (Between, Among) the three starting pitchers, Halladay is generally (considered, considered to be, considered as) the (more, most) reliable.

6. There were (less, fewer) immigrants entering the country last year than the previous year.

7. The (number, amount) of students in my class (has, have) gone up.

8. I regard the movies of Mamie Van Doren (as, to be, as being) superior (when compared to, over, to) those of Jayne Mansfield.

9. Poor Zeppo is often perceived (as, to be, as being) the least talented of the Marx Brothers.

10. According to exit polls, a majority of those who voted for the winning candidate viewed him (as, to be, as being) the lesser of two evils.

11. Adam Sandler's movies are not very different (than, from) those of Pauly Shore.

12. It was so quiet (you, that you, as a result you) could hear a pin drop.

13. Barbra Streisand and Neil Diamond (each, both) went to the same high school.

14. Dean Martin and Jerry Lewis (both had their, each had his) own take on why the two split up.

15. Some pundits like to associate the 1960s (with, and) the decline of Western civilization.

16. We held a spirited debate (over, about, concerning) the place of *Married with Children* within the pantheon of classic situation comedies.

17. I can assure you that it was not a dispute (over, about, concerning) trivial issues.

18. Charles was forbidden (to enter, from entering) the Temple of Doom.

19. He was also prohibited (to visit, from visiting) the Garden of Earthly Delights.

20. I hereby define a "baker's dozen" (to be, as, as being) thirteen.

21. Yogi Bear was clearly more intelligent (compared to, as, than) your average bear.

22. Studying grammar is about as pleasant (when compared to, as, than) going to the dentist.

23. I attribute my stunning success (as due to, because of, to) good looks and native intelligence.

24. I attribute my good looks not so much to exquisite grooming (as, but, but rather) to an inner radiance.

25. Most people credit Philo Taylor Farnsworth (as, for, with) having invented the television back in the 1920s while he was still a teenager.

26. Swing dances from the 1940s (like, such as) the Jitterbug and the Hucklebuck have recently become popular again.

27. (Similar to, Like, As with) many female supermodels, Fabio (is also, is) known by his first name alone.

28. I did not try the clam dip, (as, like) my roommate who got sick did.

29. I've finally decided (on going, to go) camping over the holidays but I still haven't figured out (whether, if) I need to buy a tent.

30. Resistance (against, to) assimilation by the Borg is futile.

Answers

1. Richard Gere portrays *not only* an officer *but also* a gentleman in this film.

2. I respect Geri Halliwell, aka Ginger Spice, both as an entertainer *and as* a humanitarian.

3. I must have either Twinkies™ *or* Ding Dongs™ for lunch.

4. You must decide *between* the hot and sour soup *and* the egg drop soup.

5. *Among* the three starting pitchers, Halladay is generally *considered* the *most* reliable.

6. There were *fewer* immigrants entering the country last year than the previous year.

7. The *number* of students in my class *has* gone up.

8. I regard the movies of Mamie Van Doren *as* superior *to* those of Jayne Mansfield.

9. Poor Zeppo is often *perceived as* the least talented of the Marx Brothers.

10. According to exit polls, a majority of those who voted for the winning candidate viewed him *as* the lesser of two evils.

11. Adam Sandler's movies are not very different *from* those of Pauly Shore.

12. It was so quiet *that you* could hear a pin drop.

13. Barbra Streisand and Neil Diamond *both* went to the same high school.

14. Dean Martin and Jerry Lewis *each had his* own take on why the two split up.

15. Some pundits like to associate the 1960s *with* the decline of Western civilization.

16. We held a spirited debate *over* the place of *Married with Children* within the pantheon of classic situation comedies.

17. I can assure you that it was not a dispute *over* trivial issues.

18. Charles was forbidden *to enter* the Temple of Doom.

19. He was also prohibited *from visiting* the Garden of Earthly Delights.

20. I hereby define a "baker's dozen" *as* thirteen.

21. Yogi Bear was clearly more intelligent *than* your average bear.

22. Studying grammar is about *as* pleasant as going to the dentist.

23. I attribute my stunning success *to* good looks and native intelligence.

24. I attribute my good looks not so much to exquisite grooming *as* to an inner radiance.

25. Most people credit Philo Taylor Farnsworth *with* having invented the television back in the 1920s while he was still a teenager.

26. Swing dances from the 1940s *such as* the Jitterbug and the Hucklebuck have recently become popular again.

27. *Like* many female supermodels, Fabio *is* known by his first name alone.

28. I did not try the clam dip, *as* my roommate who got sick did.

29. I've finally decided *to go* camping over the holidays but I still haven't figured out *whether* I need to buy a tent.

30. Resistance *to* assimilation by the Borg is futile.